Under The Mat

Inside Wrestling's Greatest Family

Diana Hart

with

Kirstie McLellan

Foreword by Stu Hart

Fenn Publishing Company Ltd.
Bolton, Canada

UNDER THE MAT

A Fenn Publishing Book / October 2001

Fenn Publishing Company Ltd.
Bolton, Ontario, Canada

Distributed in Canada by H. B. Fenn and Company Ltd.
Bolton, Ontario, Canada, L7E 1W2

visit us on the World Wide Web at www.hbfenn.com

National Library of Canada Cataloguing in Publication Data

Hart, Diana, 1963-
Under the mat : inside wrestling's greatest family

ISBN 1-55168-256-7

1. Hart family. 2. Hart, Diana, 1963- 3. Wrestling.
4. Wrestlers – Biography. I. McLellan, Kirstie II. Title.

GV1196.H373A3 2001   796.812'092'2   C2001-901726-X

Printed and Bound in Canada

*In Loving Memory of my best friend and brother
Owen Hart – 1965-1999*

Other books by Kirstie McLellan

No Remorse: A Father's Murderous Rage

Table of Contents

Foreword

Diana and Owen were my little blonde palominos. Of all my 12 kids, they had the most to offer. I remember them doing back flips and front flips right in my living room in front of Andre The Giant, Dory and Terry Funk and Lou Thesz. I was so proud of them especially because they were self-taught. That is why I am so impressed with her sharing with the world her life in the wrestling industry with this book. It's her life and she has a right to talk about it, the same right anyone else in my family has.

In my eyes Di is the perfect human specimen, no knobby elbows, thin hair or odd teeth. She was and always has been a wonderful, beautiful girl. I never knew Di to be anything but sensible and practical and she has a genuine love for wrestling. She was the first one I called when I got word that Owen had been killed in Kansas City after falling from a harness during a tragic wrestling stunt.

It hasn't been easy for her growing up female in a male-dominated household and sport. But she did end up working for the WWF with her brothers Owen and Bret and she was an integral part of the career of her husband Davey Boy Smith (The British Bulldog) – I know someday she'll end up managing her son Harry who has inherited all of our family's athletic genes and his mother's stunning looks.

Life has continued to give her a few hard knocks. Being a straight shooter in every way has got her into a lot of trouble. But Di never backs down from the truth even when people don't like it. Parts of this book may not make everyone in the wrestling world happy but it's high time someone who's paid her dues, sings the blues.

STU HART

Hart Family Tree

Edward & Elizabeth Hart

children

Sylvester	Edrie	Stewart
		marries
		Helen

Harry & Ellie Smith

children

Helen	Patsy	Betty	Joanie	Diana	Helen
					marries
					Stewart

Helen Smith and Stewart Hart's children

Smith Hart & Marla Josephson	Toby
Smith Hart & Maria Rosado	Satanya
Smith Hart & Leanne Reiger	Mathew
Smith Hart & Zoe Beattei	Chad
Bruce Ambrose Hart & Andrea	Brit, Bruce Jr., Tory, Rhett, Lara
Keith William Hart & Leslie du Berger	Stewart, Conor, Brock
Wayne Curtis Michael	
Dean Harry Anthony & Tammy Crazy Bull	Farrah

Elizabeth (Ellie) Patricia married to Jim Neidhart	Jennifer, Natty, Muffy
Georgia Louise married to B. J. Annis	Ted, Angie, Matt, Annie
Bret Sargeant married to Jule Smadu	Jade, Dallas, Blade, Alexandrea
Alison Joan married to Ben Bassarab	Linsay, Brooke
Ross Lindsay	
Diana Joyce married to David Smith	Harry, Georgia
Owen James married to Martha Patterson	Oje, Athena

Acknowledgments

Diana and Kirstie would like to thank Larry Day for his first edit and all the hard work and knowledge he put into Under the Mat, Jordan Fenn for his tireless efforts and invaluable advice, Heidi Winter for the fabulous publicity and Laura Pratt — for her watchful eye, Stu and Helen Hart and the entire Hart family including Diana's two children Harry and Georgia, James Trimble, Jason Pierce, Lynn Fisher Teruko Lewin, Michelle Burbank, Constable Bev Voros of the Calgary Police Force, Harry Forest, Caprice Ho Lem, Alison Hall, Greg Everett, Dr. Victor Ramraj, Dr. Robyn Reesal, Alberta Premier Ralph Klein and his Colleen, Betty Weis, Chris Neal, Vivian Breneol, Rich Minzer, Charlie, Lundy, Geordie, Paul and Buddy Day, Joan and Bud McLellan, Julie Sinclair, Carey Roberts, Kristin Maguire, Kyla Schmidt, Laura O'Grady, Katie Eberts, Tyler McLeod, Jeremy Brown, Warren Dubeau, John Cantafio, Jamie Polley, Arnold Goeswich, Jim Ross, Dory, Terri and Vicki Funk, Dwayne 'The Rock' Johnson, Stone Cold Steve Austin, Terry 'Hulk Hogan' Bolea, The McMahon family, Mick 'Mankind' Foley, Chris Benoit, Chris Jericho, Ken Shamrock, Shawn Michaels, Steve Blackman and the late Brian Pilman.

CHAPTER ONE

Davey Boy

I'm so dumb I didn't even know it was abuse. There I was in Florida, surrounded by crackhead wrestlers with my husband, Davey Smith, aka The British Bulldog, doping my juice every night so he could rape me, while I was unconscious. I mean I still have hemorrhoids to this day due to the sickening things he was doing to me.

I never should have married him, but even when he came to me three weeks before our wedding and told me he had just got another girl pregnant, I went ahead with it. If only I hadn't been so stupid and stubborn, I wouldn't have ended up getting suplexed by him, a 280-pound drug addict, in front of our children on the lawn of my parent's home. And I wouldn't have had to endure the pain of watching him run off with my sister-in-law and her five kids. But then I come from a long line of anything but normal. How many kids can count Andre the Giant as one of their babysitters?

I've known wrestlers all my life because I'm Stu Hart's daughter. My dad is a wrestling legend. First, an amateur champion, then a pro, then a promoter of Stampede Wrestling, an operation in western Canada that trained the likes of my brothers, Owen and Bret "The Hitman" Hart, my ex-husband, Davey Boy Smith, my brother-in-law Jim "The Anvil" Neidhart, Tom "Dynamite Kid" Billington as well as Chris Benoit and Chris Jericho, two of the biggest stars in the WWF.

For me things really started to take a downward spiral around the Survivor Series in 1997. That was the pay-per-view where Bret felt that he got the screw from Vince McMahon. Bret defended his World Wrestling Federation Heavyweight Championship title against Shawn Michaels and Shawn won within three seconds of putting Bret in a submission hold – The Sharpshooter. The referee

Earl Hebner ruled that Bret had submitted and gave the decision to Shawn, who walked off with the belt.

Two weeks before that, Davey and I were getting ready for a Halloween party. I was dressing up as Davey in his Union Jack tights, spandex shirt, boots and cape. I added a five o'clock shadow on my chin with eyeliner and pinned back my hair. Davey donned a flared spandex skirt and loose top. He couldn't fit into any stockings but he wore some flip-flops on his feet. I was almost falling over laughing at the sight of him with one of my mom's blonde wigs jammed on top of his head. We were both in hysterics and had trouble holding still as I tried to add mascara, rouge and frosted pink gloss.

It was the first time we had had any fun in weeks. He had been acting so strangely lately. As usual he was on the road with the WWF four days of the week, but instead of being his normal, active self at home he was secretive and withdrawn. The party was starting at nine and he had crawled into bed just after dinner. At first I was annoyed, but when I inspected him closer I noticed he was sweating and shivering at the same time.

"What's the matter?" I asked, concerned.

"I'm okay. Get outta the house. Go to the party."

"I'm not going without you!" I protested. "You're sick!"

His teeth were chattering. "I'll be all right. Just leave me alone for a couple of hours."

I absolutely refused to budge. After half an hour of his trying to get rid of me he finally broke down. "This is the longest I've gone without taking anything and I'm Jonesing." He began crying. "I don't think I can quit, Di."

I presumed he was talking about Percocet, a painkiller he'd been taking since 1985 for back pain, or the steroids he used for bodybuilding.

"Well take your back medication, Davey," I said. "You need that for back pain." Of course, I didn't realize he was taking 30 Percocet a day, a huge amount. I also didn't know he was addicted to morphine, Xanax (a tranquilizer), Toradol (an anti-inflammatory,) the opiate painkillers Vicodine (the drug of choice for many Hollywood addicts) and Talwin, and pain relievers Soma and Dilaudid. He was a walking pharmacy!

Trying to be Florence Nightingale, I grabbed two Percocets from his bag and handed them to him. He gulped them down gratefully and continued confessing, "I'm really scared about how much stuff I'm taking. I want to quit. I have to quit."

I looked into his bag. It was full of different colored pills, all shapes and sizes. I'd seen them before, but it never dawned on me he was a drug addict. The bottles were always full. I assumed they were steroids and medicines he had just in case he got hurt wrestling.

A light bulb exploded in my brain. I reacted immediately, "Oh my God, Davey. Are you taking all this stuff? How often?"

He hung his head. "Some of it I take every day. Some I don't take too much."

I flung my arms around him as if to protect him. "Don't worry. We'll do this together. I'll take these pills and dole them out for you, but only when you really need them. We'll get you better. We're a team, Davey."

He got up and we left for the party. Problem solved.

A year later we were separated. We hadn't had sex since June of 1998 when during a trip to England I caught him shooting up Nubain or Nalbuphine, an opiate similar to morphine used for pain in sickle cell Leukemia. I knew what it was because a friend of ours named Rich Minzer, who worked for Gold's Gym in Los Angeles had tried to forewarn me. He took me aside while Davey was working out and locked eyes with me.

"There's a really bad drug called Nubain going around. A lot of the wrestlers are taking it, Diana, and a couple of bodybuilders have died on stage right after shooting up."

At the time, I chalked it up to Rich just being a worrier. Why was he telling me this? Later I realized he was trying to let me know that Davey was a potential candidate.

By 1998, Davey was like a vegetable. He never left the couch. He had stopped working out. He didn't bother talking to me and ignored our kids, 10-year-old Georgia and 13-year-old Harry. His hands shook so badly he couldn't feed himself. He did make it to the bathroom, but that was about the only thing he did on his own, besides shooting up.

He was on sick leave from his job at World Championship Wrestling, which was WWF's biggest competitor, because he claimed he'd injured his back on a hidden steel door two months earlier at the Fall Brawl pay-per-view while tag teaming with my brother-in-law Jim Neidhardt. They were up against Disco Inferno and Alex

Wright. Watching the match on TV at home I noticed Davey struggling to powerslam Disco. Powerslamming was Davey's big move. But Davey seemed to have his hands full. It was like watching him try to pick up a wet seal. I was irritated with Disco. What was he doing to Davey? Why was he going up so heavy?

I quizzed Davey about it on the phone after the match. Davey was furious, "They had a fucking trap door under the canvas for Ultimate Warrior to burst through at the end of the match! They didn't tell Jim or me. It was two inches thick and had a solid handle on it. I hurt my damn back!"

He came home two days after the Fall Brawl, fell down on the couch and within two weeks, he never wrestled for WCW again. I dragged him to every known healing practice I'd heard of to help him get better: rolfing, underwater physiotherapy, acupuncture, acupressure, chiropractic clinics and yoga. He'd go for a session or two, then quit. I made a vow to myself to never sleep with Davey ever again unless he cleaned up. Then I tried to kill myself.

It was a Friday night in early December. My daughter Georgia was sleeping at my sister Alison's and my son Harry and I were watching the Tim Burton movie Edward Scissorhands. Davey was passed out on the couch. The movie ended and I watched, despising him as he staggered to his feet and lumbered up the stairs. I knew he was on his way up to our room for another hit of morphine. He hadn't said a coherent word all night. I was so angry. While digging through his pockets looking for money earlier that day, I'd found so many bottles of pills my mind was spinning. Since I'd found out about Davey's drug addiction the previous Halloween, I had been battling severe bouts of depression. I began seeing a psychiatrist who had me on 200 mgs. of Zoloft (an anti-depressant similar to Prozac) per day.

I heard our bedroom door close and I put Harry to bed. I sat at the computer and wrote myself a note.

"I don't know how much more of this I can take. Davey's a junkie. He doesn't even try to hide it any more. My family won't listen when I tell them. They think I'm hysterical." As I wrote I got more and more worked up.

"I mean nothing to him any more. He couldn't make it more obvious." A little while later, I made my way up to our room and stood over Davey watching him snore. He sounded liked a vacuum sucking up water. He was totally unconscious. I felt like attacking him, but I knew I could hit him on the head with a cast-iron frying pan and he wouldn't wake up.

I stormed into our walk-in closet and snatched up a full bottle of Xanax from the hollow of one of his crocodile cowboy boots. I moved back to the bed and started screaming at him.

"Look what you've done, you bastard. Look at me, you son-of-a-bitch! I'm going to take your goddamn pills so you'll know what I put up with night and day. I want you to know what it's like to live with a vegetable. You make out like I'm crazy! I'm going to take them. I'm not kidding Davey. Wake up!"

Davey slowly turned his head in my direction. "No," he mumbled. "Don't. Please don't."

"Call 911, if I mean anything to you, Davey." I dumped the entire bottle into my palm and stuffed then into my mouth, holding my hand against my lips to keep them from falling out. Chewing and swallowing I ran to the bathroom and downed a glass of water. I ran back into our room and watched as Davey struggled to sit up. He was like a turtle on its back.

The impact of what I had just done hit me. I wasn't sure about whether what I had taken was lethal or not, but I suddenly felt very frightened.

"Oh shit," I thought. "I don't want to die." I grabbed the phone and dialed 911. I gave my address and said, "Send an ambulance immediately. I just took 100 Xanax. I had a fight with my husband. I don't want to die."

There was urgency in the operator's voice. "Get dressed. Unlock your door and turn your lights on. We'll get an ambulance to you right away."

"I don't want to die. I don't want to die." I hung up.

I scanned the floor for a pair of socks. I made do with two unmatched ones. pulled on sweatpants and a loose t-shirt thinking that it would be easier for the emergency room if I was wearing easy-to-remove clothing. I slid my feet into a pair of clogs, unlocked the front door and turned on the lights. I sat in the front room in a little antique rocking chair next to our bulldog Merrilegs and my cat Dempsey. Then I passed out.

Later I learned my heart stopped four times in the ambulance on the way to the Foothills Hospital, but each time they managed to shock me back to life with heart paddles.

I opened my eyes for a couple of moments the next day and my little brother Owen swam into my vision. I reached to give him a hug and that's all I remember until I woke up two days later.

My mother was frantic because she had planned a big jazzercise Christmas Party in 10 days and as a devoted jazzerciser, I was scheduled to be there.

"Dahling, you think you will be able to make the party? Will they let you out in time?" I assured her I would try to be there, which gave her another thing to worry about. "I don't think we should mention to anyone where you have been."

The day I got home from the hospital I got fixed up for the party. Most of my family was gathered at my parents. Davey disappeared for a couple of hours. There was a lot of private speculation as to where he had gone. My brother Keith drew me aside.

"He's as bad as Elvis, Di. You and your kids have to get away from him."

My oldest brother Smith kept bringing me heaping plates of finger foods and patting me on the head. My sister Alison was as protective as a tigress and my sister Georgia squeezed my hand every time she walked past. My brothers Owen and Bret were absent as usual. My sister Ellie was avoiding me perhaps because her husband Jim Neidhart was in the car with Davey on their way to the home of Alison's ex-husband, Ben Bassarab, to get Davey a morphine fix.

Owen and his wife, Martha, invited me to their home that Christmas Day. Owen sat down with me and lectured me sternly.

"Don't ever do that again, Bearcat. If you had died you would have left Harry and Georgia with a drug addict. I've known about Davey's problem for a long time. I'm not saying he's a bad guy, but he has a real problem. I've carried him through numerous airports so he wouldn't miss his flights.

"When Davey told you about slipping in Brian Pilman's bathroom and hitting his head, that was a lie. I watched him crack that big porcelain sink in half with his head just before he passed out. You can do a lot better than him, Diana. You deserve better than this. Lots of guys would love to take care of you. Steve Austin is a big fan of yours. When a person gets to the point where they want to kill themselves because they are married to a drug addict, they have to leave. You have your kids to think about."

I filed for divorce just before New Year's Eve. Bret and his wife Julie came over to our home that night. Julie talked to me in the kitchen while Bret cornered Davey in the living room. By the end of the night it was decided Davey would check into rehab. He flew to the Alberta Alcohol & Drug Abuse Commission facility at Grand Prairie in northern Alberta the next day.

One of the conditions Davey stipulated before going into rehab was that I drop divorce proceedings. So we reconciled, sort of. Davey left rehab after seven weeks, one week before completing the program. He claimed his kidneys were failing. The doctors in Grand Prairie disagreed. But Davey flew home for a second opinion. We spent the next day in emergency where Davey underwent everything from a CAT Scan to a spinal tap. No one found anything wrong with him. He was scheduled to return in six weeks for a white blood cell count.

The wait was a nightmare. He tried every trick in the book to be checked into the hospital because hospitals administer drugs. He even passed out in a coffee shop in front of my sister Georgia and my mother and had to be transported to the hospital by ambulance. I met up with him there. The doctor recognized him and abruptly threw him out.

"You're a drug addict looking for a fix. Come back when you have a real emergency." I was incensed, why would he be looking for a fix when he had just come out of rehab?

Dr. Donna Dupuis, the psychologist I had begun seeing after my suicide attempt shook her head. "Diana, would you say your husband is one of the best wrestlers in the world?"

"Yes,' I nodded.

"Well Diana, your husband is a professional actor. He's capable of convincing 50,000 people in an audience that he is genuinely hurt, when he is not. How tough would it be for him to persuade a small gathering, say your mother, your sister and you?"

From that moment on, her words started to ring true. He would look so pitiful, lying on the bed and moaning.

"My pain is so bad, Becky, make it go away. I feel like jumping through that balcony window so I can feel something other than all this pain." He called me Becky sometimes for Becky Bear Cat, a derivative of the nickname my brother Owen gave me. Bearcat Wright was a black wrestler, who looked like an otter. His neck was the same width as his head and it was fleshy so it looked as if he was wearing rings around his neck. Owen used to tease me when I was little and it stuck.

I didn't know whether Davey was faking it or not, but six weeks later when he got the results of his white blood cell count, it turned out he had a staph infection in his back. Less than an hour later he was lying in his own hospital bed. At first the nurses could not find a vein in which to start an IV to administer ultra-strong antibiotics to prevent the infection from spreading to his spine.

Of course, he was given liberal doses of morphine to ease the pain. At that time I had no idea how much worse things would get.

CHAPTER TWO

Wrestlers I Have Known

One of my dad's most unforgettable wrestlers was Andre the Giant. His real name was Andre Rene Roussimoff. He was seven foot four and weighed 450 pounds. When I first met him in 1975, I was 12 years old, so he was beyond big. It was like looking at a huge dinosaur.

I'll never forget his gigantic hands. He was sitting in my dad's living room and my little brother Owen and I were playing around him. He let me try on his ring. It slipped right over my wrist. This really scared me because up until I'd met Andre, I thought my dad could beat up anybody in the world. I believed he was invincible. There wasn't anybody who could outwrestle my dad. What the Pope is to religion, that's what I thought my dad was to wrestling, amateur and professional. Andre The Giant was the first person- the only person – I thought my dad would have a hard time with. Then my mom compounded my fear by telling us Andre was temperamental.

Every July, Andre would come to Calgary for Stampede Week. The Calgary Stampede began as a small rodeo in 1912 and is now one of the biggest cash rodeos anywhere. Dubbed "the greatest outdoor show on earth," it attracts more than a million visitors a year. It takes over the city for 10 days every summer.

When Andre first started coming up, he was fairly humble. He'd stay in a small hotel and wrestle some local guys without complaint. But as his celebrity grew, so did his demands. He would insist on time off to watch an exotic dancer named Babette Bardot.

Babette became a friend of our family. Her kids, Bianca and Bobby, were the same age as my younger brother Owen and me. She was married to a fellow named Bob Baker. Bob was her manager and the leader of the small band that accompanied her act. Thanks to some early cosmetic surgery, Babette had the Dolly Parton chest.

She was beautiful and spoke with a sexy French accent. She showed us photos of herself posing with Joey Bishop and Merv Griffin, so I figured she was a real celebrity.

Babette and her family traveled to Calgary each year to perform at the Majestic Inn, a semi-seedy hotel on Calgary's south side. Babette had a lunchtime show and an evening show. I remember sitting in the show at lunchtime with Bianca watching Babette do back walkovers and some fairly tough acrobatics. As a finale she took off her skimpy bathing suit top, which had only covered her nipples anyway. When Bianca clapped and cheered, I was floored. The idea of my mother taking her top off in public was beyond comprehension.

Year after year this little family would stay in Alberta for a month. They'd come up for two weeks in Calgary and stay with us, then Babette and Bob would head for Edmonton and leave their kids at our house. That is until 1975. Bob was a bully and so was Bobby. Bobby was forever beating on Bianca and my parents barred them from our home forever when Owen and Bobby got into a fight and Bobby pushed Owen into the closet. Big Bob held Owen down while Bobby peppered him with rabbit punches.

In 1973 Babette billed herself as Miss Stampede Wrestling and Andre was front row center at most of her shows. This became a problem because he was reluctant to miss any of her performances, even when they conflicted with his wrestling schedule. Sometimes my dad wanted him to travel out of the city to Regina or Montana, but while Babette was in town, Andre balked at the road trips.

One time when Babette was in Edmonton, Andre did agree to go to Montana for a show, but they were late. My brother Smith loaded him into my dad's Cadillac, a gray Brougham De Elegance. Andre usually didn't travel in a car because of his size, but this Cadillac had a sunroof. With his head sticking out of it and Smith driving 120 miles an hour, they headed for the border. When they were just past Del Bonita, Alberta and the border was within spitting distance, the RCMP began chasing them.

Smith knew they'd never make it to the show if he stopped. He also knew if he could just get to the border the RCMP wouldn't be able to touch him. So he floored it and flew into Sweetgrass, Montana. Later, Andre admitted he had never felt true fear in his life until that driving trip with Smith Hart.

One of my first memories is of my dad taking a grizzly bear for a walk. I remember watching my dad's powerful body with his perfect posture, leading the hulking 600-pound animal on a thick rope around our yard. The bear's name was Terrible Ted and belonged to an animal trainer named Dave McKigney, aka Bearman, Wildman, Canadian Wildman and, the name my dad knew him by, Gene Dubois.

Dubois was born in Toronto but made his home in North Bay, Ontario. His hair and beard were long and shaggy and he looked like a bear. That was part of his gimmick. He came to Calgary at the end of June one year and stayed in our yard that winter. Terrible Ted lived under our front porch next to a U-haul trailer that Dubois slept in.

Terrible Ted wrestled on the circuit my dad set up. In British Columbia, there was High Level, Hundred Mile House, Fort Nelson and Golden. In Alberta, the stops included Jasper, Calgary, Lethbridge, Rocky Mountain House, Red Deer, Edmonton and Medicine Hat. The circuit continued with North Battleford, Saskatoon, Prince Albert, Regina and Moose Jaw in Saskatchewan and Billings, Great Falls and Helena in Montana.

A grizzly bear is one of the toughest, most ferocious animals alive, yet a wrestler called The Great Antonio used to make the bear cower due to an incident that happened at one of the matches. Antonio was a big, ugly, hairy wrestler from Yugoslavia. Maurice "Mad Dog" Vachon, a famous wrestler and promoter, sent him to Calgary from Montreal.

Mad Dog is still a folk hero in Quebec today. He came from a family of 13 children. Several of them got into wrestling, including Paul "The Butcher," Vivien Vachon and their niece, Luna Vachon. Mad Dog and The Butcher bit heads and scratched eyeballs around the world.

Mad Dog started as a legitimate amateur. He represented Canada in the 1948 Olympics in London, finishing seventh in the middleweight class. Professionally, he was always a loose cannon, sometimes the hated heel, sometimes the underdog hero. In October 1987, he lost a leg after being hit by a car near his home in Iowa while out for some exercise.

Mad Dog wanted the 400 pound Antonio to get some experience with my dad out west. Dad had trouble finding guys to wrestle him because he was so big and clumsy so he decided to put him up against Terrible Ted. The first couple of minutes of each match the bear would get really annoyed. The Great Antonio would slap its head and the bear would smack Antonio back, leaving big welts and bruises all over his arms.

During one match things got a little carried away and Antonio threw the bear out of the ring through the bottom rope and into the crowd. The fans scattered screaming and crying as the bear scrambled to its feet trying to flee. But it had a big chain around its neck and could only move forward 17 feet – the size of the ring. Dubois and all the other wrestlers on the card grabbed hold of the chain and pulled the terrified bear back into the ring. My dad said they almost ripped the poor bear's head off.

After a 15-minute struggle, Terrible Ted was mad. He was growling and spitting and ready to kill Antonio, so the match was suspended for another 10 minutes while Dubois tried to calm him. The fans were reluctant to take their seats again. Little kids were still whimpering and the adults were all shaking.

Knowing the bear loved junk food, Dubois handed him a bottle of Coke, and it swatted it across the ring like a petulant kid. The crowd began to laugh and returned to their seats. The match resumed. The crowd got their money's worth.

During that tour my dad decided to offer a $1,500 prize to anyone who could pin the bear in the ring. In 1968, $1,500 was an absolute fortune. When they got back to Calgary during the Stampede, a young girl in her twenties and weighing only 115 pounds, stepped up from the audience and said she wanted to wrestle the bear.

My dad said, "Ah, we can't have girls wrestling the bear." But the girl insisted. "I grew up on a farm. I've been around animals my whole life, horses, cows, dogs, cats, you name it. I'm really good with them. I have a special rapport with animals."

My dad held strong. "No, we are not going to have any girls wrestling the gaddamned bear. It's too dangerous." But the girl pleaded with him and finally convinced him to let her into the ring.

The bear had her pinned in less than 10 seconds. He straddled her and was getting set to crush her with his full weight when my dad lunged into the ring and grabbed her by the ankles. He yanked her out from between the bear's legs mere seconds before the bear plunked down full force.

The girl was embarrassed and accused my dad of robbing her of the chance to beat the bear. She stupidly insisted she be given another chance. This time my dad politely, but firmly sent her on her way.

Sweet Daddy Siki loved to wrestle the bear. He was charming with the animal. The charismatic African American was wrestling's answer to Little Richard. He wore high hair like Don King's, bleached white or sometimes dyed pink. He wore trunks covered in thin black and white stripes. My dad used to call him the black Gorgeous George of his day. He made dramatic entrances squirting perfume in front of him to fight off the foul odor of his opponents.

Siki had a long wrestling career, from the 1950s to the 1990s. Siki and the bear had some great matches with Sweet Daddy often making it look like Terrible Ted was getting the better of him. This really worked because Sweet Daddy was perceived as such a narcissist. He was particularly successful in Toronto and Calgary, where he had a second career as a country singer. He attracted a lot of ring rats including some high-school girls from Regina.

Terrible Ted was Dubois's first bear and far less ferocious than his second – Smokey. In July 1978, Dubois left Smokey's cage door open when he ran into his house to answer the phone. Smokey entered the house and sniffed the air. Dubois' girlfriend Lynn Orser was upstairs in bed, and she was having her period. The smell apparently led Smokey right to her and he mauled her to death. The incident made headlines and the Ontario Humane Society took the bear away. Dubois died in a car accident on the TransCanada Highway that same year when he swerved to avoid a moose.

Dubois also had an alligator with him the year he and Terrible Ted lived at our house. He would wrestle it and during the match, he'd force its jaws open and stick his head in its mouth.

That winter while the bear hibernated, Dubois took the alligator on the road. It was housed in an open cage that sat on the floor at the back of the unheated van. It was absolutely freezing in that cage driving from town to town in the western Canadian winter. Alligators are ectothermic so by the time they arrived at their destinations the alligator would be pretty damned cold. They'd work on it for over an hour, rubbing it and wrapping it in heated towels so that it could move.

When they got back to Calgary, my dad let Dubois keep the alligator under our big front porch steps next to where Ted was hibernating. But nobody knew that except my dad and Dubois. They fed it raw chicken and coconut-covered marshmallows. Dad didn't dare tell my mom. I can just hear what she would have said. "Goddamn it, Stu! I don't need any alligators! Christ!"

My dad has always insisted we protect my mom from knowing about things she doesn't want to know. To this day if we see a mouse in the house, we aren't allowed to say anything because he says she would pack up and leave.

We had all kinds of unusual animals at one time or another. Al Oeming, a man who built his own wild animal zoo in Alberta, would bring wolves and his cheetah over for visits.

We had a ferocious police dog staying at our house for a few months when Owen and I were in junior high. It was a Doberman owned by Kim Klokeied, a policeman who wanted to get into wrestling. He brought this dog down from Edmonton to Calgary while he trained with my dad, but his apartment superintendent refused to let him keep it there. So my dad let it stay in our basement furnace room.

Owen and I used to play in the basement all the time and we would approach the dog in an attempt to make friends with it. It pulled against its chain, snapping and snarling and foaming at the mouth, straining in its desire to rip our throats out. We'd come within a foot of its fangs and I remember Owen looking quizzically at it one day and saying, "Boy, that's a mean dog."

One of my dad's favorite matches was with a male tiger named Sasha. Sasha was borrowed from The Ringling Brothers Traveling Circus when it came to town during Stampede Week. My mom had no idea Dad was in the ring with Sasha. Even though she knew he was capable enough, he didn't want her to worry. He told her he was just "doing a little socializing" with the tiger in the ring, "introducing it."

Sasha still had all of his claws and his teeth and must have been a wrestler in another life because he used to head-mare my dad all around the ring. This means he would grab my dad by the back of the neck and flip him over. My dad would try to get behind the tiger to put it in a headlock or go through the tiger's legs to take it down. The tiger actually threw my dad over the top rope and dad took a bump outside the ring. They had great chemistry. Dad loved that tiger. He said it was such a good-looking cat.

Two other wrestlers who made an impression on me as a kid were Billy Leon and Benny Loyd McCrary, aka Billy and Benny McGuire, the world's heaviest twins. They weighed 743 and 723 pounds respectively. Dad billed them as two 800 pounders. They didn't like to call themselves fat. They preferred the word, 'heavy.'

The McGuires were born December 7, 1946 in Hendersonville, North Carolina and have held the record as The World's Heaviest Twins in the Guinness Book of World Records since 1968.

They usually came to Calgary during Stampede week. My dad used to arrange for all his wrestlers to participate in the Stampede Parade. The twins rode little Honda motorcycles and their fat billowed over the handlebars, past the footrests to mere inches above the ground. One year, Benny's bike blew a tire so he had to hoof it the last few blocks of the route. The effort left him a deep shade of purple.

The twins billed themselves as the undefeated tag team of the world. Their big thing was to 'splash' the guy they were wrestling. One of them would get onto the bottom rope at the turnbuckle where the padded ring post is. Using it as a springboard, he would jump up and belly flop on an opponent being held down by the other twin. The crowd would go wild.

In the early seventies, my dad and mom took their gold, four-door convertible Cadillac De Ville to the airport to pick up the McGuire twins. Knowing the boys couldn't sit side by side, my mom slipped into the backseat. When Billy sat down in the front, the seat collapsed. Dad got out and wedged a crowbar behind the seat to stop Billy from squishing my mom. Because the crowbar worked so well, he never bothered to take the car in to get it properly fixed. That's how things were in our family. Patched up.

Dad didn't know what to do with the twins once he had them in the car. He didn't want to take them home because they might fall through the floor, so he dropped them off at BJ's Gym. BJ and my older sister, Georgia, who was 20 at the time, were newlyweds. BJ was a firefighter who opened a boxing gym where my dad's wrestlers weight-trained. Wrestlers are big guys, so the equipment was all industrial strength and the gym had a solid cement floor. My dad figured both the twins and the building would be safe.

Georgia was horrified when the twins left their spittoon next to the toilet. She had never seen one before and thought they were using it as a potty. Later, Georgia whispered to Owen and me that the twins couldn't reach over their stomachs to aim at the urinals so they had strings tied to their birds. I said, "Oh, that's terrible!" But Owen thought it was really funny.

Georgia said sometimes they couldn't get hold of the string so they just aimed in the direction of the toilet. She said BJ was pretty mad because they were not very careful and they were peeing all over the floor. In addition, one of them cracked the porcelain bowl when he sat on it and there was a big crack in BJ's floor near the dumbbells where they had been standing.

As the week wore on, the twins had some good heart-to-heart talks with BJ and Georgia. They confessed they had been diagnosed with a pituitary problem. They were normal until they were four years old and contracted the German measles. They said they were really hurt when Johnny Carson had them on as guests and tried to make fools of them, having them stuff their faces with pie and treating them like big pigs.

They further told Georgia they were kicked out of school in the tenth grade. They said by that time they each weighed more than 600 pounds and had to carry special chairs from class to class. The chairs were heavy and it took them a while to do this. One day the principal made fun of them for being so slow and they jumped him, which got them kicked out of school forever. It broke their mother's heart, but there was nothing they could do. So they took off for Texas in a 1953 Chevy half ton.

After the incident with the car seat, Dad began transporting the twins in an old yellow school bus that often broke down. My poor mom and dad spent forever getting those wrestlers to the shows. They often had to get out and walk or hitchhike. Normally, the only distance Billy and Benny walked was from their dressing room to the ring or to a waiting car, but one July day they had to hitchhike in the pouring rain. Two sopping wet, 800-pound guys hitchhiking. They didn't get picked up.

Another big hit for my dad was the midgets, the little people. He brought in three of them: Coconut Willy, Roland Barriault aka Frenchy Lamonte and Wolfman Kevin. They just loved my dad. He was like Santa Claus and they were the elves. He treated them like they were regular people. That was my dad. He treated everybody the same. He'd give you a pat on the head and a peanut butter sandwich. He wasn't this side-show promoter with a big cigar in his mouth, puffing away, saying, "Yeah, do this, do that."

It must have been funny to see the midgets, the world's heaviest twins and a host of other crazy wrestlers, including Sweet Daddy Siki and The Great Antonio walking along the side of the road after a bus breakdown. Fortunately the bear and the alligator never had to hitchhike.

CHAPTER THREE

Dynamite

There was another wrestler who made a big impression on me and that was The Dynamite Kid, Tom Billington. I met him in 1978. I was 14. He was my first crush.

Tom had such a strong Cockney accent that I could barely understand what he was saying, but he seemed nice. He was a discovery my brother Bruce had made while in England. Bruce was overseas wrestling for wrestling legends, Max, Brian and Shirley Crabtree. Shirley was also known as Big Daddy. He was a big star in Britain who was famous for doing a "belly splash," which was a lot like Billy and Benny's move off the turnbuckle. Otherwise, he couldn't wrestle very well. Ted Betley – who later became famous for training my future husband, Davey Boy Smith – had trained Dynamite. Davey was Dynamite's cousin. I remember Bruce calling my dad from England insisting,

"You've got to see this guy, Tom Billington! He's unbelievable. I've never seen anyone like him in my life!"

My dad was concerned about Tom's size. He was only 165 pounds. The smallest wrestler in my dad's territory in the '70s, except for my brothers, weighed a minimum of 250 pounds. Tom would have to be pretty damned good to be able to work with people 80 pounds heavier than he was. Bruce pushed for him. He really pushed.

"Please Dad, just take a look at him!"

So Tom flew back with Bruce. They were like brothers. They were best friends. Bruce saw so much potential in Tom 'Dynamite Kid' Billington.

There was a lot of tension between my brothers Bret and Bruce after Dynamite came on the scene. Bret was wrestling as a heavyweight because he was tall – six feet. Compared to Bruce's five-feet-eight. The height gave the perception that Bret was heavier than he was. When Bruce proposed that Tom wrestle as a cousin, Tommy Hart, Bret vetoed that idea, saying that he wasn't a Hart so he could not wrestle as a Hart.

CHAPTER FOUR

Roots

My mom's father, Harry Smith, was an Olympic long-distance runner who ran for the United States in the 1912 Olympics in Stockholm, Sweden. His roommate on the boat going over to Stockholm was another legendary athlete, Jim Thorpe.

Thorpe, a 24-year-old American Indian, won the two most demanding events in track and field: the pentathlon and decathlon. And he did it with ease.

"You sir," said the Swedish King Gustav V at the medal ceremony, "are the greatest athlete in the world."

To which Thorpe is said to have replied,

"Thanks, King."

My mom's mother, Elizabeth or Ellie Poulis, was Greek and her parents had immigrated to the United States to become hard-working poultry farmers. Ellie's mother would kill the chickens with her bare hands by wringing their necks because her husband couldn't bring himself to do it. This started one day when they were starving and he was stalling. She impatiently grabbed the chicken from his hands, scolding, "Here let me!" She plucked the chickens and got them ready for sale. Tough lady.

Ellie grew up in New York City and was an excellent dancer. She danced with Arthur Murray when he was still Arthur Teichman. She was a saucy, attractive woman who would eventually fall in love with and marry Harry Smith. My brother Owen talked about going to New York to trace our roots and find out more about Harry and Ellie Smith, but never got a chance.

We do know that Harry ran in the Boston Marathon and in the Mardi Gras Marathon in New Orleans. He used to run all day. He was tall, about five foot eleven with terrific runner's legs and his deep blue eyes always twinkled with kindness. I'm told Owen looked a lot like him. They had very similar features. Owen had

Harry's "crescents," as my mom calls them, under his eyes like crescent moons. I have them too. When we were kids we heard, "Oh boy, you guys don't get enough sleep."

Like Owen and me, Harry had very blonde hair, though he used to put grease in it, which Ellie hated. She wanted him to wear his hair in flowing blonde locks, not the greased-back look that made his hair dark and slick.

Ellie had been dating a very wealthy, respected doctor who was in love with her. He said, "Ellie I want you to marry me." She had the confidence to say, "Well I don't know if I want to marry you." She had seen a handsome young Irishman named Harry Smith and fallen in love with him instead.

When she told the doctor suitor of hers, he protested.

"I'll prove he's not worthy of you! He's a playboy! I'll hire a private detective and we'll follow him."

But after two days, the private detective was exhausted because all Harry did was run. They didn't have many cars in those days and Harry ran about 20 miles a day. The detective couldn't keep up with him.

The private investigator came back and told Ellie's boyfriend that Harry was not a playboy, but in fact one of the nicest guys around. The detective followed him around New York City shaking hands with people and helping them out. He'd help old ladies with their groceries. He even helped lost animals. Everything about him seemed genuinely good. What could the doctor say? He admitted to Ellie that Harry was a good man and gave up.

Harry Smith grew up in the Bronx, which at the time housed some of the upper-class people of New York. Harry was from a very good family, but they had some pretty lean years during and after the Depression.

He discovered he was a runner while playing craps in the alley with some of his friends at the age of 12. A policeman spotted them and yelled, "Hey, you can't be doing that! Gambling is illegal!" The kids scattered like a flock of startled birds when the cop fired his gun in the air.

The officer was fast and caught all the kids except Harry. He had never seen anything as fast as Harry. He could not believe the speed of this boy. He spotted Harry a few days later and before he could bolt, the cop grabbed him by the collar and said, "I'm not trying to catch you because you were gambling. I'm trying to catch you to tell you that you should pursue running. You're gifted. I have never seen anyone run like you." It was that experience that inspired Harry to begin practicing. He went on to the Olympics and was a true hero in New York City.

After the Olympics he became the city treasurer. But Harry had a bipolar disorder like his brother Frank. They could be having a great day and then just one thing, one thing that no one else would notice, could send them spiraling down, unable to lift their heads for the rest of the day.

I have noticed that trait in so many people in my family. I see it a lot in my brother Bret. He'll be having a great day with everything going his way. Then a relatively small thing will really disturb him and it may take days to bounce back. I've seen that happen with my mom, and I see it happen with me too. People think, "Oh, what is it now? What's bothering you this time? Do you ever quit complaining?"

But it isn't because we want to complain. It's just that we look at things differently. We over-analyze everything. A psychiatrist once told me it's called cognitive hurt. That is, we focus on the negative things people say and do to us and it is hard to see the positive things. It is an illness.

When Harry Smith's daughters were young adults, he tried to kill himself. He tried to hang himself in a room from a light socket, but someone came in and found him before he was dead. All he said was, "I can't even do that right." He was so upset about it. He really did want to die. I can understand that, due to my own experience in the ambulance on the way to the hospital after taking an overdose of pills.

My dad says that Harry was one of the sweetest men you could ever meet. He was the father my dad never had, and my dad was the son Harry never had.

Harry and Ellie married and had five daughters: my mother, Helen Louise Smith, Patricia, nicknamed Patsy, Elizabeth, shortened to Betty, Joanie and Diana. Ellie was crazy about boys. She wanted a son so much and Harry did too. So when their first grandchild Smith was born, a boy with blue eyes, they adored him. They doted on their big, healthy half-Greek, half-Irish grandchild.

Ellie the one who choked the chickens was demanding and temperamental like her mother. Harry was the opposite. This worked for them for a long time, his sweetness and passiveness and her aggressive willingness to call a spade a spade. I see that with my own sister Ellie. In fact, I see it in most members of my family. No one pulls punches.

My cousin Harry Forest, Aunt Patsy's son, is a lot like that too. Aunt Patsy's husband Jack Forest was a great, great, great-nephew of Nathan Bedford Forest, founder of the Ku Klux Klan. Nathan's contribution to the army was strategy in combat. He was one of the great leaders of the Civil War.

Of course people primarily remember him for founding the Klan. According to my Aunt Patsy, his diaries and letters demonstrate that the Klan of today is not what he intended it to be. Nathan had envisioned an order dedicated to upholding the highest principles of American heroism and justice. He was disappointed when the Klan veered off course into racist attacks on blacks and other minorities.

My uncle Jack Forest was a highly decorated general who was one of General Schwarzkopf's superiors. I am close to his son, Thomas Harry Forest but his friends mostly call him Tom. He is the tenth of 11 children and the second last in his large family, as am I. Harry and I are soul mates. I haven't seen him in a long time, but know that when we next get together, we will pick up as though we haven't missed a day. He is another family member who I think suffers from depression and is very hard on himself. Extremely talented, bright and handsome, Harry is a male version of me and one of my best friends. I haven't spoken to him in a while because I'm ashamed of what's happened with my husband and my marriage.

I think our grandfather Harry Smith was an obsessive/compulsive person. He would run and run and run, sometimes up to 30 miles a day. When he wasn't running, he was washing his hands and worrying himself sick, often about the state of the country. He was brilliant in math. He could add up a list of numbers as long as a grocery bill in his head. He was a genius. And in my opinion he suffered.

I bet he was good natured like my brother Owen was. I know Owen falling from a harness 90 feet above a wrestling ring in Kansas City in 1999 was an accident. And even though my brother Bret has threatened to kill me and burn my house down for saying this, I still maintain that Owen was like a son to WWF boss Vince McMahon because that's how Owen was. Just like Harry Smith, Owen was so damn appealing and endearing. His humor and his work ethic and his talents carried the whole team.

When my mom was in her late teens, some teenage driver knocked my grandfather down and left him lying on the road. He and his wife Ellie were so destitute they couldn't afford the proper surgery for his leg. The doctors said the best thing to do was amputate, but he wouldn't let them. Instead he let his leg atrophy and it was so damn painful for him, all he could do was lie around.

He spent the rest of his life on a couch and became an alcoholic. He could hardly stand the pain and Ellie had little patience with him. It hurt her to even look at him. She became angry with everyone. Why did this happen to her? Why did the Depression happen? Why did they go from rags to riches to rags? She was so upset and critical of him that he couldn't handle it and stayed drunk all the time.

Their five girls tried their best to act like nothing was wrong. They were among the five most beautiful, charming, intelligent, sexy girls in the whole city, but Harry's decline took its toll on all of them. During the Depression, my mom weighed less than 80 pounds, because there was little food. They ate from a big pot of never-ending stew that was kept warm on the stove 24 hours a day. They just continued adding water and vegetables and whatever meat they could get their hands on.

Mom and her sisters were all thin and would share each other's clothes. They'd have one outfit for each girl and they'd mix and match. To this day my mom worries sick about money and always fears that she and my dad are going to go broke. They don't throw anything away. Everything is recycled: wrapping paper, ribbons, old tires, cars, everything. Like many others, my mother is a child of the Depression and that never goes away. All these crazy fears that she has, are now mine.

CHAPTER FIVE

My Dad

I don't actually know what fears my dad ever had. He has never shown any, except maybe that his kids are going to lose it, lose it all.

Just before World War II, my dad was named to two different Canadian amateur wrestling teams bound for international competitions. One trip to the British Empire Games was cancelled due to a lack of funding and the second to the Olympics was cancelled due to the outbreak of the war. Had that not happened, I believe my dad would have won a gold medal representing Canada.

During the war, when he was on leave from the navy, my dad would slip in and out of the New York area to wrestle in small matches for cash. He had to be careful because he wanted to keep his amateur status in case he did get a chance to wrestle for Canada in the Olympics some day.

He used to tell me stories about that time in his life. "I would work out in New York. I'd get on the exercise machines and wrestle. There were a bunch of these old crowbars down there waiting for the young punks like me to come and wrestle and they'd crank us up pretty good.

"One of my bunkmates was a fellow named Max Summersville. He slept on the cot underneath me on the ship. I got to know him a little bit. He had seen me in Edmonton because I was playing a lot of sports up there – basketball and soccer. I played pro football for a season with the Edmonton Eskimos at the time. I played cricket against John Bradman – the greatest cricket player of all time. He was even knighted.

"Anyway, Max Summersville and I had a two-week furlough and he wanted me to go with him to Washington, D.C. to visit his sister. So we hitchhiked from Cornwallis down through Boston and New York and Baltimore into D.C.

"Joe Carter was the light heavyweight champion of the world and he had a restaurant there. I saw posters of a wrestling match in the window, so I went in to have a cup of coffee and thought I'd have something to eat. I passed by this big fat guy in his fifties with these big cauliflower ears. He looked up and said, 'Hey kid, have you ever wrestled?' I said I had won the Canadian wrestling championship. Then he said, 'I knew you wrestled by the size of your neck.'

"He introduced himself as Toots Mondt and asked me some questions about what I was doing. So I told him I was from Edmonton. He said, 'Did you ever hear of a Jack Taylor up there?' I said, 'Yes, I watched Jack Taylor wrestle in 1932 in Edmonton. He wrestled Tiger Dooligan.' The old bastard smiled, 'You know, Jack Taylor? Jack gave me my first wrestling lesson in Greeley, Colorado in 1916.'

"I said I was in the Canadian Navy. He asked me to sit down for a bite to eat. We talked for about 10 or 15 minutes, and then he asked me to join his wrestling operation. He said, 'I could use you here in Washington, D.C. You could wrestle in Joe Turner's arena.' I said I couldn't right now because of the navy. So he said, 'When you get out of the navy, come and join me.' We kept in touch and when I got out, I met him in New York and he put me to work."

When my dad came into my mom's life in 1947, he was fresh from the war. He was 30 years old in New York City and a Canadian. She had just turned 17 and he thought she was "a pretty little devil." He also thought her sisters, Patsy and Betty, weren't bad looking either.

He regaled the girls with his war stories. He had witnessed some horrific events. One of the worst was watching a man decapitated on D–Day. The guy got drunk the night before and was terribly hung over. He belonged to the shore patrol. The next day they were making their rounds in the shore patrol car and he stuck his head out the window and started vomiting. He drove too close to the shore where there were lifeboats parked on the water, close to the edge of the street. There was a hook on one of the boats hanging off a long pole. It was sharp and sturdy, strong enough to hold a thousand pounds. It caught him around the neck as he drove past and pulled his head right off.

Dad met Mom through a friend of his named Paul Boesh, who was a lifeguard at Long Beach. When Paul spotted my grandfather

Harry and his family, he went over and introduced himself. My dad used to go to Coney Island to work out. But Paul convinced him to come to Long Beach one Sunday instead and that was where Paul introduced my dad to my mom.

Tar from the ships had come in off the tide coating the bottom of her feet as she waded in the water. My dad gallantly offered to remove it for her. She said okay. So sitting side by side on a blanket, my dad gently scraped the tar off the bottom of her feet. I've always thought this was such an appropriate way for them to meet because he has devoted his life to watching over her in the 53 years since.

My dad's family were farmers, transplanted from North Dakota. His grandfather, Donald Stuart, was a senator there. My dad was born in a little farmhouse on the southern edge of Saskatoon, Saskatchewan in 1915. His full name is Stewart Edward Hart. His father was Edward and his mother, Elizabeth. He had two sisters, Sylvester and Edrie.

When he was four years old his most treasured possession was a ball that he had made out of salvaged scraps of string or rags. Day after day he'd roll them together until it was the size of a small baseball. His father found him playing with it one day and snatched it away admonishing him that there was no time for toys on a farm.

That's how his father was. That hard old man lived into his 90s. My dad went to Mayfair School for grade one when he was six years old, then moved with his family to a farm at Forgan. Squatters burned their farmhouse down, driving the family into a tent on the outskirts of the property.

They stayed in that tent through the harsh Saskatchewan winter of 1929. Temperatures dropped to 40 below zero. To stay warm they kept their cow inside the tent with them. Most of the time she provided the family with milk, but it was so cold on some mornings it was impossible to milk her because her teats were frozen. They cooked on stones gathered for a fire pit outside the front flap. When they were done eating, they'd bring the hot stones inside to heat the small area. The harsh conditions were too much for Elizabeth who suffered from diabetes and died that winter. The rest of the family persevered.

When Dad was 11, he hunted for rabbits and squirrels with a slingshot in order to feed the family. His best friend was a pet hawk he'd raised from a chick. The hawk would retrieve the small animals he shot down. School was not an option. He had no shoes, just rags tied around his bare feet. Finally the Salvation Army stepped in. The Salvation Army has been a good friend to our family through the years. They fed and clothed my dad while he was growing up and he turned to them again for our clothing through some of the lean years when I was little.

In 1946 my dad had heard a lot about Harry Smith, the former treasurer of New York City. After he started dating my mom, my dad would take Harry for rides and Harry would call my dad, "son." My dad would be driving in a big, big old car. Harry Smith wasn't used to cars as he had always walked or run everywhere, so they would be driving down the street and Harry would say, "Turn here son," just as they had passed the turn. Harry didn't understand you needed more notice in a car than on foot.

My dad felt privileged to be in his company. He used to take Harry to the Atlantic Ocean. No matter how cold the water was Harry would dip his bad leg in the water. It felt so good that he would wade into the surf time and time again. Harry's leg was pretty well black and should have been amputated years before, but he refused the operation.

Harry had a lot of respect for my dad too. He recognized that my dad would have been in the Olympics had it not been for World War II. My dad was modest about what a great amateur wrestler he was. He still is today at age 85.

My dad and mom, Stu and Helen, married on New Year's Eve, 1948, during the worst blizzard of the century. Helen turned to her new husband and asked, "How long are we going to be in wrestling, Stu?"

"Only two years," he promised.

CHAPTER SIX

Growing up Hart

I was seldom allowed to go to the arenas to watch wrestling. My dad was adamant that none of his daughters would get involved in the business. We weren't even allowed to go down into "the dungeon," the training ring in the basement of our house, until the "fresh" smell from the wrestlers had dissipated. I also didn't know anything about "predetermined matches," (a match where the outcome is decided ahead of time) or the terms "heel" (bad guy) and "baby face" (good guy). My dad got really mad at me once because I asked Owen in the car ride home from school, "What's a heel? What's a baby face?"

My dad growled, "I don't want you two discussing that. Do you understand?" He had too much respect for wrestling. He wanted everyone to believe in it, not just wrestling fans and not just the people who paid to see it. He wanted his family to believe it too.

I inherited my dad's passion for wrestling, as did my brother Bret. This led to the only fistfight I've ever had in my adult life – me against my 230-pound brother, who was in peak condition.

My mom and dad had 12 kids. Smith Stewart Hart was born November 28, 1948. Bruce Ambrose Edwardious was born January 13, 1951. Keith William was born August 21, 1952. Wayne Curtis Michael was born November 19, 1953. Dean Harry Anthony was born January 3, 1955. Elizabeth Patricia was born February 4, 1956. Georgia Louise was born May 21, 1957. Bret Sergeant was born July 2, 1958. Alison Joan (Joan for my mother's sister,) was born December 7, 1959. Ross Lindsay, honoring one of my dad's Negro friends Luther Lindsay, was born January 3, 1961. I, Diana Joyce Hart was born October 8, 1963. And Owen James Hart was born May 7, 1965.

All the boys except Owen had single-syllable names. My mom wanted it to be that way. She thought it sounded better with Hart. My dad had liked the name Owen and my mom liked James because it was her father's second name. Ellie was named for her grandmother. Many of the girls' names came from my mom's favorite writers, Kathleen Norris and Edna Ferber the woman who authored So Big and Showboat. Smith was my mom's maiden name.

Smith was the first grandchild and he was a big boy. He had blue eyes like the shoe buttons women wore at the beginning of the century. His nickname became Shoe-y. My mom's mother just adored him. Actually Mom's parents, Harry and Ellie, raised Smith. Mom was expecting Bruce and was in a car accident in Montana. A woman had escaped from a mental institution in a stolen car and was making her getaway when she ran through a stop sign. She hit my mother's car while Mom was getting driving lessons from my dad.

Mom went right through the teak dashboard. She was in her seventh month of pregnancy and every bone in her face was broken. There was a flat of jars full of strawberry jam in the back seat. The flat hit my mom in the back of the head but she refused painkillers at the hospital because she didn't want to hurt her baby.

To this day she is devoted to Bruce because she worried so much about him from that day, two months before he was even born. While she was in the hospital recovering, she had to have her jaw wired shut and her face reconstructed. They were concerned that she would lose Bruce.

At the same time, my dad was trying to get his wrestling company going. So they all thought the best thing was to have Smith go live with Gaga (Ellie) and Harry. When the time came for my mom and dad to get their son back, my mom's mother didn't want to give Smith up. She said, "No, no, we're attached to him, we can't give him back." And she was serious about it.

So there was a tug-of-war over Smith. I don't think Ellie ever forgave Mom for insisting she give him back. As I said before, she was a little bit saucy. It was either her way or the highway, and she would criticize you forever if you didn't go along.

CHAPTER SEVEN

Smith

Smith is quite warped, but he's not a pervert.

Like my parents he never likes to waste anything. Years ago he was cruising along in his Cadillac, the one he used to transport himself and his crew for my brother Dean's landscaping business, when he accidentally ran over a pheasant. Minutes later, he hopped back in the car shaking his head sadly. He turned to Owen and said, "No point in having the bird die a senseless death."

He spent the next day in the kitchen chopping and cooking, getting this big feast ready. We all sat down to pheasant under glass. Well, after we dug in, Owen opened his big mouth and told us it was really road kill. We all put down our forks and Smith was really hurt.

Smith's first child was illegitimate. I was ten when Smith impregnated Marla Josephson a girl my dad called "an arena rat." He hid the pregnancy from my parents, until during her eighth month my dad saw Marla and Smith together. When my dad questioned Smith about it, he was defiant and answered, "Yeah she's carrying my baby. So what?"

My mom and dad were shattered. Apparently Marla had been sleeping around, but Smith took full responsibility for the baby. When Toby was born, my mom and dad were so disappointed and disgusted they could never accept the baby girl, especially because there was always doubt as to whether Smith was her biological father.

She is grown up now and she turned out just like her mom. None of us ever sees either of them. Smith brought Toby around when my brother Dean died and she made a brief appearance when Owen died. I'm not saying my dad isn't nice to them. He just doesn't think of her as his granddaughter and will always feel that she was born because Smith was an ass and Marla was a tramp.

Smith has had two other children out of wedlock, Matthew with a girl named Leanne Reiger and Chad with a girl named Zoe. When Matthew was born, Smith was no longer seeing Leanne. He had moved on to a relationship with Zoe, after first dating her mother. He started sleeping with Zoe when she was just 15 years old.

Smith lost custody of Chad when Zoe became a prostitute and gave the baby up to her great aunt, Jan and her husband Doug. Smith launched a custody battle and Chad became a foster child with a prominent Calgary gynecologist. In fact, the gynecologist and his wife tried to adopt him, but the aunt fought it and won custody. So Chad now lives with Jan and Doug.

Smith is consumed with a lawsuit to regain custody of Chad, but so far he hasn't done too well in court. My brothers Keith and Bret were subpoenaed by the court to testify. Chad is a handful due to attention deficit disorder.

Neither would consider letting Smith baby-sit their own kids.

In fairness, Smith has done a lot of things to bury himself and cast aspersions on his reputation. He's lost his license due to several unpaid traffic tickets, but hasn't made any attempt to pay them off because of his anti-government-authority stance. He drives my dad's car anyway. And my dad always says, "I don't know what I'll do if the police catch him. If something happened to him and he had an accident and he doesn't have a license, what will I do?"

I just hope someone in heaven is watching over Smith, maybe our deceased brothers Dean and Owen. Right now, the court is trying to reduce the four hours per week that Smith spends with Chad to four hours every six months.

Zoe is dead. Her life as a prostitute killed her. Smith worked hard to try to get her off drugs. The police are not sure whether it was suicide, an accident or murder. She may have overdosed on drugs or someone may have injected her.

Smith lives with my mom and dad up in their big mansion on the hill on Calgary's west side. They have given him the entire top floor. He doesn't bother with housekeeping, but then neither does anyone else in the house. His place is wall-to-wall dust, cat fur, books and chaos.

When Matthew visits, he runs around the house dirty-faced and shoeless, like a wild animal. My dad is in his eighties and he is the only one who ever seems to be able to get Matthew to sit and eat. Maybe Smith is crazy, I don't know.

My dad says Smith was the best wrestler of all his sons and a particularly good villain. He had all the right facial expressions. I think it came from being so cynical. He didn't used to be that way.

On one of Bret's first wrestling tours, Smith wanted to go to the beach in Puerto Rico and suntan. There, he spotted his future wife, Maria Rosetta. She was a bikini model.

I remember Bret telling me that Smith was mesmerized. He could not take his eyes off of her. He told Bret he was going to marry her and that she was the girl for him. It turned out she didn't speak a word of English.

Maria, her sister Rosa, and her mother were very poor. When Smith first dated her, she would wash her clothes on a washboard in the ocean with a rock. For drinking water, Maria would go down to the well and fill a ceramic jug, then carry it back to her home on her head. Years later Maria still had bumps on her head from carrying the huge jugs. Smith quickly learned enough Spanish to communicate. They fell in love and she moved to Calgary.

When I first met Maria I thought we would become good pals because we were both the same age, but Smith pulled the wool over her eyes and that got in the way of any friendship that could have developed.

No one in our family spoke Spanish and Smith communicated with her in a butchered version of the language. When he first brought Maria to visit, he wanted to marry her so desperately; he represented himself as owning our house, our business and all of our property. Because he was such a wrestling sensation in Puerto Rico, she believed him. They married when she was 17 and still a virgin.

At first, Maria seemed puzzled that we were all living in her home. She thought that we were all a bunch of freeloaders living off Smith's generosity. Finally, she became annoyed. She began to lock herself in her bedroom. When was her husband's family going to leave? Smith would bring heaping plates of food and leave them outside her door. She'd respond by smashing the dishes on the stairs.

My dad didn't mind her antisocial behavior but when she threw the food away he got angry. "That was a gaddamn good dinner and she broke the dish too!"

Her behavior became more and more erratic. She and Smith would take two-hour showers together. They would sing duets and laugh and fool around. I remember pounding on the door begging them to get out so I could get ready for school. Maria would always respond with a "fok off."

When I would report this to my dad, he would barge into the bathroom, flick the lights off and on and order them to "finish up." This would lead to a major fight.

"This is my house! Go to hell! Why is your father ordering us out of our own bathroom?"

I think I preferred hearing them fight to listening to their make-up sessions, which always culminated in a noisy, passionate reunion in their bedroom on the floor above mine.

My dad and mom begged Smith to get Maria psychiatric help, but he refused. Sometimes she would strip off all her clothes and climb up on the balcony railing off our second-floor landing and wave at the airplanes. One time when it was 40 below outside and the snow was hip deep; she walked over to our neighbors' and tried to rescue them from an imagined fire.

The last summer she lived with us, in 1987, she made an unprovoked attack on Alison and Ellie's mother-in-law, Katie Neidhart. Alison was having tea with Katie. Katie offered Maria a candy bar. Maria didn't respond. Then suddenly she turned from the stove where she had been cooking rice and pounced on Alison.

Alison was holding her newborn baby girl, Brooke, so she couldn't properly defend herself when Maria began tearing Alison's hair out in clumps. It was as if Maria were fighting for her life. Katie tried to pull Maria off Alison, but Maria, screaming like a wildcat, kept clawing and scratching. Finally, Katie got her in a bear hug.

Desperate to escape, Alison bit down on the hand closest to her. Unfortunately, it was Katie's. The pain was so intense Katie couldn't even cry out to let Alison know she was biting the wrong person. Meanwhile, my parents were in their bedroom watching television. There are 18 stairs, a long hallway and a solid oak door between the kitchen and their room. My dad was 72 at the time and hard of hearing, but my mom thought she heard something.

"Do you hear that, Buffy?" she asked my dad.

"I think I did, Tiger." he replied. "I better go see."

When he opened their bedroom door, one of Maria's wails cut through the house. He sprinted to the kitchen and separated Maria from Katie and his battered daughter. My dad confronted Smith that night.

"You're gaddamned lucky Maria didn't crack baby Brooke's head open on the tile floor!"

My dad ordered Smith to take Maria to the hospital, but again he refused. That night our family had a meeting. Enough was enough. Since Smith and Maria would not take any steps to deal with Maria's mental illness, she would have to return to Puerto Rico. We basically voted her out of the country. Within a week she was gone.

She was diagnosed with schizophrenia and last year she died of pneumonia. It is debatable whether she went crazy because this was common in her father's side of the family, or whether she lost her mind from so many hits of the bad acid she took in Calgary in 1984.

Maria and a wrestler named Mike Hammer and a hired hand named Kevin Trembley dropped acid from the same batch just before a wrestling trip to Regina and they went nuts. That night, Mike Hammer went out and hired a prostitute to whip him, burn his back with lit cigarettes and walk all over him wearing spiked heels.

He was so whipped and burned that he couldn't sit down properly in the van on the way to Regina. Instead he knelt on the floor with his elbows on the seat. This was far less painful than missing the match and having to explain why to my dad. The acid made Mike's eyes so weird, they shivered. Mike's future claim to fame was that he gave Chris Benoit, WWF's "Rabid Wolverine," his initial instruction in wrestling.

The day after dropping this same acid, Kevin tried to hang himself in the horse stalls from one of the beams in the back of the arena in Regina. Before they cut him down he had already messed himself. He was close to dead, but my brother Wayne and my brother-in-law Ben Bassarab, found him and resuscitated him.

According to Smith, Ellie's husband Jim Neidhart, my other bastard brother-in-law, made several passes at Maria, which she ignored. Maria had become quite dependent on pot. She was a hot-blooded Spanish girl so Smith gave her plenty because he thought it would calm her down.

Smith is a staunch pot supporter. He doesn't think it should be illegal. I do, because I think it alters your mind and destroys your brain cells like crazy. I never found it did much for me, except make me paranoid.

When Maria lost her mind she became quite a minus. Like so many drug addicts she was not the same person and you could never get her back. She would sit and rock back and forth, crying one second, laughing hysterically the next. Then she'd threaten to kill you and cry again, all within 20 minutes. She gained over 30 pounds and shaved her head.

Maria and Smith had a baby named Tanya. Tanya was born after Maria started to lose her mind. When she was pregnant, Maria ran back to Puerto Rico. We didn't see Tanya until she was about a year-and-a-half old. When she returned, Smith raised her largely with the help of my mom and dad.

Tanya's real name is Satanya after the devil. Satanya Ecstasy Hart. At the time Maria and Smith had lost their faith in God because of the way their lives had turned out.

Smith's life philosophy shows in the way he treats cars. He'd pick us up from school or he'd drive us out to the beach and he would floor it all the way. He wrapped one of my dad's limousines around a telephone pole and managed to walk away. He has always taken his frustrations out on his cars.

In Smith's eyes, a good-quality car will hold up to the abuse. But if it's a car of lousy quality, then it deserves to be driven "like the piece of shit it is." The same thing with people. If they can put up with Smith's treatment, they survive. And if they can't, they die a slow or painful death. To Smith, it makes no difference whether it's a car, a telephone, an old pair of pants or a person.

CHAPTER EIGHT

Owen's Ribs

I see a lot of Owen in Smith. They have the same laugh lines, the same voice, the same cheeks and the same salty humor. I wonder how Owen's widow Martha, could not want her kids to see Smith when he and Owen are so much alike.

When Owen was tag-teaming with Davey and it was his turn to wait in the corner while Davey wrestled with say, the Smoking Guns, Billy and Bart, Owen would be shouting all kinds of foul things just to get Davey laughing.

He'd scream, "Scratch his box! Scratch his snatch!" Things like that. Well Davey would start chuckling and so would the Guns. They'd all be ordering Owen to stop it.

Owen was always up to something, either messing up his hair or spiking it up as high as he could. Sometimes he'd comb it straight down flat against his forehead before a TV taping. He was a great joker and a real showman.

In 1993, Christina Neal from the British magazine Gladiators, became a really good friend of mine. She started out as rock star journalist, writing profiles of bands like Oasis and The Verve. Then she became quite a wrestling fan and decided to do an article on Owen.

Owen set it up by phone from the States. He arranged to meet her at his hotel when he toured England. She came into his room at the appointed time and he emerged from the bathroom wearing a tee-shirt and trunks that bulged obscenely at the front. He had rolled up a big bath towel and shoved it down his shorts.

It looked ridiculous, but he acted very nonchalant. Smiling and shaking hands he asked, "Okay what did you want to talk about?"

She thought, "Oh, my God, is he for real?" because she didn't know him.

Owen had a gift for keeping a straight face, so he sat down cross-legged on the end of the bed and proceeded to answer her questions. When the interview was over he let her in on the joke. She thought he was hilarious and they became good pals.

Smith got up to similar antics when he was in Germany in the late '70s. All the wrestlers had to come down to the ring in parade fashion before the matches started so that the fans could see who was wrestling on the card that night. The wrestlers would come out one at a time to get introduced in their gear, then they'd wait in the ring until the last person arrived then leave the ring in the same order they had arrived.

Each night during this tournament, Smith would come out in a different outfit. One night, he did a mechanical robot walk, another night he came out with a towel stuffed down the front of his trunks. And one night he got bored and came up with a scheme that nearly got him kicked out of Germany.

The tournament was held in a big tent on the fairgrounds in Hanover and it was several weeks long. The pay was bad, but the upside was the experience gained and the opportunity to meet other wrestlers, which could lead to more work in other countries.

Smith had been growing a mustache, a bushy one. The last night of the tournament, he shaped it to look like Hitler's. He parted his hair over by his ear, and slicked it down with Vaseline and rubbed it with black shoe polish. He waited until mere moments before the marching music so nobody would stop him. Once in the ring, he raised his hand in a Heil Hitler salute and the entire arena, which had been buzzing with excitement over the impending match, went totally silent. Only the wrestlers were cracking up. The promoter was furious.

Owen's impressions were awesome. He could imitate my dad perfectly. Even Owen's best friends didn't recognize it was him on the phone if he didn't want them to.

In 1986, Owen was on the road with Mr. Hughes, a huge African American wrestler. Owen was in the hotel room when Mr. Hughes was unpacking his stuff. He noticed Hughes had lots of stolen hotel towels and ashtrays and soap in his suitcase. Later, when Owen was back in his own room he called Hughes.

"This is the hotel manager. It has come to our attention you are stealing things from our hotel."

"Uh no, I don't know what you mean," replied Mr. Hughes.

"Don't play coy with me sir," Owen scolded. "I happen to be aware you've taken towels, washcloths and even an ashtray! I am calling Mr. McMahon. I want you people out of my hotel. Now! Out! All of you!"

"Sir, sir..." Mr. Hughes stuttered. "I was planning to put it all back. I need the towels for work tonight. I wasn't planning to steal anything."

"You bunch of thieves," Owen ranted. "Pack your things, or I'm calling the police. I'm ordering you all out."

Mr. Hughes was really upset. He didn't want Vince to get word that he was causing all this trouble, but he had to get ready for the match that night. So he promised to meet the manager in his office first thing in the morning. Owen, playing the manager, reluctantly agreed.

The next morning as the wrestlers were getting ready to board buses and taxis for the airport, Owen had a good laugh as he watched poor Mr. Hughes slink into the manager's office with two cups of coffee in hand. The manager must have wondered what in the heck Mr. Hughes was talking about.

Davey wrestled together with Owen as a tag team for 15 years, spending countless days on the road together. Most of the TV footage of Owen includes Davey with him horsing around. Owen would always encourage Davey to walk ahead, muscles bulging in a strongman pose, and then as Davey neared the ring, Owen would race in front and strike a pose of his own. They were inseparable.

In fact, the last conversation Owen and Davey had was in April 1999 a month before Owen died. Owen visited Davey at the Rockyview Hospital in Calgary. Even though Davey was affiliated with the WWF's rival, WCW, and Owen was a WWF star, they were determined to wrestle together again. Owen said he was working it out with Vince.

When they traveled together, Owen loved to pull the ribs on Davey because he would get so mad and yet would be unable to stop laughing. One time they boarded a flight back to Calgary after a show in Atlanta. Owen and Bret upgraded to first class, but Davey was late and got stuck in coach. That was really uncomfortable for such a big guy.

Owen and Bret got comfortable and Davey walked by. Owen whispered to Davey not to worry. He would help him move up front. But just before the plane took off, Owen called the male flight attendant over and confided in him that there was a passenger in coach who was a big wrestling fan.

"He follows us around. He really believes he's a wrestler and is always trying to act like he is one of us." Owen told the attendant that this guy would probably try to sneak into first class.

"I don't mind him coming up and saying hi, but can you make sure he takes his seat back in coach after a few minutes?"

The flight attendant said, "Sure, just give me a signal."

A little later Owen visited Davey at the back of the plane and told him he had it all set up for him to move up to first class. So Davey moved all his stuff to an empty seat in front of Owen and Bret. They chatted a while then Davey settled back for a nap. Owen gave the flight attendant the signal.

"Sir?" said the flight attendant as he leaned over Davey and shook him awake, "I think it's time for you to go and take your seat."

Davey opened one eye. "What are you talking about? I'm s'posed to be 'ere. I'm a wrestler. These are my brothers-in-law." He jerked his thumb back toward Owen and Bret.

The flight attendant looked over Davey's head to Owen who shook his head and circled his ear with a his forefinger indicating that Davey was crazy.

The flight attendant turned back to Davey, "Yes, okay sir, good enough. But you still need to take your seat."

Embarrassed, Davey stood up and gathered his things. As he passed them, Owen burst out laughing.

"Fuck you Owen! And you too Bret. Fuck the both of you." Davey blustered and stormed off down the aisle.

Ribs were pulled on Owen too, even ones that weren't funny. Owen first got into wrestling in 1988. He never drank or took pills or any kind of drugs. He was on the road with Bret and Jim doing a coast-to-coast WWF tour. Owen was wrestling as the Blue Blazer. Bret and Jim were riding high as The Hart Foundation.

Owen was very conservative and careful with his money. He couldn't fathom going out to a bar and spending $50 to get drunk, then having to deal with a hangover the next day. But one match in Chicago was held on Jim's birthday, so Owen relented because he wanted to fit in with the guys. That night he accompanied Jim, Davey, Dynamite and Bret to a blues club.

Unfortunately for Owen, his compatriots had a hidden agenda. They had planned to get him wasted as part of his wrestling initiation.

When Owen wasn't looking they dropped halcion in his beer. Of course it didn't take very much to get him totally bombed. First, he began slurring his words. Then he fell down. He was stymied. What the heck was going on? He'd only had one beer. Owen said he didn't remember much after that. But the guys made fun of him for days, telling him he'd passed out and had to be carried out from the bar.

Owen got Bret back in 1995. He and Bret used to wrestle each other in the "Brother vs. Brother" feud set up for the WWF main event. Bret was the baby face and Owen – the jealous little brother – was the heel. One night Owen snuck into the ring before the show started and concealed a handful of sardines in the turnbuckle. Then in preparation for a quick exit after the show, he packed his bag and left it beside the door.

When his match with Bret was nearing the finish, Owen passed by the turnbuckle and secretly scooped up the sardines. Then he slammed Bret and put him in a camel clutch, as they had previously agreed. This placed Bret flat on his stomach with Owen squatting on the small of Bret's back. Owen grabbed Bret under the chin and pulled his head. But this time he stuck his fingers inside Bret's mouth as if to pull his cheeks apart.

Bret wondered what Owen was doing when an odd salty taste filled his mouth. Then Owen clamped Bret's mouth shut with both hands. Bret continued to try to be professional and sell the hold while puzzling over what was in his mouth. His eyes widened as he realized it wasn't just the taste of Owen's sweaty fingers on his tongue, it was a mouthful of raw fish!

Owen refused to let go. Bret bucked like a bronco throwing Owen to the mat. Spitting and choking, he put Owen in a particularly rough Sharpshooter, his signature move. Owen tapped out, jumped up and ran through the curtain past Davey and a group of agents who were all wiping tears from their eyes after watching what Owen had done. Bret was hot on Owen's heels screaming at him about his unprofessional behavior, which made everyone laugh even harder.

Even Dad wasn't exempt from Owen's phone shenanigans. Twelve years ago when Dad was in his 70s and still a strong athlete, he, Bret and Jade, Bret's daughter, were at Wrestlemania. They were watching the show from a suite when the phone rang. Bret picked it up. It was for my dad.

The guy on the other line said he was Reg Parks, a retired wrestler and long-time friend of my dad's. Reg was into jogging and light weight training. Puzzled over why he would need to speak to my dad right then, Bret handed him the phone.

Bret watched as Dad nodded and chuckled into the phone. "Hiya, Reg. Ah yeah, I'm here with Bret watching the show. What can I do for you?"

Suddenly my dad frowned and said, "What's that Reg? What are you saying?"

My dad got madder and madder until he was yelling into the phone. "I'm a what? Oh really!" Then he stood up.

"If you really think you can take me, Reg, we should just go down in the lobby right gaddamned now and we'll just see!"

Then the caller said something and my dad slammed the phone down on the cradle and sat down.

"That little bastard Owen got me again," he muttered.

CHAPTER NINE

Growing up Hart: II

My mom calls my dad Buff, for Buffy, and he calls her Tiger or Tigerbell. Other than that, I have never heard him use a pet name. He would use them to be sarcastic of course: honey, shitbird or farto, if you wouldn't eat your cereal and the school bus was honking. Between running the wrestling and doing all the cooking and cleaning for 14 people, he had no time to be delicate. If we were stalling, it was, "Get on the gaddamn bus, shitbird." If anyone at the table ever said, "Do you have a sore tummy?" it wasn't out of concern. It was an accusation and caused instant heat at the house. If my dad ever said it to anyone, they got little snickers from everybody at the table. My dad would admonish anyone who left food on a plate.

"Make that disappear while I watch."

If you heckled, you'd get a thunk on the head with a metal serving spoon. "That goes for you too." One of the worst things he could call you was a "softie toffee."

"Eat up shitbird. Do you want some softie toffee to rot your gaddamn teeth out?"

We had to eat our oatmeal, weevils and all. My dad figured they added protein to our diet. Sometimes those bugs would still be alive and kicking, even after the cereal had been boiled for 15 minutes. We would watch them swim around in our milk, if there was enough milk. It never seemed to hurt us. What's worse, that or eating a dead cow?

Though we lived inside the city limits, my dad owned 25 undeveloped hillside acres so he often bought farm animals. My dad loved our cow named Daphne, which the City of Calgary ended up accidentally killing. They picked her up with a backhoe when they where digging a roadway called Sarcee Trail, which was to pass in front of our house. They never mentioned the accident and as far as we knew, Daphne went missing. We called everywhere, but the humane society had no reports of stray cows.

Daphne had been dead for about a month when a neighbor reported seeing her body lying at the end of the road the city was building. My dad was saddened by her death. She was a lovely cow, she really was. And he was so impressed that she gave milk only having calved once.

Bruce and Smith used to compete milking her. Smith hated to lose so during one competition he topped up his pail with water to make it to look like he got more than Bruce. But compared with the rich, thick, frothy cream that Bruce handed to my dad, it was pretty obvious what Smith had done. My dad put the fear of God in Smith for that one. He snatched Smith up off the ground by his Adam's apple and warned him not to try that again, gaddamnit.

We also had goats. Cicero was a goat who used to pee everywhere, even on its own whiskers. One time Cicero wet on Daphne's head and she got so mad she turned around and kicked him so hard he flew up in the air and bounced off the carriage house door. We had a rooster and hen given to us by a Mexican wrestler, Jess Ortega who wrestled under the name Mighty Ursus. We named them Mighty Ursus and Edna.

Mighty liked to crow at the crack of dawn which woke Smith up and annoyed him to no end so he decided he would try to break Mighty of the habit. One morning he snuck up on Mighty just as he was about to crow and startled him. This scared the crow right out of the bird and he strutted around for the rest of the day trying to cough it out.

In 1973 when my brother Owen was eight years old, we had a cat we found as a stray out at the beach. We named her Mom Cat, because she had so many litters. She was a great little hunter and, while playing with Owen one day, she caught a gopher in the yard. The mayor of Calgary, Rod Sykes, was over for a visit. While my dad and he were having a chat in the yard, Owen came up and tugged on my dad's sleeve. He was concerned that the cat was going to take the gopher into the house.

"Dad, Mom's got a gopher and it's still alive and she's got it in her mouth!"

The mayor's eyes widened in horror when my dad told Owen not to worry, she'd probably just eat it on the porch. We eventually donated the bigger animals to the Calgary Zoo, including our big horn sheep and our horses, Ricky and King.

Animals always figured highly in our upbringing. Even today, people take stray cats up to Stu Hart's. They know they will get the best home possible, including the best of everything, from milk, to food, to discipline.

We had a Siamese cat named Heathcliff, who helped Owen a lot with his wrestling. Owen developed quite a relationship with the cat and practiced wrestling holds on it. It was his guinea pig and Owen knew if he could do pile drivers and knee drops on Heathcliff without hurting him, then of course he could do them on a person. That's one way Owen got to be so good.

When Heathcliff got irritated about something we did to him, or if we brought a cigarette smoker into the house, he would retaliate by wetting in the toaster. My dad loved his big commercial electric toaster. It looked like a wall safe. It had six slots and made a really loud ticking sound. When my dad smelled what Heathcliff had done in his toaster, he got so mad he grabbed the cat's head and shoved it in the toilet. He flushed, yelling, "You bastard!" He'd done it to some of us kids before, but never a cat.

When I was a baby, former world heavyweight boxer Jack Sharkey was in town. My dad had invited him to appear as a celebrity attraction at the wrestling. En route to the airport, Jack and his wife stopped by the house for a visit. Jack was dapper in his knee-length yellow cashmere coat, but he was a real blowhard. My dad had suffered silently the entire weekend through Jack's recounting over and over all his wonderful accomplishments in and out of the boxing ring.

At the time my dad was breeding dogs. He owned the best dog of its breed, a grand champion boxer named BF of Rosscarack. BF was a huge animal and he had the run of the house. That night, BF was lying at my dad's side listening to Jack as he launched into yet another story about his athletic prowess in the ring.

BF stood up, yawned and studied Jack for a moment. Then he moved over toward the ex-champ, lifted his leg and urinated all over him. Jack reacted as if he'd been electrocuted. He jumped up in shock, shaking with fury. He kicked at BF fiercely in an attempt to castrate the dog on the spot with his boot. But BF was too fast for him.

"You people have no respect for a great athlete and world champion like me. You Canadians are all the same, so jealous of genuine heroes. I promise you I will never set foot in this hell hole again!"

"Ah, Jack."

My dad was on his feet helping Jack shuck off his urine-soaked coat. "I'm so sorry about that. Don't know what got into BF. Git, boy!" My dad gave the dog an affectionate nudge with his knee.

In the end, Jack was forced to board the plane sans cashmere coat, which was wrapped in plastic and tucked in his suitcase. My dad gave him money to dryclean the coat, but Jack never spoke to him again.

My sister Alison was a picky eater. She would cry or whine or wretch if she didn't want to eat any more sauerkraut which always seemed to be in abundance. Alison would clamp her teeth together, and my dad would force her mouth open with a fork or spoon, digging it right up into her gums under her lip.

"What's the matter? Do you have a sore tummy?" He was imitating my mom, because when my mom was there, she always came to our defense. "Oh Stu, don't do that, don't make them. If they don't want to eat, don't make them."

This would frustrate my dad. Not eating what was put in front of you was one of the few things that made him furious. He'd shout, "Gaddamn it, eat up!"

We knew through my mom that he had had to eat worm-infested rabbits and gophers when he was our age in order to survive. Like Scarlett O'Hara he was determined that neither he nor his children would ever go hungry.

My dad continued to feed Alison, even into her teens. She would cry and my dad would say, "Eat up dahling..." really sarcastically. This would make everyone crack up. She would take forever. She'd chew it, pretend to swallow then secretly spit it out and give it to the dogs. Someone would catch her and tell my dad and he'd force her to fill up her dish again. "Don't be wasting the gaddamned food!"

We never visited the dentist. There was no need. My dad's strict policies limited candy and sweets. He insisted that we brush our teeth faithfully even when we were out of Pepsodent and had to resort to soap. We all had strong, healthy teeth.

Another thing my dad would never tolerate was sickness. That came into play when my brother Dean first became ill and eventually died. We were all in extreme denial throughout. "He couldn't be sick. We're the Harts. We don't get sick. Even when we're sick, we're not supposed to be sick."

One morning, poor Alison was really nauseous. She was 10 years old, but still a tiny little thing. She was so sick that while digging her clothes out of the big industrial clothes dryer in the basement, she fell right inside and passed out. My dad came down searching for her. He told her to get her gaddamned head out of the dryer and get the upstairs and he made her go to school.

When she got there she had to deal with her miserable teacher, who was particularly hard on her. She was a witch. She used to pull Alison's hair if she asked a question that had already been asked. Sometimes she'd make Alison sit in the corner in front of the whole class. She'd drag her by the hair and put her there.

Owen's grade one teacher, Miss Rubenstein, wanted to make Owen repeat the grade. My mom was just sick about it. She would not let Miss Rubenstein keep Owen back. She was adamant.

"If you keep him back, he will think he's a failure and he'll never regain his confidence." My mom was right. Owen became a good student and went on to university.

Georgia did well in most subjects, but Ellie had real trouble in math. She got 4% in math one year with Mr. Falk, the math teacher at Ernest Manning. We all did best in social studies and English, thanks to my mom. She'd check our work and make sure that our grammar and punctuation were correct. She always came to the rescue if she found a dangling participle or a problem with conjunctions.

She found it excruciating to watch the wrestlers interviewed. Sometimes she'd pause before the television set for a brief moment while they threatened to tear each other to pieces. She'd shake her head in disgust. "Ugh! Listen to that grammar!"

My mom hated bad grammar. She could barely stand talking to Mrs. Carr, one of Ross' teachers at Vincent Massey High School, due to her atrocious grammar. Ross thought Mrs. Carr was impossible. He was a good student except in her class. It seemed no matter what he did she would get on his case. When Ross was 27 and working as a substitute teacher, he got a call from Vincent Massey to work. He was late, so he hurried into the school. As he passed by Mrs. Carr she barked, "Ross! Stop running in the halls! And get rid of that baseball cap!"

The one kid among us who legitimately had a lot of trouble in school was Bret. He was handled very badly by his teachers. Some threw books at him and called him stupid and told him he would never amount to anything. Now he writes a weekly newspaper column, which includes his own cartoon drawings.

Mr. Marks taught art to both Bret and me. He was warm and encouraging and recognized talent in both of us. A few years ago when Ernest Manning High School was being renovated, Mr. Marks refused to let them sand the wall where Bret had carved his name.

Maybe some teachers picked on us because we were so poor. I remember not having any socks. My mom and dad didn't have any socks either. One year for Christmas, all the boys got was a hockey puck, socks, a mandarin orange and homemade chocolate cookies. The girls got paper dolls in lieu of the pucks.

Lunch at our house consisted of stacks of enormous corn beef sandwiches, dripping with mustard and mayonnaise on rye bread. I can still see the cats gingerly licking the meat and blood residue off the blade housed in the huge industrial meat slicer. I remember opening the fridge and seeing a huge cow tongue sitting on the shelf. We had a large cuckoo clock hanging on the wall beside the fridge covered in a fuzzy film of cooking grease. On the counter by the window there was a large wooden chopping block made of hardwood. It was at least 100 years old years old and eight inches thick. It was scarred like an old tomcat. Behind it sat an industrial-size milk machine.

Numerous sounds would fill the kitchen at lunchtime, dishes clattering, phones ringing, dogs barking, children yacking and frolicking, horns honking outside and someone yelling "Hurry up! I gotta get back to school!" Oh, how I envied the children who brought tidy little paper bag lunches to school.

When I look at old pictures of my mom, I see a prettier version of Rita Hayworth. She had long chestnut hair and an hourglass figure. Even now there is no hint of the 12 children she bore. She used to wear pretty Doris Day-type gingham dresses and sandals on her feet. She still has an upper-class Long Island accent.

She spent most of her day working on the books for Stampede Wrestling in one of the upstairs bedrooms converted into an office. When my parents met, she was a private secretary for the superintendent of the New York City School Board.

My dad used to say she was "the best gaddamn office manager in the whole city." She handled all the finances for our house and business, while his job was to promote the wrestling and take care of the kids. That included all the cooking and cleaning. I remember my mom's desk blotter. She never wanted anyone writing on it. Once, Smith drew a swastika on it and she got so mad. My dad got mad too.

"Smith, did you draw that gaddamned swastika on your mother's desk blotter?" Smith shook his head innocently, though of course he did it.

My mom used a real fountain pen, a Schaeffer White Dot. Nobody ever touched her pen. You didn't even use it to write down a phone number. Each week she had to get the weekly wrestling advertisements ready. She'd type them out, add the photos by cutting out pictures of the wrestlers' heads, add the headlines and the stars in the right spots, underline what was most important, center everything and finally tape it to a piece of paper. It was like preparing camera-ready copy for newspapers without any of the usual editing equipment. Then she had to schedule the separate lineups for each town. My dad would drive the ads to the Greyhound bus for his different partners in each location. They had to keep an eye on everybody. The Lions Clubs and the Boy Scouts always did a good job, but my parents would often work with somebody that they thought they could rely on and that person would take off with the money. That happened a lot. We never knew who we could trust.

My brother Dean was always pulling ribs and sometimes when my dad went to take out the garbage or start the car, Dean would call upstairs in my dad's gruff voice.

"Dear?"

"Yes Stu?" she would answer in a sugary tone.

"Where are those gaddamned posters for Greyhound?" he'd demand.

This would really upset her, "How dare you talk to me that way!"

Then she'd slam the bedroom door as hard as she could, sending plaster sprinkling down on my dad as he came back into the house. He'd shake his head, "Why did she do that?"

But all he'd get was the muffled retort, "Go to hell!"

He'd turn to all 12 of us, sitting innocently at the dining room table. "What got your gaddamn mother all keyed up?"

I have the utmost respect for my mom and dad. I got enough attention. I got encouragement. I mean maybe they were more concerned with keeping me fed than whether I had good self-esteem, but I do remember them telling Owen and me we had so much to offer and we were the best in the world.

"Don't sell yourself short. You are so smart. You should be modeling. You should be in the Olympics."

Beginning when I was seven years old, I practiced in the gym with Owen. We taught each other nip-ups and somersaults and flips. It was just the two of us putting each other through these little workouts that we had designed. "Okay, we've got to do 100 squats now." Owen and I did everything together.

When we started school we were two dirty-faced, unkempt-looking kids. A six-year-old boy and a seven-year-old girl dressed in Salvation Army clothing, with uncombed hair. Sometimes we were climbing from rags to riches and sometimes falling from riches to rags. Riches brought Cadillacs, clothes and new toys. But more often than not we were poor and the kids at school constantly heaped scorn on us.

Owen was an awesome marble player and always accumulated a bagful. At lunchtime while we waited for my dad or Dean or Bret to pick us up, we'd shoot marbles in the powdery playground dirt.

One day, three grade 10 boys – Ken, Scott and Martin – approached us. They were privileged kids who looked down on us. Scott, the ringleader, called out, "Hey, it's the Hart farts."

Martin joined in. "Little bastards. Their brother Bret is in my homeroom. The teacher says he's retarded."

Then Ken began a singsong chant, "Tar-doe. Tar-doe. Tar-doe."

Martin laughed, "The other day, she threw a book at him and told him he'd never amount to nothing."

Ken was close enough now to kick some dirt at us. "Lowlifes. Have you seen their shitmobile?"

Only Scott hung back. "I dunno, Bret is kinda tough."

Ken spit on the ground beside me. "Bullshit! Wrestling is fake. Everybody knows that, even the rummies who spend their weekends at the Pavilion." He narrowed his eyes at us. "Hey, Hart farts!"

Martin leaned in close to Owen." Hart farts, nice clothes. Where'd you get them? Green Acres? What're you waiting for? The Shitmobile?"

Owen swallowed hard, but ignored the taunts and kept focused on the marbles. I felt my eyes stinging, but pretended to concentrate on the circle in the ground Owen had made with his index finger.

Ken leaned in and grabbed up the whole sack. "Gimme your marbles."

He kicked dirt at Owen and tossed the marbles in the air. Owen stood up, wiping the dirt from his eyes.

Ken patted him on the head. "Hey a cat's eye! Thanks, Hart fart."

Although Owen only came to his waist, he stood toe-to-toe with Ken and growled menacingly. "Give it back."

Ken laughed and shoved Owen roughly and started making his way past him.

Head down like an enraged bull, Owen leg-dived and threw Ken into a headlock. The other two jumped on Owen using him as a kicking bag. Owen managed to land a kick and Ken stumbled. He held Owen's head back with one hand, debating what to do. He snarled, and then began slapping him with his free hand.

Though none of his blows were landing, Owen continued to flail away at Ken. Martin and Scott were laughing. I was on my feet and kicking at Ken's shins.

"Let go!" I shouted.

"Gimme back my marbles!" Owen screamed.

Ken shoved Owen so hard he tumbled to the ground, taking me with him. The three boys ran off laughing, tossing our marbles into the field as they left.

When Bret arrived at the school to pick us up, he could tell something was wrong with Owen. He was usually not so subdued. We were conditioned not to whine or tell on people, but Bret got it out of him.

The next morning just before noon hour, Bret's 1965 gold Brougham Cadillac came to an abrupt halt in the school ground parking lot. He waited outside his Caddy as we tentatively readied our marbles in the dirt. Ken and his buddies were headed our way and Owen made eye contact with Bret indicating they were the bullies.

As soon as Ken came within 10 feet of us, Bret started toward them. His tee-shirt sleeves were tight over his impressive biceps as they pumped through the air. He was on them as quick as a cat. He held all three tight in his grip. With one arm he caught Ken's neck in the crook of his elbow while he twisted Ken's arm up behind him at a painful angle.

All three fussed and swore at him. "Ow! Let me go!" Ken demanded.

Bret smiled." I hear you like to play marbles."

"Let me go." Ken sounded a little less sure of himself. Frightened, his buddies backed off.

Bret twisted Ken's arm up a little higher. "I think you have something to say to my little brother and sister here."

Now Ken was almost crying. "I'm sorry. I'm sorry."

Owen piped up, "You should say sorry to Bret too, for calling our car a shitmobile."

Bret's face grew dark. "What?"

Owen nodded. "He called your car a shitmobile."

Bret goosed-stepped Ken over to the Cadillac and pushed Ken down in front of the bug-covered headlights.

"Kiss it," was all he said.

Ken was almost passing out from the pain. "No way."

Bret twisted Ken's arm so high it looked like it would break. His voice was quiet. "I'm not asking again."

"C'mon. No!" Ken pleaded.

Bret made a quick, sharp move and I heard a terrible cracking noise accompanied by Ken's scream. Then I watched a slow smile spread across Bret's face and I heard Ken kiss the grill.

It was particularly hard for us at school. The teachers were usually unsupportive and the kids teased us constantly. Every day we heard, "My dad says your dad is a fake." Owen would answer, "Yeah well that's because your dad is too much of a chicken to ever wrestle my dad."

Then they'd say, "Your dad doesn't even buy you decent clothes," because we always had holes in our knees and elbows. But when you only had one pair of pants, what could you do?

Some kids would mock us about our dad's cars. "What kind of dad buys a limousine but doesn't buy his kids clothes?"

Owen would reply, "That's because my dad can afford a limousine. What does your dad drive, a Datsun?"

This kind of exchange always turned into a fight. Owen was brilliant at saying something that really got to them and the kid would try to grab him. He and I always backed each other up. I remember one time I was trying to help Owen and I got kicked right in the groin. Later, my brother Dean got a lot of these assholes back. If he knew they had been a jerk to one of us he'd bide his time. Then when they were looking for a vehicle he'd screw them so bad. He would sell them one of his cars he knew was on its last legs, or he'd take out new parts and replace them with worn parts.

Dean had a long memory.

51

CHAPTER TEN

Cats, Mint Jelly & Sunday Dinners

To this day, my dad says Owen and I showed the most promise of all his kids. If he were to have favorites, it would be the two of us. We were his little blond palominos.

We would run around the big mansion on the hill where we lived, naked. Both of us had pretty, long blonde hair. Owen's was especially white. In the summer we had dark suntans and we were free and happy.

Ellie and Georgia doted on Owen and me. We were like their little baby dolls. They changed us, gave us affection, fed us and pushed us around in our baby carriages.

Saturday nights were the only opportunity my parents had to spend time outside the family. They didn't have much money, but they were often invited to charitable events such as The United Way Gala. My dad would dress up in his dark gray cashmere suit and my mom had a wonderful sense of style. She would arrive on his arm looking like Jackie Onassis.

Ellie and Georgia at 16 and 15, would be left to baby-sit. Bret always objected to their being in charge. Georgia was only a year older than Bret and he didn't want her telling him what to do. Besides he was bigger. At 14, he had just gone through his first growth spurt. He was around five foot ten and strong as an ox. On top of that, he wrestled with his seven brothers all the time.

As soon as my parents were out the door, Ellie and Georgia would begin ordering everyone around.

"Okay, Georgia is going to make toasted egg sandwiches, then we are all going to watch Peyton Place and then everyone has to be in bed by nine o'clock!"

"No, I hate Peyton Place!" Bret would argue. Georgia would remind Bret that Mom and Dad had put them in charge and the fight would begin. It would often escalate to physical blows. I remember watching Bret holding Georgia in a tight headlock and knuckling her on the head repeatedly as hard as he could. Ellie would have Bret's hair in her fist, trying to pull him off Georgia. On several instances he grabbed Georgia by the hair and yanked her down all 18 stairs that led to the kitchen. You could hear her body banging against each step as she screamed bloody murder.

As soon as my parents returned home, Bret would disappear and Ellie and Georgia would carefully chronicle the events of the night and show my parents all their injuries. My dad would become incensed. His sons were taught never to hit girls. Bret was the only brother who repeatedly had to be told, "Keep your gaddamn hands off your sisters."

Dad would order a search of the house and Ellie and Georgia would inevitably find where Bret was hiding.

"Here he is!"

He had some pretty clever hiding spaces, like the top shelf of the closet in the boys' bathroom, or behind the five vacuums in the huge broom closet.

My dad would snatch him by his chin, lift him off his feet and cuff him in the head. My dad was good with his cuffs to the head. They made one hell of a whacking sound and scared onlookers and the person being punished. They stung too, but didn't do any real damage.

"If I hear about you laying a hand on your sisters again, I'll knock your gaddamned head off."

Owen and I were the last two kids that my mom and dad could have. They were heartbroken that they couldn't have any more. The doctors told them they had to be responsible parents because my mom was in her 40s and had already had 12. The doctors couldn't be sure she would survive another pregnancy. If she didn't, my dad would be left with 12 kids to raise without a mom. So they did their best to keep us young as long as they could.

My mom and dad gave Owen and me a bottle every night until we were five. She mixed our milk with a little bit of vanilla and sugar and heated it. Owen had his little blue furry blanket. I remember my mom saying asking in her Long Island accent, "You want your furry blanket, Owen?" She was smitten with him.

My dad didn't get into the silly stuff like that. He did tuck Owen and me in every night. He'd kiss us on our heads and say, "Seepy bye." He would brush my hair out with his comb, which hurt like hell, but he tried to be gentle.

He was affectionate, but he would rarely give you a kiss or anything. Dad was more comfortable with hugs. He can see the beauty in things and animals and furniture and houses and trees and a nice dinner. When you were crying you could bury your head in his shoulder and cry, and he would pat you on the head and somehow it would be all right.

My dad displayed his artistic side redesigning his house. His favorite thing to work on was the kitchen. He converted it into a commercial kitchen with stainless-steel appliances and a brick tiled floor. The walls were covered in beautiful yellow tiles from Italy with a fleur-de-lis design. It's such a pretty kitchen, so useful and so masculine.

We lived in a beautiful house. The Hart House, originally known as Crandall House, was built in 1905 by William Hextall for Edward Crandall. There were three buildings: the servants' quarters, the carriage house and the mansion. Crandall moved to Calgary from Ontario and set up the Crandall Press Brick and Sandstone Company. His bricks were used to construct most of the big houses in Calgary in the early part of the century. The Crandall House was built on a hill overlooking the city and the Bow River. He chose the location because he speculated that the downtown Calgary core would spread west toward the mountains.

In the 1920s and during World War I, the Red Cross used the building as a hospital. After the war, Judge Patterson bought the house and then sold it to my dad in 1951. When the judge and his wife moved, they left my dad their cat as my dad was desperate to get rid of all the mice before my mom moved up from New York. He had bought the house before she had a chance to see it. He paid $25,000 for it.

I'm sure the house is haunted due to all the soldiers who died there when it was a hospital. At night, the chandeliers will sometimes rock and doors will slam. Each one of us has seen some strange happenings. Ellie has watched curtains blowing although the windows were closed and a lot of us have had the same dreams at night. Now, since Owen and Dean have died, I can feel their presence.

When my dad saw this house he fell in love with it. He added 24-karat gold borders around the ceilings. He chose the 100-year-old Persian carpets and the chandeliers and the china in the dining room. He wanted a Florentine turquoise china pattern with a place setting for each of us, but my mom would not let him get it. She said it was a horrible investment.

"I don't want you buying 144 dishes, Stu!"

He went ahead and placed an order with Birks anyway. The sales lady knew my mom and informed her of the order, which my mom cancelled instantly. This was the late '70s. Wrestling was doing a lot better and my dad wanted to capitalize on the small fortune that he was making, buying the best of everything. From 1957 to 1981, he bought over 30 mint-condition Cadillacs.

In the '70s, he acquired a limousine and he'd transport us to and from school with the glass partition down so he could eavesdrop. But often one of the boys, usually Bret, would roll it up to talk about something he didn't want Dad to hear, driving my dad nuts. My brothers would torment the hell out of him sometimes.

My dad hated gum. If he smelled it in the car, he'd demand to know who was chewing the gaddamned gum or the Thrills or Tooty-Fruity! Then, if that partition came up, he'd pull the car over and throw open the door. Everyone would dive-bomb over each other trying to get away from his grip. He'd catch someone by the scruff of the neck and shake him or her.

"Do you understand, gaddamnit? I don't want you to do that ever again. Do you understand?" Though it was just a stern warning, it would put the fear of God into us. My mom never, ever spanked us. She never even laid a finger on us. My dad admits that he did, but my mom never did.

Mom and Dad always took in strangers and animals. Right now they have four dogs and 10 cats. The house itself is worth a million dollars. The land it sits on is probably worth more. And some of the furniture and antiques are priceless. Unfortunately, there is a lot of cat pee around.

If you know what cat pee smells like, it's easily noticeable when entering my dad's house. If one of the animals has been sick or unable to get out, you might have to step over the dog mess on the hand-knotted antique Persian carpets in the foyer. Although my parents are no longer able to keep house they do not want strangers there cleaning, so everything is falling into disrepair.

People have moved in and my parents are too polite to ask them to leave. Bob Johnson was a prime example. He was an itinerant wrestling fan and moved in 1989 ostensibly to help my mom out with the office work. He was still there eight years later.

Bob claimed he was Icelandic. He had thinning silver hair and false teeth and blue eyes. He was built like a pear so he had a big back yard with a little head. His hands and feet were tiny too and he was allergic to cats. He slept on a Salvation Army cot in the basement next to the furnace.

He was a sick, perverted person. He kept child pornography magazines and horrible, disgusting triple-X-rated video cases lying around. He was obsessed with pornography. They were all out in plain view and if anyone complained he was defiant.

"This is my room where Stu and Helen Hart said I could stay. If I want to have my literature out, I will."

When my own two children, Harry and Baby Georgia, and my sister Alison's daughter, Brooke, were four and six years old, they went down to his room and threw all of his stuff out. They were disgusted with it. They put socks over their hands because they didn't want to touch the filthy books and magazines. Then they poured sticky green mint jelly, which had been a Christmas present to my mom and dad, all over his bed. Finally, they sprinkled saltine cracker crumbs on top of the jelly.

Everyone was so proud of them. But Bob raised hell about it. He sobbed to my dad that someone – he didn't know who – had poured mint jelly all over his bed and he wanted justice.

But my dad didn't react. "Well better clean it up, Bob," was all he said.

I remember Harry and Brooke and Georgia were wide eyed, like the three bad little kittens, but everyone supported them. We had warned my parents a million times that Bob Johnson was leaving his pornography around the basement and they did nothing to stop it. They never stood up to a guest in their home. They were determined to be gracious hosts at any cost.

The basement also houses a running machine. This big treadmill looks like something you'd put a racehorse on to get it in shape. My sister Ellie's husband, Jim Neidhart, ran on it when he was with the Oakland Raiders. It's a big, noisy, cumbersome machine, but God, can it get you in shape. It's on a two-foot-wide conveyor belt. The tread is made of twine and jute and sandpaper so your feet can get traction. There are ball bearings in every single roller. It was shipped up to my dad's basement in the '80s and everyone trained on it.

I loved it. My greatest physical achievement was running on that thing for 90 minutes straight. I still have the record. I would get on there and think about things and run and run. There wasn't a hill I couldn't tackle after that. I built such strong hamstrings from it too. I try every so often to run on it now. Your throat burns so bad you feel like you swallowed a Christmas tree.

Next to the treadmill is the incinerator room and beside it, the shower that has so much force it feels like it's ripping your skin off. The spray is so forceful and fine it's like sharp quills piercing you. It is the same shower that we all used when we were little. We had an assembly-line approach. There was just time to get in, get rinsed off and get out. We kids would line up in our birthday suits. Nobody was really thrilled to be standing there naked waiting their turn, but there was no embarrassment.

A bubble bath was practically unheard of. The only way we would get bubbles would be to use dishwashing liquid in the tub, but it was expensive so we seldom had it. We always had dishwashing powder because it was cheaper. The odd time we would have lemon Sunlight liquid, but God it was hard on your skin. After using it we'd come out of there with skin like parchment paper. To pull out the tangles from our hair, we'd use Fleecy or Downy whenever we had it. It was really nice but it hurt like hell if you got it in your eyes. We used Cascade or Sunlight bar soap or Castile. That was our shampoo too.

The basement stairs leading to the shower are made of iron. They look like those grates you see on the sidewalks with the solid iron footprints. These stairs are heavy duty and quite steep. My dad made them steep because he refused to let them curve. He wanted them to run straight up and down. As a result, they are brutal. I've got so many dents in my shins to prove it. They're deep too. Most stair steps are a standard height. These are double that. Many times hurrying to get my clothes out of the dryer, I'd skin my shins running up and down those goddamn stairs.

Sunday dinners have been a regular part of our lives ever since I can remember. Even as grown-ups living elsewhere, we always make sure to arrive at our parents' house for our dad's Sunday dinner no matter what, no matter who you're fighting with. It's an unwritten law. You must attend Sunday dinners.

By the time everyone got married the dinners had degenerated into hostile get-togethers. Everyone was always at each other's throats. If you have ever witnessed what happens with chickens when one gets injured, you'll have a good idea of what happens at our Sunday dinners. If a chicken has a cut or injury, the other chickens peck at that injury, one by one, until it becomes a huge wound and the injured chicken bleeds to death.

If I was the one getting picked on at Sunday dinner, it might begin with Davey sniping. "Di 'ad a hard day, she broke a nail unwrapping 'er clothes from 'er shoppin' spree." This would bring gales of laugher at my expense.

"Whatever Baby wants, Baby gets," my sister Georgia would chime in. Alison would be busy showing off by listing all the latest books she'd read. "And just what have you read lately Diana, besides People Magazine that is?"

On the rare occasion Owen's wife Martha happened by, she would contradict everything anyone said. I remember remarking how pretty I thought Christie Brinkley was. Martha shook her head and rolled her eyes, "Ugh, that woman is as homely as a mud fence."

Week after week we would get into the same altercations. Smith would load up dishes for his kids, giving them more than they could possibly eat so there would not be enough left for the rest of us. Then he would force-feed his kids at the table while everyone tried to look the other way.

Bruce would talk non-stop about trying to get Stampede Wrestling off the ground again. After Dean and my nephew Matt died, my mom started drinking more and more at these family get-togethers. She would sometimes rise to her feet, fist raised and rail at the ceiling, "Dean and Matt we miss you!"

Martha and the kids didn't join us too often, but when they did, if things got the least bit chaotic they were gone. As soon as it started to get crazy, Owen would just get up and leave, "Yeah well, I've got to get going." Maybe he figured he went through enough fighting when he was growing up so he wasn't going to go through it anymore.

The rest of us would jump all over him. "What's the matter, Owen? Are you losing your connection with the family? Why? Because of Martha?"

My mom would always act surprised. "Dahling where are you going?" She would be sad to see him leaving, but she wouldn't have spent any time with him. Meanwhile, my dad would engage him in a conversation the minute he stood up to leave.

"Have you had any luck talking to Vince about taking Jim back? I would like to talk to him about getting Jim working for him again." And Owen would nod, "Yeah, okay."

Despite all this, my dad is still proud of his Sunday dinners. Saturdays are his Sunday dinner shopping days. He goes to Safeway and shops the aisles and leans over the shopping cart carefully inspecting each item. He buys enough food for 40 people, cooks it, serves it and cleans it up every week.

As a kid, I'd love going to Safeway with my dad. He'd usually buy me Sesame Snaps or if I were especially lucky I'd get to go to the Old Smoothie and buy a big ice cream. Dairy Queen was also a rare treat. We'd get big vanilla chocolate-dipped cones. This was reserved for only a few times a year, after church. There was no rhyme or reason to our church-going. We'd go to St. Mary's Cathedral, the big Catholic Church downtown, but only if someone happened to suggest it.

Of course, fitness and muscle-building figured heavily in our upbringing. My dad had nickel weights, beautiful weights. He had "Hart" engraved in big letters on every single one of them. A lot of wrestlers who used the dungeon thought it was a novelty to steal my dad's weights as souvenirs. Thus his collection has diminished quite a bit.

My dad even built his own equipment. His pulley cables were hooked up on two walls across from each other with thick ropes. His neck-building machine had wrestling rope threaded through two holes in the wall, the top rope was attached to a 20-pound weight and the bottom rope was attached to a helmet made of cross straps. It looked like the shell of a football helmet. The idea is to put on the helmet and rock your head back and forth.

Dad built his own leg press. You would lie on your back, place your feet on the bottom of a board covered in weights and push your legs upward. My dad had these big wooden blocks put between the floor and the board to hold the board above ground so you could squeeze yourself into position.

One time Owen wanted to move the blocks so he would have more room to position himself. He was 12. My sister Georgia and her boyfriend Howard Zerr were downstairs watching Owen do a few reps. He loved to perform. He got the middle finger of his right hand caught under the blocks in it and just about chopped it off. It was terrible. He came upstairs crying but not sobbing and my dad took him to the hospital. Nobody made a big fuss. That wouldn't have gone over very well.

My dad's squat racks were made from PVC piping and the sides of the shelves were made of rusty cast iron soldered to the pipes. It was all very raw looking. There is a 17-by-17-foot wrestling mat in the basement, covering the floor of an entire room called the dungeon. Falling on that wrestling mat is like falling on sand. We used to wind ourselves when we didn't land just so. The bottom half of the walls in the dungeon are covered in pine wainscoting.

We played so many games in the dungeon. I remember the resounding thud the pine paneling would make when someone ran into it playing British bulldog down there. The game involved running from one end of the gym to the other trying to duck the big, heavy leather medicine ball coming your way. Someone would always get hit. It was a good lesson in learning how to fall. Ross would throw it at us to try to knock us right off of our feet as if he were bowling. So we learned to jump pretty high.

We had three of these big, heavy leather medicine balls. My favorite game with them was when we'd stand in a circle, eyes closed, and throw the medicine ball at each other. With your eyes shut you didn't know who was throwing it, but you had to be prepared to catch it because dropping it meant being expelled from the game.

Other times we'd use it like a football, throwing it back and forth. We called this game Stampede Wrestling, because those are the letters we'd call out to keep count of who made the most catches. We'd get into a big triangle and throw the ball to the person across from us. It had to be a fair throw, but if you missed it you would get S, then T and so on. Whoever got the words Stampede Wrestling spelled out first was out of the game.

We used to have contests to see who could do the most squats in a row and who could skip rope for the longest period of time without stopping. We would try to get the contestant to laugh so they'd lose control.

The board game Risk was Bret's favorite. He would goad us into killing Ross's men just to watch how mad he got. We would all kill poor Ross's men and he would blow up, kick the whole game over and run out of the room crying. I feel bad about it now. But it was typical of Bret. It was about ruling the world.

CHAPTER ELEVEN

Dean

Gradually, I found the ceiling was getting too low for cartwheels. At five-feet-eight and 110 pounds, I was a 16-year-old beanstalk who'd just got her period. I wore my hair in braids and looked like one of the girls from The Sound of Music. This growth spurt gave me stretch marks everywhere: on my calves, kneecaps, hips, seat and chest. No stretch marks on my stomach though. That happened when I was pregnant.

As a teenager, my chest hurt and I lost my edge. I gave up on all my dreams of being an athlete. I thought, "Well, what's the point?" Where would I ever go with this anyway? I was just so pathetic at times. My brother Dean recognized this and, just like in the song, To Sir With Love, he took me "from crayons to perfume."

I would lounge in the hallway with my chin in my hands, spying on my older sisters Ellie and Georgia as they applied their makeup. They really plastered it on. Heavy dark liner and bleached blonde hair. Cher was a major influence. They also had a daily exercise routine. They had a little chart on their bulletin board that demonstrated the correct technique for twists, pushups, sit-ups and squats. It was a good 10-minute workout. In most homes it was the guys who practiced isometrics, not the girls. They were way ahead of their time.

They were fashion conscious too and managed to pull themselves together quite nicely, no thanks to my mom. She never voiced an opinion on how we should dress or groom, although she was very particular about how she looked. She would simply pull us each aside and say, Take this five dollars and go out and buy yourself a wardrobe."

Naturally, you couldn't get much for five dollars, but my mom seemed to have no concept of the price of clothes. If my sisters complained that five dollars was inadequate, my mom would tell them, "Five dollars can do you very well. Maybe the two of you can put your money together and buy one outfit. Hat to shoes. Combine your five dollars to make it ten dollars, and surely it will cover makeup and bus fare and something to eat." She was completely clueless about how far money would stretch.

My dad knew. He'd slip Ellie and Georgia a little more money. And when things started getting better, my dad always gave more. There were times he'd give Ellie and Georgia $100 so they could buy crushed velvet cords in all colors: purple, gold, turquoise, blue and burgundy. They'd come home with cashmere sweaters and really nice belts. The best deals came from The Bay bargain basement or the Army and Navy store.

My brother Dean would drop by the house between trips to Hawaii and girlfriends and spend time with me. He'd show me how to put on makeup and advise me on what to wear. He was lovely to me. Dean was eight years older than I. He shared a birthday with my brother Ross. They were five years apart. They even looked alike, but you could not find two more different people. Dean was open and notorious for his ribbing. Ross is serious and secretive. He still harbors big secrets.

Dean was so handsome with his gigantic, beautiful brown eyes that were always twinkling. His hair was a luxurious curly chestnut and he had teeth as white as freshly cracked coconut. Of all my brothers, he was the gutsiest. This is what endeared him most to my father. Dean had more nerve than anybody I know. He was fairly compact, which added to his personality. Five-feet-eight, excellent legs and big hands, good for working on cars or fixing the stove. His nickname was Biz because he was always so busy. Even when he was dying he wasn't lazy.

Dean was barely out of school when he organized the very first rock concert in Calgary's McMahon football stadium. He brought Charlie Rich to Calgary. Charlie Rich was hot. He had two hit songs on the radio at the time, "Did You Happen To See The Most Beautiful Girl In The World?" and "Behind Closed Doors." He was known in the country music circle as the Silver Fox. Rich had a beautiful, rich voice and he was a good-looking man.

Dean was 18 years old. He did all the promotions himself. He designed and ordered the fliers, and recruited Owen, Alison, Ross, Ellie, Bruce, Georgia and me to put them on windshields all over Calgary. We'd go out late when the bars were full of people on a Friday or a Saturday night and run through the parking lots placing these fliers under car wipers.

Dean also ran concerts out at Clearwater Beach, which belonged to my dad. The beach was about 100 acres of beautiful foothills property on the Elbow River. I remember sitting right on the platform where the three-man Canadian band, Chilliwack, was playing. I sat right behind the drummer and listened to them sing "California Girl" and "Monkey on Your Back."

Things got more hectic out there with Dean because throwing concert after concert the city health inspectors tried to close the place down. There was broken glass in the sand and inadequate bathroom facilities. Wrestling would close down after Stampede Week and we relied on whatever income the beach brought in until the matches started up again in the fall.

Every year we had six weeks of pretty lean times. My mom and dad made money at the beach by charging five dollars a car. Families would cram as many people as they could into their cars. No charge if you walked in. It was located out by what is now called Elbow Valley Acreages, where my brother Owen was building his house and where Martha his widow lives now. I think Owen wanted to build out there because he had such good memories of the beach.

My mom and dad would do well at Dean's bookings. Dean and Bruce branched into hiring bands to play at graduation parties. They would charge admission to see the band and they would run the concession all night long. This was another thorn in the side of city health inspectors – the submarine sandwiches. I remember making hundreds of them the night before each high-school grad. They were good sandwiches too. We used real butter and mayonnaise. My mom would package each sandwich in Saran Wrap along with potato chips and a cookie. We went to so much trouble for these people and I doubt they ever appreciated it or cared. We put more money into making the sandwiches than we made.

One night Dean and Bruce accidentally booked grad parties at the beach for the same night and the two high schools got into a fight. That night, a fire burned everything to the ground. It wiped my dad out. All the buildings went up in flames because the change rooms and patio barbecues were all covered with canvas. The concession was torched. The locker rooms were gone, including the toilets. People were screaming and fleeing.

It turned out that some high-school kids, angry because their rivals were celebrating at the same location, had poured gasoline on everything – trees, buildings, even in the water – and then lit matches.

The health board refused to let my dad re-open. My mom was freaking out. She was hysterical. "We're going to go broke!" she screamed. "How are we going to survive?"

My mom was really worried about money. As it was, she only had $100 for the entire month to get by. Every night, Owen and I would hear how we were going to lose everything.

Dean was a genius and very charming. He was especially smooth with older women, much older women. They would lend him cars. He drove a fifty-thousand-dollar Jaguar for a while. People also loaned Dean money, and he used it to buy what is now Eau Claire, an exclusive part of downtown Calgary along the Bow River. He owned the Riverside Auto Body Shop there. Calgarians would park their cars on his lot and walk downtown to go to work while Dean had their cars cleaned or serviced.

He also had a landscaping company, Kleen and Green Landscaping. He'd put the biggest ad in the yellow pages and people would think, "Oh, it's the biggest ad, it must be the most professional." They'd call Dean to come out to their homes and give an estimate and no matter what the job was, Dean would say, "Yup, we can do that. Yeah, that won't be a problem."

Then he'd hire kids like me and my friend Alison Hall, who were both 14 and didn't know anything about rototilling or air raking or power raking. I could pull weeds and mow lawns, but that was about it. We had different jobs every day. "Guys," he would say, "we've got a fence to paint today." And we'd paint the fence although we had never painted a fence in our lives.

In a way, it made me a more capable person. Mind you, a lot of customers complained about the quality of the work. A week after we were there, their grass might be burned because we had applied the fertilizer improperly. Or we might have planted shade flowers in the blazing sun. We got a lot of callbacks.

Sandy Scott was a Stampede Wrestling heel; he played a Scottish referee who always cheated. His gimmick was to play a corrupt referee who has been paid off by another heel named John Foley. During the day Sandy worked as a receptionist at Riverside Auto Park. He was very pleasant. It was funny because he was so polite on the phone and then on Friday nights you'd see him grabbing my brother Bruce by the hair, tossing him around and disqualifying him and fining him a thousand dollars for not playing by the rules.

Then Monday morning he'd be back on the phones, "Hello, Riverside Auto Body or Kleen and Green, how may I help you?" You know, nice and polite. Dean would send Sandy Scott out to take care of our irate customers. Sandy would pour on his Scottish charm and manage to calm down the unhappy housewives. We were honorable and always went back to correct our mistakes.

Dean was not only enterprising but he was also a heartthrob. He dated a lot of girls who were the cream of the crop at his high school. On the other end of the spectrum were my sisters Georgia and Ellie. They were being picked on and bullied at the junior high school, Vincent Massey. Ellie was in grade nine, Georgia in grade eight and Bret was in grade seven. Georgia had cheap, big black-framed glasses that were terribly unattractive. Later she turned heads, but back then she and Ellie were on the heavy side.

Ellie's best friend at Vincent Massey, Gwen Cooper, had no arms. She was a Thalidomide baby. Ellie was always helping her out. The kids at school would tease Gwen and call her "the vegetable." Gwen had funny-colored skin and she wrote everything with her toes, which made matters worse for her. But she was no Simon Birch. She used to boss Ellie around and treat her like dirt. "Get this for me. Get that for me."

Ellie and Georgia got no fair treatment at Massey. For Bret, it was even tougher. Some days it would be 30 below and he would only have shorts to wear to school because that was the best thing my dad could get at the Army surplus store or Salvation Army. This really made him stand out.

The only bras Ellie and Georgia owned were the black ones that they got from one of my mom's friends Isabelle Grayston, who used to be Ralph Klein's secretary. At that time Ralph was the mayor of Calgary. Now he is the Premier of Alberta.

Isabelle was very nice to all of us. She and her mother Kitty made their own clothes and gave them to us new or as hand-me-downs. Ellie's first bra was this great big – well big for her because Ellie was just young – black bra. On top of which, she wore dresses with darts.

Their teachers were aware of how badly they were treated by some of the other students, but did nothing. Some of the teachers at Vincent Massey never lifted a finger to stop it. They looked the other way when kids were tried to jam Georgia into her locker or pull her glasses off her face and break them. And they pretended not to notice when kids beat Ellie up.

One day Ellie and Georgia were standing in the schoolyard after school when they were attacked by some of these rotten kids. My brothers Dean and Wayne from Ernest Manning Senior High were driving by at the time. The boys brought the car to a screeching halt. Then Dean and Wayne got out and cleaned house. They beat the hell out of all these kids. The next day, Georgia and Ellie were called into the office and warned that their family had better not darken the schoolyard again.

The only good thing that came out of that incident was that Pat Seigers, a popular girl who wasn't a part of the teasing, took one look at Dean and fell hopelessly in love. She was in Georgia's grade and she was pretty and full of confidence. She came from a nice little home in Westgate with little lunches and normal walks home from school. Nobody ever picked on her. The next day she wanted to be friends with Ellie and Georgia and eventually did date Dean.

Maybe if she had married Dean like they had planned, Dean would be alive today because she would have taken care of him. But Dean left her for another girl, Sue Berger, who was popular but heavily into drugs. Dean got her off drugs and took her under his wing and promoted her like she was a movie star. She was the very first Calgary Sun Sunshine Girl of the Year (the tabloid's most popular page-three pin up girl.) Dean always dated the most popular foxes.

In 1977, Dean was downtown waiting for his ride and got hit by a transit bus. The bus hit him in the back from behind. There was always speculation that it was the bus accident that caused Dean to die of kidney failure. Dean got a pitiful settlement from the City of Calgary for the bus accident. Ironically, Ed Pipella, the lawyer who represented Dean, also happens to be the lawyer Martha hired to sue Vince McMahon and the WWF in the wrongful death suit over Owen.

CHAPTER TWELVE

Dean & Hawaii

Dean decided to move to Hawaii in the late '70s. He was fascinated with the TV show Hawaii Five-0 and slightly resembled the show's star, Jack Lord. Once there, he recruited these big Samoans to come up to Calgary and train to wrestle. He would put them on our Stampede Wrestling TV show and then put our show on the Hawaiian TV stations so that the Samoans would gain celebrity status in Hawaii. It was an excellent idea. In fact, Vince McMahon does that now. He'll run tours in England, Germany, Singapore, India, the Middle East, South Africa, Japan and Hong Kong, capitalizing on wrestlers in his lineup with local appeal.

Dean knew he would be a king over there because there were a lot of Samoans who would be treated like royalty if they were seen on TV, especially since the show was coming from another part of the world.

Many young Samoans were involved in marijuana dealing. Their parents would come to Dean and say, "We want our son to focus on something else." They trusted Dean. They treated him like one of their own, like he was a fellow Hawaiian. He went very far on his looks and personality because initially he didn't have much money.

One of the first guys Dean brought to Calgary was part of a syndicate and his name was Sui. He was a big, hard working, honest guy. But he bought and sold marijuana for a living. Dean brought him to Calgary in the wintertime and the freezing Hawaiian thought he'd moved to the tundra.

When he returned to Hawaii, he actually saved Dean's life. Dean was body surfing on the water and got caught in a vertical whirlpool. Sui grabbed him with one hand and pulled him out. He was that strong. Sui was the first wrestler that Dean used as a vehicle to show what he could do for other Samoans and Hawaiians.

My parents were close with a Hawaiian couple named, Neff and Ola Maiava. When my mom was pregnant with me, Ola was expecting too. My mom said Ola made her own maternity clothes—crisp, cotton gingham dresses – and Ola generously shared them with her. When Ola and Neff's son was born, my parents were honored as his godparents and when I was born, Ola and Neff became mine.

Dean was working closely with Neff's relatives, Peter and Leah Maiava, who happened to be the grandparents of Dwayne Johnson, an ex-college football player turned wrestler. Most people know him better as Rocky Maiava or The Rock. In Dwayne's book, 'The Rock Says,' he dedicates a whole chapter to Owen and talks about how Dean set up the ring and venues for his grandparents and sometimes refereed for them. Dwayne also writes about how accessible and friendly Dean was.

Peter Maiava had tribal tattoos appropriate for a high chief. Only the highest-ranked warriors could wear the green tattoos up their legs as he did. His wife, Leah, was a very tough Hawaiian. She was almost as big as Peter and they would often have words. She wouldn't back down from him and he wouldn't back down from her, but they had an obvious love for each other and made for a quite an unusual couple. They were almost mirror images of each other. They ran their wrestling at the Blaze Dale Arena in Honolulu.

My very first trip to Hawaii was in 1980 during spring break. I had been working in the jewelry department at Woolco, diligently saving my money. Owen went with me. I was 16 and he was only 14 when we met up with our brothers Bruce, Keith and Dean. Our brothers were wrestling and because they were foreigners, they were considered the villains. The local Samoans were the heroes, of course.

In one particular match the boys were wrestling Peter Maiava. When Keith and Bruce entered the ring with their black cowboy hats, the fans went wild. They played up their roles by cheating and acting bad. There was a huge Samoan guy in the crowd named Fast Eddie, a gangster. He picked up a bottle and went to clobber Keith on the back of the head with it. Although he was just a kid, Owen didn't hesitate. He grabbed Fast Eddie with a forearm around the neck to stop him.

Fast Eddie turned around in a fury and nailed Owen right in the eye with his brass knuckles. Owen got stitches all around his eye. My dad had been good to a lot of the Hawaiian gangsters' kids.

Many of them had come up to Calgary to learn to fight and when they found out what Fast Eddie had done to Owen, well, nobody ever heard from Fast Eddie again.

I remember Dwayne Johnson's grandparents lived in a big hotel apartment building called the Chateau Blu and Dean lived there too. He became really good friends with the owner, Tommy Wong. There were a lot of unusual happenings there. It was there I met Hans Schroeder, this huge Viking wrestler.

Hans was a big German with unsuccessfully bleached hair. It was yellowy-orange and crispy in texture. He had a big nose, large, watery, bulging blue eyes and dry lips. He looked hard, as though he lived a life of partying and drugs. I don't know how tough he really was, but because of what he later did to his wife, I know he was a big bully.

I never gave him much thought. But back then, I just thought he was a big wrestler and he was marrying this girl named Jane. Jane was your typical biker girl, quite raunchy. Bleached blonde hair, a lot of it, about shoulder length. Big pores in the skin from drinking a lot, black eyeliner, overly suntanned skin, kind of chubby, but full breasted. She must have figured she looked pretty good, because she didn't hesitate to prance around in a bikini.

There was also a little magician living at the Chateau Blu who made his living doing small shows at the hotels. He'd do tricks with a ball or a deck of cards or a coin for Owen and me. He was a nice guy.

The night Hans and Jane got married, the magician came down to Dean's crowded room on the 17th floor where we were all staying. He said, "I know a trick, a magic trick, and it will show if there is true love between two people." It was just a silly little trick, like swearing by your horoscope in the paper. But that was the kind of logic that Hans Schroeder used.

The magician held this pendulum watch on a long gold chain, over Jane's stomach. Then he instructed Hans to hold his hands over her belly. If the watch swung north/south it meant she loved him and they would be happy forever. But if it swung east/west it meant the marriage was doomed and she didn't love him. Well, the watch moved east/west and Hans just went berserk. He grabbed the magician by the collar and dragged him out over the balcony and dangled him by his feet. Jane was crying and begging Hans to put the poor guy down. She was from the American Deep South and had a thick accent.

"Hans, honey, pull 'em up. Y'all are gonna drop him."

I saw Dean take his glasses off, which always meant there was going to be a fight. Meanwhile Hans was demanding to know if this was just a trick or if it was real. The magician knew that if he admitted it was a trick Hans would kill him. If he said it was real Hans would kill Jane. So he tried to convince Hans to let him try the trick again. But Hans would have none of it. Finally, Dean persuaded Hans to bring the magician up and we all left, except my brother Keith's future wife, Lesley, who got so scared she hid in the bedroom closet.

The closet had one of those slatted doors so she could see what was going on and she sat in there for about five hours watching Hans and Jane beat the hell out of each other. It was mostly Hans beating the hell out of Jane. He threw her hard into the pullout bed and smashed her face into the steel frame. Her nose was squashed flat as if he had whacked it with a small ax. She wound up with a permanent divot on the bridge of her nose, about half an inch thick. The next day, her eyes were black and blue and bloodshot and there were lumps all over her face. Her toes were broken while trying to defend herself and as a result she couldn't even walk.

When I saw Jane by the pool the next morning, I felt bad for her. And I didn't understand. I thought, "Oh, maybe she's just a rough biker type who likes fighting." But now I realize she didn't deserve that at all, nobody deserves that. Poor Jane, in an attempt to be hopeful, turned to me. "Well, my momma always told me that the best marriages are the ones that start out fightin', so Hans and I should be married forever now."

Another thing Hans did which really bothered me was to stick his whole head in Tommy Wong's fish tank and snap fish in his mouth, then swallow them. Or he would catch them with his hands and squeeze them until their eyes popped out.

I don't know what it was that caused Dean's kidney failure, but one time he was almost beaten to death in Hawaii by mobsters. Ronnie Ching spent time in jail for murder and drugs and while he was there, he stored a lot of his things including rubber bullets at an apartment in the Chateau Blu. It was all on a hidden floor that the elevator slid past unless you had a key. When I went to visit Dean a second time, he got me to help move these boxes for Ronnie. We had no idea what was in them but our fingerprints got all over them.

The Honolulu city prosecutor Charles Marsland felt his son had been murdered by Ronnie in 1975, but couldn't prove it. He was out to get Ronnie. It was 1981 and the chief of police called a wrestler named King Curtis Ikea, who had played college football with him. He told King Curtis, "Get hold of Dean's father and tell him to get his son off the island because I'm taking no prisoners."

The police found the boxes we'd moved and they traced the fingerprints back to Dean and brought him in for questioning. Ronnie Ching was convinced the police coerced Dean into giving them information on him. In his mind's eye he was sure the police had threatened Dean, "Dean, if you don't give us something on Ronnie Ching, we'll hold you responsible because your prints are on these boxes." Nothing like that happened, but it was Ronnie's perception. It looked even fishier because on King Curtis Ikea's advice, Dean suddenly left town. In March 1981, Ronnie was indicted on 11 counts. The police said those boxes contained 11 handguns, a silencer, a shotgun and a third of a pound of military C4 plastic explosive.

Dean waited until things cooled off, then returned to Hawaii. Ronnie got wind of this and he and his people found Dean and beat him until he was almost dead.

CHAPTER THIRTEEN

Shaved Ice

Not long after that, Dean came home for good. He was so sick. His kidneys were shutting down. Dean used to open up my dad's big oven (it was big enough to cook 20 chickens,) turn the heat up to 500 degrees and just sit in front of it chewing shaved ice.

He was freezing and thirsty, but he couldn't drink anything, even water, because his kidneys couldn't flush it out. So he'd eat the shaved ice. Then he'd get so cold from eating the shaved ice. And he was so thin. He'd sit in front of that oven with his heels tucked right underneath his seat, right up underneath him. He'd just sit there eating shaved ice.

He must have wondered, though he never talked about it, why none of us ever gave him a kidney. There were 13 potential donors including my parents, not even counting the nieces and nephews or his own kids. None of us was even tested. I still can't explain why nobody gave Dean the kidney he needed. There was a lot of talk about it, but no action. There was no deadline. The doctors never called anybody. We were so caught up in our own worlds we didn't recognize that Dean had a limited amount of time.

One day, as he was readying for a shower in the boys' bathroom on the second floor of the house, his heart just gave out. Alison's daughter Brooke popped her head in to use the toilet and saw him lying naked on the floor. She ran down the stairs crying, "Dean's dead!"

Georgia and my dad hurried upstairs and pulled Dean into the adjoining office, trying to shake him awake and get him dressed at the same time. Alison called 911.

I was at Bret's house. I had gone over there trying to bury the hatchet with his wife Julie. She hadn't accepted my calls for a year because she thought I told people Bret only married her because she was pregnant with their first child, Jade. She had been pregnant at the time, but I believe they would have gotten married anyway.

It was a Tuesday morning. The phone rang. Julie answered and after listening for a moment, she got a grave look on her face. She hung up and told me to call home. Alison answered and gave me the bad news. Dean was dead. He was pronounced dead en route to the hospital. (In Calgary, when the paramedics arrive they work on you until you are loaded into the ambulance, even if you've been dead a while, because if they pronounce you dead at home they have to leave the body there until the medical examiner arrives.)

I was in disbelief and in denial. How could this be? I had just seen him two days before.

"How are you doing, Dean?" I had asked.

"Barely functioning," he had answered. But I hadn't taken him seriously. I thought it was just his dry sense of humor.

Then he died and we were all in shock.

Owen was wrestling in Germany when Dean died. I got the message to him through Jockam Herrmann. He was a German immigrant who came to Calgary and became a referee for my dad. Jockam had worked for the police force in Hamburg. He was with the vice squad there and moved to Canada when the work became so dangerous he was afraid he would be killed. He brought his wife and son Dennis, who now wrestles, over to Calgary. My dad sponsored them. They bought a farm out in High River, a town 30 minutes south of Calgary.

Owen and his new wife Martha were touring around Europe and Martha's mother was staying at their house on Siricco Drive in Calgary, taking care of their cat and watering the plants and stuff.

Jockam got hold of Owen and told him to call home. I gave Owen the sad news. He was calling from a pay phone and I could hear him adding change every few minutes. He was crying and crying and repeating, "No, No, No." It must have been just awful for him to be so far away. Then we got cut off and he had to call back again because he ran out of change. He just didn't know what to do.

Martha must have convinced him to stay in Germany, as he did not come home for the funeral. Instead, Martha's mother and sister came and brought a card and read it at the funeral. Quite frankly, Martha's sister Virginia was fine. I always thought she was pretty nice, not too complicated, not looking to have a fight with anyone, just kind of blindly loyal to her younger sister who's a bitch to her all the time. Martha's mother, Joan Patterson, read some sappy card about our sorrow, signed, "love Owen and Martha." But she pronounced Martha's name "Marta."

At the wake she began throwing back the liquor, one glass of red wine after another after another, and she was delivering them just as fast to my mom. I got really uncomfortable with this and so did my sister Alison.

We were thinking, "What the hell is she doing? We don't want our mom bombed." I went to say something, but Bret moved between me and my mom and said, "Don't say anything. It's not the place, it's not the time."

"Well, Bret," I said, "Mom has got diabetes and it's not good for her to be getting drunk and, you know, we might need her too. She is our mother, and Dad might need her. He just lost his son. Dad doesn't go get bombed."

I was so upset about it. I never could really understand addictions. But more than anything, I was really pissed off with Martha's mom for encouraging my mom to get so drunk.

We went out across the highway to the acreage that my dad owns, across from our house. It's this beautiful parcel of land on the ridge in Edworthy Park where we used to play when we were little. We thought it would be symbolic to have Dean's ashes thrown there on this cool November evening. It turned out that throwing ashes was like throwing that fine sand you see in ashtrays. It was the first and only time I've ever grabbed hold of ashes. When we threw them they sort of swirled around in the air in a mystical way.

Smith read a very heart-wrenching speech about Dean, saying goodbye to our most beautiful brother. Ross' eulogy was more upbeat, chronicling the funny parts of Dean's life. It even brought us to the point where we were laughing and cracking up about Dean's pranks and his love of horseback riding and mechanics.

Then Wayne sang "Hallelujah."

Everyone but Bruce's wife Andrea joined hands and made a circle. Wayne was quite religious and still reads the Bible faithfully. He's a good person and he has a good heart. He just never really had the relationship with my dad that he had with my mom.

My dad could never really tolerate that Wayne smoked and wore his hair long. My dad attributed this to peer pressure and that is something he cannot tolerate.

Wayne and my dad had a terrible row when Wayne was in high school. I think it affected their relationship forever. Wayne wanted to run for president of the school. Elections were always held before the school year was over so that when the new year started in the fall, they had their president already in office.

But Wayne was a rebel; the teachers really disliked him and his attitude. One teacher lowered Wayne's math mark so he wouldn't have the 65% average needed to run. Wayne's disqualification caused such a protest around the school that the students decided to have a sit-in. The school called my dad and said, "Your son is causing problems," and would you please come down and get him.

While my dad was talking to the principal on the phone, he caught the television news out of the corner of his eye and saw Wayne in the back of a green half ton shouting through a megaphone. He had long hair and love beads and a cigarette dangling out of the corner of his mouth. Enraged, my dad stormed down to the school. He grabbed Wayne in front of his peers and told him to get the hell home and straighten out.

Wayne figured he had been embarrassed for life by his own father and I think that incident poked a hole in his love for my dad. I see a lot of similarities between Wayne and my other brothers. It's just that Wayne went out a little farther than the rest of us. He was a little more daring and tried a lot more things than any of us were willing to do.

So we threw the ashes. Dean's old girlfriend Pat Seigers was there, heartbroken. I always thought somehow that she and Dean would get back together and she'd marry him and she would become one of the Harts. A sister to the Hart girls. She had been Ellie's best friend, but they hadn't seen each other in a couple of years. She was so well liked by our whole family it's a shame they didn't marry.

Keith said Lesley was never the same after the Hans beating Jane incident, because she sat there and watched the whole thing and heard the screaming and the crying and the shouting and the accusations. She was traumatized and had nightmares for years. However Keith and Lesley did eventually get married.

Keith claims that that incident caused a lot of turmoil in their marriage and eventually led to their divorce. She never got over it. She could not accept wrestlers after that and Keith being from a wrestling family and loving it didn't help.

Keith and Lesley had some luck. They won $100,000 in the Western Express Lottery on New Year's Eve a few years after they married. A lot of family members resented them for that. They were jealous. In 1994, when Keith ran for provincial politics, he put quite a bit of that money into his campaign and that became another point of friction between Lesley and him.

She was in there pretty strong for the beginning of the campaign when it looked like he might have a chance. I think if he had won maybe she would have stayed with him as a politician's wife, not a wrestler's wife anymore. But by the time he lost the election, Keith said she felt that politicians and wrestlers were cut from the same cloth. They were all dishonest and she had no regard for any of them.

Keith's job as a firefighter was noble enough, but he wouldn't quit wrestling. According to Keith she became agoraphobic and would clean the house for days refusing to take off her rubber gloves or touch anything. But that's not what I saw. Lesley looks a little like Pamela Anderson before all the surgery. She entered university to become a geologist but ended up with a business degree. She's always behaved lovingly toward me and never caused any trouble in the family. Because of her quiet demeanor I think she was overlooked by all of us.

She filed for divorce in 1995 and Keith says she got the house, $2,500 a month alimony, plus $1,800 for child support and custody of 13-year-old Stewart, 7-year-old Conor and 4-year old Brock. She and Keith are still wrangling over child support issues today so their divorce isn't final but Keith moved across the street and they remain friendly for their boys' sake.

CHAPTER FOURTEEN

Horrible Happenings

In 1978, when I was in grade ten I had my first crush and it was on The Dynamite Kid. I thought he was so much better than any boy at my school. He wrestled hurt. He wrestled with bad knees. Whether there were 15 or 1,500 people in the crowd, he wrestled his heart out every match. I had no interest in anybody my age because they didn't measure up to Dynamite.

But that all changed in 1981 when I met the Dynamite Kid's cousin Davey Boy Smith. He wasn't much older than I and seemed to have all the qualities Dynamite had. I decided he was the person that I wanted to be with.

My friend Alison and I used to go over to the apartment building where the Dynamite Kid lived and eat lunch in the stairway. We could smell cigarette smoke coming from his apartment and I was sort of horrified. I really did live a sheltered life. I could not believe that the phenomenal athlete that he was, could be a chain-smoker. I grew up detesting cigarette smoking, as did everyone in our family except my brother Wayne.

Dynamite, or Tom as we called him, turned out to be a sadistic, masochistic bastard. He started using steroids big time because he was always trying to stay big and his skin eventually became in-fested with boils. One time as I watched, he sliced boils right off his arms with a razor. He couldn't be bothered squeezing them and he didn't want to look at them.

Tom's dad, Bill Billington and Davey's mom, Joyce Smith were brother and sister. Both Tom's parents were alcoholics. Tom's mother, Edna, was constantly beaten by her father so she married Bill to escape her family. But Bill's mother Nellie used to say her daughter-in-law jumped from the frying pan into the fire because Bill was even rougher with her. He learned to beat his wife from his father Joe. Tom and Davey's grandfather Joe Billington frequently thumped their grandmother Nellie.

Joyce and Bill had an older brother named Eric Billington who eventually became a professional boxer. Eric used to stick up for Nellie and got into several fistfights with his father while trying to protect her. He and Joe would nearly kill each other. Finally Eric moved all the way from England to Edmonton just to get away from it.

Joe eventually died of lung cancer. He sucked back 90 hand-rolled cigarettes every day, one after another after another.

The family tried to make some money in a lawsuit by saying he died because he fell down the stairs getting some money for one of his grandchildren to go to the ice cream truck outside. They claimed the fall caused cancer in his hip. But it was soon uncovered that he had been a chain smoker since he was ten years old. In addition, he worked in a coal mine and spent the rest of his time in a pub.

It's no wonder that Tom, the spawn of this severely dysfunctional family eventually became such an evil man. When his ex-wife Michelle told me about the following incident involving his best friend's daughter, I was disgusted, offended and scared.

After Tom married Michelle, the sister of Bret's wife Julie, they hung out with John Foley, a wrestler who used to work for my dad. John was a Liverpudlian. Fans would jeer at him and shout that he must be from "Cesspool, England." When John finished wrestling he became a manager. He was always a "heel," a tough guy.

John had thick red hair, a broken nose, cauliflower ears and watery blue eyes. Tom considered John his best friend. Their kinship began as a result of being the only two British blokes in the middle of all these Canadians. My brother Bruce changed John's name to John Rex, but when the television show Dallas became such a hit, Tom suggested he shorten it to JR and he did.

To become more detestable in the ring, JR wore an army helmet, dyed his moustache black and shaped it like Hitler's. Part of JR's gimmick was to ask, "Would you like to come to a party? Ha! You're not invited anyway!"

When they got into the suds, John used to sing his favorite song, "My Sonny Boy," to Tom. Tom was so fond of John he began insisting people call him Sonny.

JR Foley was always first in line for his paycheck Friday mornings at our house. He would wait patiently for hours on one of my mom's Chippendale dining chairs as Mom and Dad finished up the payroll. One morning after JR had waited for what seemed an eternity, I watched my brother Owen emerge from the kitchen bearing a crystal bowl full of pebble shaped cat treats called Sea Nips. "Ellie made 'em," he said, chewing vigorously on a concealed carrot.

JR grabbed a handful. "Don't mind if I do."

Before moving to Canada, John had lost a son in a car accident and used that as an excuse to drink. His second marriage was to a sweet little lady named Vera Lynn who still resides in Calgary. She was an accountant for Woolworth's and, because she was honest and good with numbers, she used to do the income tax returns for a lot of wrestlers. But John drank away everything they had.

John and Vera Lynn had a daughter Michelle who was in a car accident when she was about 20. When this happened, John thought his prayers were answered. Certainly a big insurance settlement would be in the cards. But she wasn't as seriously injured as he had hoped. He dragged her over to Tom's begging for his assistance.

"Tommy, I need yer 'elp." He was drunk and sobbing. "I need yer 'elp," he blubbered. "My Michelle was in a car accident and we thought we was gonna get some money from the car accident for 'er injuries, but they says that the x-rays don't show anythin'. They says there's nothing wrong with 'er."

So John Foley asked Tom to break his daughter's legs, and Tom did. With poor Michelle's permission, they trussed her up to the bed just like Kathy Bates did to James Caan in the Stephen King movie, "Misery." They gagged her with a towel, so she'd have something to bite on. Then Tom whacked at her kneecaps with a mallet. John was crying and Tom's wife Michelle was crying, and John's daughter Michelle Foley was crying and Tom broke her legs right at the kneecaps. The insurance company awarded her twenty thousand dollars, but she could never walk right after that. I hear she is quite heavy now and her knees are turned in almost like those Barbie dolls with the bendable knees. John Foley ended up dying of cancer. This story came out after Tom's wife Michelle Billington was rid of Tom. She was too afraid to go to the police at the time. Tom used to beat her up. He used to click a gun in her ear and whisper, "It's gonna be loaded one of these times."

Michelle Billington and her sister Julie have had to reinvent themselves. They are the products of a really horrible childhood. They lived in foster homes because the whole family was split up when their mom and dad were found unfit to parent.

Julie and Michelle Smadu were from Weyburn, Saskatchewan. A French-Canadian family raised Julie. When she grew up, she got a job working security at the wrestling matches. That's where she met Bret. They fell in love and moved into a little house in Ramsey, a run-down area behind the Stampede grounds. Michelle and Tom lived in a four-plex nearby which they shared with my brother Wayne and his girlfriend Sandra.

Michelle got very thin because she was always worried about Tom. After Davey and I were married, she would call us up in the middle of the night and say, "Tom's got a gun and I'm afraid he's gonna use it this time. Can you come over here?"

Davey and I would drive over there and wonder, "What's going to happen? Is one of us going end up dead? We've just left our kids alone. They are sound asleep 45 minutes away at our house in Springbank. Now we are on our way to save Michelle from Tom who's drunk and got a loaded gun. What are we doing here? Maybe we should call the police."

But we'd rush over there, and Tom would greet us with a smile, "Hey Dave, how are you? Nothin's wrong. Michelle's just nuts again."

When Michelle decided to leave Tom for the first time, it was due to an incident that took place just before Christmas 1985. Tom and Davey were a tag team in the WWF and Tom was getting into the coke. Who got him into the coke? Hermish Austin, along with Ben Bassarab. They were selling Tom coke, and he was getting pretty hooked on it. Combined with all the steroids he was on, he was a time bomb waiting to explode.

Michelle and Sandra, my brother Wayne's girlfriend, were best friends. Tom threw a cocaine party for them and spiked their drinks with sedatives and they were rendered unconscious. Tom then proceeded to have his fun with Michelle. A little later she began to come to and she told me she witnessed Tom raping Sandra who was still completely senseless.

Michelle waited until Christmas. She spent a lot of their money on really nice Christmas presents. She gave everyone she liked cashmere scarves and $50 earrings. Then without a word, she loaded her children in the car and drove to Regina. Michelle never told anybody except Julie why she was leaving Tom. So tongues started wagging when she left.

"What's the matter with her? He's got all that money and she has nice clothes and she came from Weyburn, which is "Nowhere,

Saskatchewan.' The poor guy, he's one of the hardest working wrestlers you could ever meet."

Bret and Julie threw their full support behind Michelle every time she left him and gave her the nerve to finally hand Tom a one-way ticket back to England after he declared bankruptcy. She told him to get the hell out and she kept the kids. She got the house and heartache, but he left and he's never been back. Now Michelle's a teacher and she's gotten on with her life. She has remarried a younger man and is the mother of twins. I'm really happy for her. She's one example of how somebody can turn her life around.

Tom on the other hand is a bitter, broken man resigned to a life of oblivion. According to London's News Of The World, January 2, 1994, Tom blames Davey for "leaving him in the lurch when he was forced to quit the ring after breaking his back." The article goes on to say that Tom "now sleeps on the floor of a one-bedroom flat which has no carpets and is riddled with dry rot." The last I heard, Tom is in a wheelchair and is so incapacitated he urinates in a tin can that he keeps by his side.

CHAPTER FIFTEEN

Bruce and Andrea

About the time Tom and Michelle got together, my brother Bruce met his future wife Andrea, the woman who eventually left him for my husband Davey. Andrea was in the seventh grade and he was her substitute teacher. She was 14 years old. He was 37. The school kept her back a year because she so seldom attended and her marks were horrible. She used to hang around the wrestlers at the Pavilion on Friday nights. She was what they call a "ring rat. Like a groupie who hangs out at rock concerts, ring rats are low-class people who dream about sleeping with wrestlers and ultimately marrying one.

At that time, Bruce was doing quite well with the wrestling. He was one of the top stars. He was also the booker. It was like being the director, or the principal, or the navigator. He decided who was going against whom and who would win and who would lose. Bruce also developed the angles. He would plant the angle and water it. Then it would grow into a drama and that's how he built his talent. It's what Vince McMahon does so well – create talent. He has an eye for which guys fit the different roles best. Some guys can transform naturally from baby face to heel, and others don't want to or can't.

In the 1980s, Bruce had the power to make himself a star. And he did. He was making a lot of money for my dad and he put himself against very good people, like the Dynamite Kid. Dynamite made Bruce look invincible. He flew around the ring for Bruce. They had good chemistry too. Bruce made Tom look like he was the worst heel ever and Tom made Bruce look like a sympathetic hero.

Fans felt sorry for Bruce, but they always counted on him and rooted for him. He had naturally curly blonde hair. Not tight Afro curls, but big soft waves. He was always suntanned and that accentuated his deep blue eyes. So of course, the girls loved him and they hated Dynamite. It was a very good match.

Bruce was always getting cheated by the referee, Alexander (Sandy) Scott. The angle was to make it look like Sandy was being paid off by Foley's Army to purposely screw the Harts, especially Bruce. Bruce would have Dynamite covered for the pin and Sandy would go to the corner and pretend to inspect the turnbuckles or bend down to tie his shoe. He was always conveniently distracted in tag team matches when Bruce had the opponent covered. This drove the fans crazy.

I remember Bruce and Keith in a tag team against Dynamite Kid and the Cuban Assassin. Bruce had Dynamite covered and the referee turned his back on this to make sure Cuban Assassin was holding the tag team rope. If Bruce or any of the Harts tried to fight back, Sandy would order them back into their corner. Just after this, we got a bomb threat from some fan. He said he was going to kill Sandy Scott and bomb the Victoria Pavilion because he hated him so much. We tightened up our security that night.

This angle really bothered my dad because he would be watching from ringside and fans would be screaming at him to go in and help poor Bruce. My dad would get so agitated because he knew he couldn't do anything about it. His interference would mess up the end of the match even though it would be Bruce getting screwed. That set up the next week for a different kind of match against the same guy.

The wrestling formula had Bruce work every Friday night with the same guy for two months, building to a big finale. The first week was a regular match, the next week was a no-disqualification match and the next week a 60-minute time limit. Then maybe there would be a Lumberjack Match in which nobody would be allowed to escape the ring because of wrestlers guarding the ring apron and rolling the escapee back in until he was pinned. The matches would culminate in a special event like a cage match in which the wrestlers would go up against each other in a cage with a special referee.

Cage matches were rare, maybe once a year, but Stampede Wrestling's ultimate was the ladder match. We only had one every few years. There would be a sack of money or a belt hanging from the ceiling, and the wrestler had to climb the ladder to fetch it. Stampede Wrestling had the North American Heavyweight belt. It would be attached to a chain or a rope and hung down from above the ring. The objective was to clobber the other guy, then climb up the highest ladder we could find and grab the prize. The wrestlers would pulverize each other to be the first one up that ladder and when the ladders tipped, they fell into the crowd, not back into the ring. That's how high the ladders were.

One time they used a rope instead of a ladder and Keith grabbed a set of dangling keys and won a car. It was a Trans-Am like the one in Smokey And The Bandit. It was a 1978 model, brown with a gold eagle on the hood. Keith was with the fire department so he was an excellent climber.

With Vince McMahon's help, Bret was groomed to be the same person Bruce had been, where the girls were crying for him because they felt he'd been screwed. It was a page out of Bruce's book.

But in the 1970s Bruce was the heartthrob, the baby face. In England they call them a "blue eye." A heel is a "black eye" or a "brown eye." Bruce looked more like my dad, only shorter. His music was "Heartache Tonight" by the Eagles. He'd come down to the ring and get beaten and cut by five or six wrestlers and a cheating referee, then manage to rally.

Bruce was teaching school and appearing on TV every week. He was a celebrity in Calgary. The Calgary Flames had just recently been established. We didn't have a baseball team or a soccer team and wrestling was more than surviving, it was thriving. The Pavilion was packed every week and the show had great ratings.

Bruce was a hero to tens of thousands of people in Alberta, Saskatchewan, BC and Montana, and the Harts were really loved. It was a really great time. But behind the scenes, Bruce's heart was broken over his breakup with a girl named Sue Cowie. She was so pretty. She looked a little like Faith Hill, except her eyes were blue. She had flowing blonde hair and big white teeth.

Sue Cowie was the lifeguard out at my dad's beach and she loved being in the tall lifeguard chair and whistling. She'd stick her fingers in her mouth and belt out this piercing whistle followed by, "You, on the dock, quit pushing out there!"

Sue Cowie and Bruce dated for a long time. She was bubbly, good in gymnastics and smart. Bruce helped her with her essays in school because she was still in grade 12, six years younger than he. They'd go on trips to Hawaii. Bruce was crazy about her and they were very much alike. They both had hot tempers, loved to be tanned, and liked taking good care of themselves.

When Bruce and Sue eventually split up, Bruce was absolutely devastated. My mom and my sister Ellie thought he was going to end his life. They were really worried about him. My mom sent Bruce to her doctor, Dr. Otto Spika, who had delivered Bret, Alison and Ross. He didn't do cesareans and I was my mom's first cesarean, her eleventh child, followed by Owen. After she had Ross they told her, no more. She waited almost three years before she had me. Ross was born in the beginning of 1961. I was born at the end of '63 and Owen was born in May of '65.

Anyway, Bruce went to see Dr. Spika, and he was very unsympathetic. Back in the '70s, mental problems were regularly dismissed as being "all in your mind."

Dr. Spika was a German who didn't believe in any of these mental illnesses. He told Bruce, "You need a kick in the bottom. Go out and live in the forest for a month and eat only brown bread and peanut butter. That's what you need." Bruce left there feeling even worse than he had before.

It took him a long time to get over Sue Cowie.

She ended up marrying an ex-Calgary football player named Tom Forzani. Tom and his brothers own a chain of sporting goods stores, including Sport Check and Foot Locker. Tom and Sue have divorced and apparently they have two kids, one named Chelsea. Sue was crazy for that name. We had a dog named Shep, but Sue insisted on calling him Chelsea because she loved the name so much. I remember her calling him.

"Chelsea, come here. Good boy."

I know Sue has a soft spot in her heart for Bruce. She came to Owen's funeral. Bruce and Sue spent so much time with Owen. It was as if he was their little boy.

After Sue, Bruce started dating Brenda Bowie who was on the national gymnastic team. Brenda was adorable. She looked like Ashley Judd. A phenomenal gymnast, she traveled all over the world competing.

She taught Owen and me a lot about the sport: poise, balance and back handsprings. She said, "You've got to throw your weight behind you in order to get over."

Then Brenda went to Germany and Bruce said she was raped over there. When she came back he said she was never really the same. She put up a barrier.

Bruce dated some pretty noteworthy people. He dated a stunning blonde named Donna Rupert who was picked to be the face of the 80s for the Merle Norman agency. She eventually moved to Los Angeles and made several big commercials including one for Tropicana.

Bruce also dated Nancy Southern, a champion equestrian rider whose family now owns Spruce Meadows, a huge horse competition center south of Calgary. Nancy's dad Ron was a fireman who bought Atco Trailers and turned it into a huge business that provides temporary housing for oil and construction crews around the world. The family now owns a large natural gas utility company as well. Nancy now runs the corporate empire.

But Bruce never really got over Sue Cowie. So when he met Andrea, this 14-year-old ring rat, I guess he thought she might be a good distraction.

Andrea originally went to wrestling because she had a crush on Owen. She saw Owen amateur wrestling at her school. Her mother Bunny Finch used to work at a coffee shop across from a local hotel – the Palliser. She was a waitress, who was always hitting on the wrestlers. My dad didn't say anything too nasty about her, just he mentioned she was a single mom and that she was always hoping to win the affection of a wrestler. She'd come over and rub the back of their necks and fawn on them.

When Bruce met Andrea at the wrestling he put two and two together. "This girl at the wrestling matches is the girl I'm teaching at school." Pretty soon Bruce was living that like that the Police song that was so popular at the time, "Don't Stand So Close To Me." Ironically it was popular when Bruce and Andrea started to bat eyes at each other.

Andrea had the Sun In hair. You could tell by the distinctive orange color – almost pumpkin – it turned after she sprayed in her naturally dark locks. Andrea hated school, but she didn't want to get a job either – she just wanted to get married. She was really thin, built like a boy. She hadn't even developed yet. She had 32-inch hips, a totally flat chest and a kind of vacant look in her eyes. She wasn't beautiful. She had a dull face with a long neck. The only plus she had going for her was her height. She was about five feet four. Bruce was a weakling. In his quest to get over Sue Cowie, he should have had more sense, but he got involved with Andrea. He never promised her anything, but he did tell her he loved her.

The next thing anyone knew she was riding in the back of the wrestling vans, making out with Bruce instead of going to school. The wrestlers would take day trips to Edmonton, or Cochrane or Morley, somewhere close. Bruce violated my dad's ironclad rule – girls were not allowed in the vans with the wrestlers.

So here she was having sex with Bruce in the back of the maxi cab van while all the wrestlers sat stiffly staring straight ahead or out the window. None of them ever said anything because they were afraid that Bruce would fire them. One time Davey and Bret glanced back and she blasted them, "What are you looking at?"

She and Bruce would lie down in the rear of the vehicle and Andrea would giggle and groan and, lo and behold, when she was 15, she told Bruce she was pregnant.

He was shocked. "Pregnant! What the hell? I thought you were on the pill!"

"Well I guess it didn't work," she replied.

I don't believe she was taking the pill. I think it was her plan, and maybe her mother's too, to get pregnant by Stu Hart's son and then blackmail them. Bunny came to my dad and said, "If your son doesn't marry my daughter, I'll take it to the newspapers. How will it look that this 30-something-year-old substitute teacher has gotten his 15-year-old student pregnant? One of the Harts, and he won't marry her?"

Bunny was totally loopy, just nuts. She was one of the stupidest people I've ever met. But she was pretty conniving too. She saw the potential. This guy shouldn't even be looking at her daughter, let alone getting a quick feel in the hallway. Andrea would slip into the school bathroom during cigarette breaks and giggle to her friends, "He just pinched my bum."

Bunny later admitted to our family that she ordered Andrea to get into the Hart family. "I said Andy, you're not married yet. Well what are Bruce's intentions? You've been dating him a year!"

Just before Bruce found out Andrea was pregnant, he and Owen had taken a road trip down to Montana. Bruce had admitted to Owen that he had absolutely nothing in common with her, and confessed he didn't have any feelings for her and he didn't think she had any feelings for him. He also complained that she was immature. "Well," said Owen, "she just turned 15. Of course she's immature. You're twice her age." Bruce said he couldn't stand her mother or anyone in her family. He called them "stupid" and "trailer park trash" and he claimed he was embarrassed he had gotten himself involved with her. But at the same time he wasn't willing to break away from whatever the hell they were doing.

No one knew who Andrea's father was. Bunny had several different stories about him and as many explanations as to why their family had so many different last names. She was Andrea Finch sometimes and Andrea Redding other times.

"Oh my little Andy's part Swiss. Her dad was Swiss," she would sniff.

One of Bunny's stories that my sister Alison and I loved hearing was when she claimed Andrea's father died in the Korean War. That war was in the '50s, which would make Andrea closer to 30 than 15. Sometimes Bunny would say he died missing in action. Of course we couldn't figure out how she knew he was dead if he was missing in action.

By the time of the wedding, Bunny had changed jobs and was working in the deli at an All West Supermarket. If my mom accidentally bumped into her, she'd come home practically sobbing.

"That Bunny is such an ass. She's so stupid!"

Let fools rush in where angels fear to tread. That was Bunny. She had frizzy permed hair, with sparkly blue eye shadow, coral lipstick, high-heeled black vinyl boots and tight jeans. I guess she thought, "I've still got it." She was rather uncouth. When you get to a certain age, jeans that tight aren't cricket.

It's one thing having kids out of love with your lifelong partner and it's quite another to be in Bunny's situation. One night Bunny had been drinking and she was cackling, "Helen, you and I should have had our legs tied together by a two by four." My mom nearly died, "Oh My God, I can't believe Bruce is bringing this into our family."

Bruce did the right thing and married Andrea. They had a quick June wedding. Their baby Brit was born in November 1983. Andrea called her Brit because Andrea fancied she looked like Brit Ecklund.

Just after Brit was born, Bruce went on a big tour of Singapore with Keith. Andrea was 16 and while Bruce was gone she began having parties at their house in the community of Deer Run in south Calgary. She would invite guys into her bedroom.

Steve Wall, a 19 year-old English kid, used to chauffeur Davey and Bret to matches in Edmonton. He even let them use his car, which Davey ended up buying. It was a light blue Caprice Classic, Davey's first car in Calgary. Steve called me one night and said that he had been at one of Andrea's parties and he thought Bruce should know that Andrea was having sex with several people each night. He said it was horrible because the baby was in the next room.

So I called Bruce in Singapore and I told him. Bruce of course told Andrea and Andrea denied it. And that's when the feud got started between her and me. She didn't have another child for four years. When she had Bruce Jr. we all suspected he was Brian Pilman's son. Brian had come came up to Calgary to try out for the Stampeders football club, but didn't make it. The day he was leaving he ran into my brother Keith who suggested he give our training camp a whirl. Brian ended up becoming friends with Bruce and moving in with him and Andrea.

Ten days after Dean died while we were all still grieving, Andrea threw a huge birthday party for Brit and invited everyone's kids except mine. I didn't care that she didn't invite me, but why did she have to target my kids?

After the party incident I felt betrayed. How could my brothers and sisters be willing participants in something that excluded my kids? I drove up to my mom's crying.

"I don't like the way she treats me and she does it in front of you and you never say anything."

My mom replied, "Well, I'm so worried, her mother is such an ass, she might cause problems for the family."

A month later, we were having our first Christmas dinner without Dean. I was still hurt over Andrea's unkindness toward me the night of Dean's funeral. She had been standing off by herself because she never liked Dean. He was always on to her. He told me he despised her. Nevertheless I took pity on her. I touched her arm to guide her into the fold and she shook me off angrily.

At this first big holiday meal without out him, Andrea and her mother got really drunk and Bunny told me to eff off at the table. She added in a slur, "The world doesn't revolve around Diane Hart."

She couldn't even get my name right. Without missing a beat, she turned and kept yapping at Bret's wife, Julie, who was rolling her eyes with a "get-a-load-of-this-old-drunk" expression. I was steaming. After the dishes were cleared and cleaned, I cornered Andrea in the doorway and said, "You and your mother cannot talk to me like this in my dad's house on Christmas Day."

Andrea had spent a couple of days in the hospital that fall under the guise of having a miscarriage, but my mom had confided in me the real reason and it came tumbling out.

"We all know you weren't in the hospital with a miscarriage. You were having breast implants that my parents paid for. We are

sick of walking on eggshells around you people because you and
that mother of yours are blackmailing us over your affair with
Bruce. You aren't part of this family. You aren't a team player. You
didn't care about Dean or support your husband in his grief. I
know of your antics when he is out of town.

My mom had been drinking and when she heard us, she ran up
the stairs to get away from the conflict. Andrea was so ticked off
she ran home and tore up all her wedding photos and her wedding
license. Of course it had nothing to do with Bruce, but she blamed
him because I'm his sister. The next day my mom told me that
Andrea was filing for divorce because of me. My mom said she
hadn't realized Andrea was so ungrateful and how little she loved
Bruce.

"Dahling never again will I let her upset you in this house. I am
so sorry," she said.

But as Mary Poppins would say, it was a piecrust promise. Easily made, easily broken. On New Years Day, Andrea came over
with her friend to collect her birthday money and I happened to
answer the door. Testing my mother's new promise, I held the
kitchen door open for her and gave her a look.

"What are you looking at?" she sniped.

My dad turned from the kitchen sink. "I didn't think she was
looking at anything."

Andrea ignored both of us and stomped up the stairs to rat on
me. "Helen! Helen! I need to talk to you!"

A few minutes after their confab, my mom called down the stairs.
"Dahling, you can't talk to one of our guests like that!"

That was the straw that broke the camel's back. I said, "That's it.
I'm out of here." I was already stewing because Alison told me my
mom was writing cheques to Andrea. I went through my parent's
chequing account stubs even though I knew it was wrong. I found
out Andrea was getting $800 a month spending money, plus her
and Bruce's mortgage was paid. In addition, Bruce was getting
$1,000 a week for handling Stampede Wrestling. I had asked my
mom for Davey's wrestling paycheque and she said, "Well Dahling,
we just don't have enough money to give it to you." I didn't argue
because my mom was threatening to kill herself all the time. Mind
you she had threatened to do this since I was little.

It was due to our lack of funds that Davey joined up with a
criminal named Hermish Austin and our bum brother-in-law Ben
Bassarab. I know that Davey borrowed money from them to help

us pay our mortgage and in return he let them use our house as a dumping ground. Hermish would store cars and motorcycles in our yard. These vehicles were stolen from people who didn't pay up on their drug deals.

I don't know the extent of Davey's involvement with Hermish and I don't want to know. One time when I was driving along in our Bronco with my two babies Harry and Georgia strapped into car seats and we were following a group of bikers, Davey and Ben among them, I remember thinking, "What the hell am I doing? I should just turn around and get the hell out of here. I don't need to be a wannabe. I don't even fit in with these people."

CHAPTER SIXTEEN

Ben and Alison

All of us girls have married athletes associated with wrestling.

Ben Bassarab left Alison before their second daughter Brooke was even born. He didn't want Brooke. He wanted Alison to get an abortion, and Alison made a point of letting Brooke know that almost as soon as she came into the world.

"Your dad never wanted you. He wanted you to be aborted. He never took care of us. He chose to hang out with ring rats."

Ben was always a wild type. He grew up in Elbow Park, a pretty good area in southwest Calgary. His family belonged to the Glencoe Club, an exclusive golf and country club with a great facility that included pools, gyms, a bowling alley, even a figure skating rink. His parents Betty and Rusty Bassarab were well respected. Alison met Ben at a Halloween party at BJ's Gym. Alison was there as Pocahontas, decked out in braids and a fringed chamois miniskirt. I always thought Alison looked a little like Vivien Leigh, a petite Scarlett O'Hara. She resembles my mom more than any of us. Ben was intrigued and asked if he could drive her home. She had come alone so she agreed.

As she stepped out of the car, he asked her for her phone number and she said, "Look it up in the phone book. It's under Stu Hart." He reached across the seat to catch her arm. Could he have a kiss goodnight?

She slipped into the darkness calling, "If you call me, I'll give you a kiss next time."

This was 1981. At that time, BJ's was a pretty hard-core gym for people who wanted to get strong. There were a lot of steroids being used and bodybuilding champions were coming out of there. Ben was pretty strong. He was one of the few people who could bench press double his body weight. He was 200 pounds and he had over a 450-pound bench press. That's phenomenal weight. I don't know how he did it. I don't think he had dabbled in steroids until after he met the Dynamite Kid and Davey.

Anyway, he had become a pretty popular fixture at the gym. He was working in the juice bar a little bit and playing with Georgia and BJ's kids. Little Ted was the young one then. Benny wore army fatigues while he trained. The guys called him "the jungle cat."

Alison was older than Ben by a couple of years, which gave her an edge. He was flummoxed. Within two months they were very serious about each other. They were inseparable. She flew to Las Vegas to watch boxing with him.

They seemed like such a good match. My mom had schooled Alison in proper etiquette and Ben's parents had taught him social graces. Members of the Glencoe Club went to certain parties and churches. Alison fit in well. Our family always did everything together and we were respectable, but we never went anywhere. We never went to restaurants. Where would you go with 12 kids when you couldn't afford it?

Ben and Alison fell in love fast. Alison started saying, "It's love and I want to marry him." She was working in the accounting department at an upscale steak house called Pardon My Garden and waitressing when they were short staffed.

Ben was trying to get on with the fire department, but he kept failing the test where they put you in a room full of smoke and you only have so many seconds to get out. Ben couldn't make it out in the time allotted. He kept panicking.

Alison became very close to Ben's two sisters and his mom who was dying of cancer. Ben's sisters Whitney and Wendy weren't snobs, but they were really into the Glencoe Club scene. When Betty got really sick, Alison started to see things in Ben that worried her. He was drinking a lot and his friends could get him to do stupid things.

"Hey, Ben that guy looked at you and gave you the finger!" they'd tell him. If he were drunk Ben would want to go over and punch the guy out. Alison would plead with him, "Don't. Don't." It was a tug of war. Who was going to control Ben Bassarab? Was it going to be his responsible girlfriend who had only known him a little while or the Elbow park gang who he grew up with?

More often than not the gang won out. He'd end up getting in the fight and going home with Alison, so she'd have the worst of it. She'd have the mess to clean up.

"I hope they don't press charges. I hope there's not an assault charge," she would fret.

"Alison, I get into fights all the time," he'd tell her. "Quit worrying."

I remember during the winter of 1981, Ben was coming up to the house quite often and Alison was protective of him. She didn't want him getting into wrestling and didn't want him getting mixed up with anything shady. She was desperate to preserve this wonderful new love she had. She was so happy with him and he was so happy with her.

But he started hanging out with Davey because both trained at the same gym and Davey got Ben onto the steroids. Davey would say to Ben, "You've got to get into wrestling. You're a good athlete." Ben was in hockey and football and all the sports that the kids at the Glencoe Club played. He even rode in some rodeos.

In the meantime, Ben's mother passed away. She had a horrible death and Ben was really upset about it. Still, he wanted to marry Alison and they wed on May 21, 1983. Ben had a good job as a delivery driver for Bridge Brand, a food wholesaler, and they were doing okay. But through his association with Davey, he started to believe he could become a wrestler too.

Alison loved him so much she said, "Okay, I'll support you. I'll quit fighting you on this."

My brother Ross and Ben were the same age, 24, but they were opposites so they complemented each other. Ross was conservative and rigid and Ben was a clown. Ross had an excellent eye for wrestling technique. He had been obsessed with the sport since he was little and knew more facts about it than any of us. When he was in high school he had learned to edit the television show. He was reliable and dependable and never overstepped his bounds with my dad. He did as he was told.

Alison approached Ross and implored him to train Ben. Ross gladly agreed but said they needed to recruit someone for Ben to lock up with. They dug through some of my dad's potential students and found a guy name Phil Lafon, the same size and age as Ben. Phil later went on to the WWF as Dan Kroffat.

Phil and Ben adapted well. Ben had a great drop kick. He patterned his style after Dynamite. Unfortunately wrestling wasn't the only thing he did like Dynamite. He copied his lifestyle too. He became a heavy steroid user. The steroids made Ben really aggressive. He began snapping at Alison and calling her names.

One night he smashed her face into his plate of food screaming, "Learn to cook, you cow!" A little while later he shoved her through their slatted wooden closet door, and broke her nose and jaw. Alison was five-feet-four inches tall and 115 pounds. He was six inches taller and at least 100 pounds heavier. He could have killed her. My parents had no idea he was beating her. She avoided the family until her bruises faded. Her jaw never set properly because didn't seek medical help at the time and to this day as a result of the abuse, Alison has to wear a Hannibal Lechter-type mask to bed every night because she suffers terrible headaches from Temporomandibular Joint Disorder, better known as TMJ.

Dr. Spika told Alison she was pregnant and then another doctor told her she wasn't. He said she had a large ovarian cyst. She was just sick about it. She ended up having surgery. Both doctors were right. A surgeon removed the cyst – which was the size of her fist – and found out she was indeed pregnant.

Alison recovered completely from the operation, little Lindsay was born and Ben started wrestling. Things seemed to be going along well until two things happened. Ben failed to get on with the WWF and he began cheating on Alison. He claimed that everyone else was doing it, why not him?

In 1986, Ben got involved with a girl named Lisa, who was 17 years old. He got her pregnant while Alison was pregnant with their second daughter Brooke. Lisa had an abortion so Ben insisted Alison get one too. Alison refused. My dad was still giving Ben wrestling jobs tagging with Owen or Chris Benoit.

Ben left Alison and moved in with another girl named Monique. She was the same girl who had claimed Davey got her pregnant just before our wedding.

Ben went down to Montana to try out for the WWF. They were lukewarm on him and asked my dad what he thought. Should they hire him? My dad approached Ben.

"If you work it out with Alison, support her and try to reconcile, I will recommend you to Vince."

Ben refused. He said he would take the job, but he didn't want his wife and kids. So my dad didn't support Ben's application to the WWF.

Alison moved into the carriage house on my dad's property and lived there until 1998. She raised her girls there rent-free. She went to the Southern Alberta Institute of Technology and got her librarian certificate. My dad and mom took care of their utilities and food so her only expense was her phone bill. Ben was a deadbeat dad and seldom sent child support or alimony.

CHAPTER SEVENTEEN

Hermish

After Ben left Alison he hooked up with a very bad man named Hermish Austin. He was the guy who got Dynamite hooked on coke. Hermish was a Calgarian of Persian heritage. He was born in Africa. When he was a teenager he went down to the Smiling Buddha Tattoo Parlor and spent thousands of dollars having the entire map of Africa tattooed on his back along with an elephant, water buffalo, lion, rhino and tiger. He loved his mother and hated his father and brother. He said his father was abusive, which may be the reason Hermish became a psychopath. It's hard to figure out why he went wrong. He was nice looking and a good athlete.

When he was 17 he was the Alberta Heavy Weight Junior bodybuilding champ. He trained at BJ's Gym and ran the juice bar. He also worked as a bouncer at a popular nightclub called Papillon's in the early 1980s. Hermish got into taking and then selling steroids and became more and more violent. The owners of Papillon's repeatedly warned him to stop being so aggressive with the customers.

Hermish loved to do people favors so they would owe him. He claimed that his first hit was in Germany. He apparently managed to board a plane with a concealed knife and slit a guy's throat there. In Calgary, he hung around with another bodyguard named Mark Gibbons-or Gibby. Both were heavily into drugs.

The story goes that Gibby ripped some people off and Hermish was asked to take care of it. Hermish bragged that he and some other tough guys hung Gibby by the arms a few feet off the ground in a warehouse and beat him while they interrogated him about the whereabouts of the missing drugs and money. When Gibby finally told them, Hermish said, "We can't just let him go." He calmly walked over and chopped Gibby's foot off with an ax.

Hermish began working at a steel factory and claimed he used to get rid of the bodies by chopping them up and throwing them in the blast furnace. By the time Ben joined him, Hermish was buying cocaine in Central America, shipping it to the Bahamas and sending mules over to bring it back-a couple of kilos at a time. One of his mules was his girlfriend Wendy Milligan. Hermish was so jealous when it came to Wendy and other men, that he was said to have slit a guy's throat in front of her because he placed his hand on her knee.

Hermish eventually got caught and went to jail in 1994 due to Wendy. Her brother Darrin got involved with Hermish but something went wrong and Darrin disappeared. The police found his clothes and glasses in a downtown dumpster. It is said that Hermish killed him in Vancouver, welded him to a 45-gallon oil drum and dumped him in the ocean.

Wendy went to the police and told them Hermish was responsible for a lot of the disappearances of various low life drug addicts they were investigating. This included a case involving 24-year-old Greg Kungel. Court documents show that Hermish picked up Greg as a hitchhiker somewhere in Vancouver. Greg was living on the streets so Hermish brought him back to his house in Deer Run in Calgary and let him work for him. Day after day, Greg watched all this money roll in and out and one day he pocketed $15,000 and took off.

This was 1990. Darrin helped Hermish hunt this kid down and when they caught him it was awful. They cut off his ears with scissors and they beat him with a baseball bat. They took a blowtorch to his feet. Then transported him outside of Calgary where Hermish shot him in the back of the head and slit his throat while taunting him, "Tough to breathe, huh?"

All in all, Hermish is said to have killed 50 people and plenty of the people who asked him to do some of these killings still owe him favors.

Anyway this is the lovely person stupid-Davey and Ben got hooked up with. In 1989, Hermish fancied himself a cross between the Hell's Angels and the mafia, but he needed some muscle to look dangerous. So he recruited Ben and Ben recruited Davey. Davey was more of a mascot. Hermish gave Davey a brand new Harley Davidson Soft Tail. Davey rode it all through the summer of 1990 with Hermish and his gang. But they showed Davey no respect.

One time they rode out to Cochrane to try out some new guns. Some of the guys grabbed Davey's helmet and propped it up on the fence and shot it to pieces. That winter Davey got a call from

Ben in jail. Hermish was arrested and needed money for his defense. Davey was to take the bike to a retailer, Kane's Harley Davidson, for resale. You didn't fool around with these guys. Davey did what he was told.

Davey

Davey was born in Golborne, a rough neighborhood near Manchester, England. Kids there were always up to no good, breaking windows, writing on walls, kind of like Harlem in New York.

Davey's dad Sid was a natural gas line fitter. Unlike the other dads who'd spend their paychecks in the pub, Sid would head straight home after work and drink his beer there. He was a big man, six foot, one inch, 240 pounds and strict, though he never hit Davey. There was no need. Davey was inattentive at school, but otherwise he kept his nose clean.

Sid was proud of his only son's athletic ability. Davey wasn't big, but he was acrobatic and fearless. When Davey was 12, Sid approached Ted Betley. Ted ran a mobile grocery store and trained wrestlers. He had trained Davey's cousin, Tom 'Dynamite Kid' Billington.

Ted was building a new house and Sid offered to trade the pipe fitting work for a few lessons for Davey. In addition, Davey would deliver groceries for Ted. So Davey spent his days bicycling all over Manchester with huge loads of groceries hanging from the handlebars. He'd do 30 to 40 deliveries a day. Sometimes, the bags were so heavy his bike would almost bend.

By 15 years of age, Davey was ready to turn pro, even though promoters didn't usually start their people until they were 19 or 20. Thanks to diet, exercise and training, Davey had increased in size and strength dramatically. At five foot nine, he was now a good grappling weight, 145 pounds. He won his first match against a 20 year old named Bernie Wright. When Bruce scouted Tom, he also saw potential in Davey, but considered him too young. Four years later, they called him over. Davey didn't hesitate. Dynamite was his hero.

When he arrived, Bruce and Dynamite picked him up in Bruce's big Buick Riviera. Davey was so awestruck he barely noticed the look of surprise and slight envy his cousin gave him. Davey had grown to almost six feet and weighed about 180.

"Wow this is a neat car!" Davey exclaimed, patting the soft leather seats. He'd never seen a Riviera up close. As they made their way from the airport to Dynamite's house, Davey was impressed by the size of the city. Everything was so spacious compared to Manchester. Life would be grand in Calgary.

He woke up the next morning and made himself a huge breakfast of bacon and eggs. Dynamite stumbled into the kitchen, his head throbbing from a big night out. He brought a glass of orange juice to the table and plunked it down.

"Drink this," he ordered.

"Thanks!" said Davey grabbing the glass and downing it in a single gulp. A few minutes later, as he scraped the last of the egg of his plate, Davey started to feel woozy. He'd never taken a pill, not even aspirin in his life and had never been drunk, yet he could barely stand and he was slurring his words. As he stumbled over to the couch, he could hear Dynamite laughing.

The next two weeks were a nightmare for Davey. Dynamite had given him chocolate bars, which turned out to be Ex-Lax and continued spiking his food with Valium. Dynamite was jealous of his young cousin, who was bigger, stronger and more likable so he kept up the mean pranks.

Tom's favorite pastime was drugging people by putting things like laxatives in their coffee. Tom's wife, Michelle, watched all this happen. She sat by, too frightened of Tom's vicious temper to warn Davey about the poisonings. Davey would get debilitating diarrhea with piercing abdominal pain for the three days.

He finally wised up and stopped accepting any sort of food or drink from Tom, so Tom insisted Michelle give him spiked food.

"He'll take it from you," Tom would cackle. Finally, Davey couldn't take it anymore. He no longer trusted any of the food at Dynamite's house and began losing weight. He confided his problem to my brother Bret. Bret was seven years older and a bit of a big brother figure to Davey. Bret opened his door to Davey and immediately welcomed him in as a roommate. Mom and Dad instilled that quality in all of us.

When it came to romance girls, Davey was as inexperienced as he was about drugs and at 17, so was I. Dynamite warned him off Stu's daughters. He wasn't to go near us or Dad would send him packing. But I had seen Davey's photo in a Stampede Wrestling program and developed an instant crush on him. I kept the picture in my high school binder. I'd stare at it while my teachers droned on and on. I found out through the grapevine, when Davey's day off was and contrived to drop by Bret's on that day.

I had sort of made up my mind Davey was the man for me even before I met him.

Davey's manner is and always has been kind of remote, so when he answered the door he merely left it open and ambled back to his game of solitaire. I'd brought along my girlfriend Alison Hall for moral support and because I knew my dad would kill me if I saw Davey unchaperoned. I had intended to invite him to a movie with us, but he seemed so distant, I lost my nerve. I picked up Bret's phone and pretended to dial home and ask for Owen.

Davey suddenly barked. "What're doin'? Yer ruinin' my game!"

"I'm trying to get hold of my brother Owen to ask him to a movie. We have an extra ticket," I gulped.

"Oh." He shrugged.

"But," I continued, "I can't get through and it's going to start in an hour. Do you want to come along?"

Davey's eyes lit up. He loved American movies. They were so exciting. He envisioned Burt Reynolds chasing through the streets in a souped-up semi. "Sure."

We went to Excalibur, a romantic epic about King Arthur, which included stars now famous, Liam Neeson, Patrick Stewart, Gabriel Byrne and English wrestler, Pat Roach.

Partway through, Davey leaned over and yawned. "What's this supposed to be about anyway?"

We started going to movies and playing racquetball together, always carefully monitored by one of my brothers or a sister. As our relationship progressed, Dynamite became madder and madder.

"I told you to leave Stu's daughters alone!" he'd growl at Davey. Tom didn't want Davey to have a stronger foothold in the Hart family than he had.

Half a year later in October of 1981, I turned 18. My dad loaned me his 1981 red Cadillac Seville. I picked up Davey and we made our way up Scotchman's' Hill, the local make-out spot to 'watch the sunset.' We'd kissed a little in the past, but nothing too heavy.

That night we climbed into the back and made love for the first time. It was not wonderful sex because I felt a terrible sense of guilt, but I was in love. Davey opened the door for me and I slid into the front seat on a cloud of happiness and turned the key. The car wouldn't start. I'd left the lights on. The battery was dead. Davey looked at me in horror.

"Holy God, here I am with Stu's daughter, on top of Scotchman's Hill. Holy God! How are we gonna explain this?"

I put the car in neutral and he pushed me down the hill to the 7-11. My brother Wayne lived just across from it. We would say the car stalled there while we were buying Slurpees. No one would suspect a thing, I assured him. I could hear Davey grunting and groaning as he pushed. We made our way from the bottom of the hill toward the store. The Caddy weighed a ton and we were on flat land. He stopped for a breath.

"Di, I dunno if I can keep goin'!" he panted.

"I could always call my dad for a boost," I replied. Davey starting pushing with renewed vigor.

My dad had a big wrestling show with New Japan Pro Wrestling. They were the WWF of Japan. It was a big invitational tournament. Antonio Inoki, Japan's prince of wrestling, ran the promotion. Two heavyweights wrestled the main event, Bret and Seiji Sakaguichi. Davey was up first with Kobiashi. I watched with pride. Davey's match was loaded with strategic high spots, good psychology and terrific pacing. They didn't speak the same language, and they had never wrestled each other before, but they had great chemistry. It was an important career match for Davey.

Bret and Dynamite watched Davey's match from the curtain. I saw them exchange looks. Davey was becoming a contender. New Japan and Stampede Wrestling had scheduled a big meeting after the show. They were going to determine which Stampede wrestlers would be invited to Japan for a return tour. Bret and Tom intercepted Davey and me on our way to say hi to Inoki and told us to meet with everyone at the Sushi Hiro restaurant in an hour. We were pretty excited.

Davey smiled at me, "I've never 'ad sushi before, but I'll sure as hell have it tonight."

We waited at the restaurant for a couple of hours before we realized we'd been double-crossed. Meanwhile, Bret and Tom joined the meeting over at the real location, the Four Seasons Hotel. Antonio and his agents including, Seiji Sakaguichi and Tatsumi Fujianmi, Bret, Bruce, Dynamite and my dad all reviewed the talent and matches.

I told my dad what Bret and Tom had done. It wasn't fair. He said he thought Davey had a hell of a match and not to be too concerned. He made the decisions.

"Keep your nose to the ground, Di. Don't get wound up."

I was still stewing so I went down to the running machine in the dungeon to work off some anger. Bruce found me down there. He said Bret and Dynamite buried Davey at the meeting.

They told Antonio Inoki that Davey was too young, too green, too small, too stupid and didn't have enough experience to wrestle in Japan. They complained Davey had too many high spots in his match and that he tried to overshadow the main event."

This implied Davey wasn't a team player. Bruce claimed he defended Davey and had words with Bret.

"Now Bret is mad and he is here looking for you, so you'd better make yourself scarce." My dad always said Bruce was just like Bugs Bunny. He liked to stir things up then step back and enjoy the show.

I figured Bret was probably trying to find me to set me straight on the hows and whys of wrestling. I got off the machine and headed over to Ellie and Jim's for refuge.

Bret spotted me on the pavement between the two houses and bolted out of the kitchen toward me. He grabbed the collar of my tee shirt in his fist, choking me. I struggled to get free and he ripped the tee shirt right off my body. He was livid.

"What's this you telling dad that Davey deserves a shot in Japan?"

I felt so vulnerable standing there in a bra and pair of shorts, but I didn't back down. "You're jealous of Davey. You and Tom kayfabed (deceived) Davey. He deserves a chance just like you two! You're so jealous you told us to go to the wrong restaurant!"

He stood over me, his huge knuckles white with fury. "You don't know what the hell you're talking about. Davey is so stupid and unprofessional! If he knew anything about wrestling he'd know you don't have 20 high spots in the first match. How's the main event supposed to follow that?"

I maintained Davey was bigger than him or Tom and that Dad made the decisions not him.

"Shuttup or I'll pull your blonde hair out by its black roots!" he countered.

I socked him in the mouth, splitting his bottom lip. He grabbed my wrist.

Meanwhile, Jim was working out with Davey in the carriage house, enjoying a joint and a Pilsner. "Do you hear screaming, Ellie?'

"It sounds like Diana," she said as she opened the door. Seeing Bret's hand on my wrist she yelled, "Let go of her, Bret!"

"Take a number, Ellie, you're next!" came his reply.

Beer in one hand, joint in the other, Jim pushed Ellie aside. "You can't talk to my wife that way."

Davey followed Jim out the door. "Let 'er go Bret."

"This is all your fault, you stupid ass! As long as I'm in charge, you are never going to wrestle in Japan. That's a promise not a threat. Tom and I are going to run Japan. You'll be lucky to pump gas into our cars."

Ross had heard the commotion and rushed to my defense. He leg-dived Bret, forcing him to let me go. Ross and Bret were down on the gravel with Ross trying to restrain him. I ran over to Davey. My dad bolted from the kitchen, "This is the ugliest gaddamned thing I've ever seen in my life. I want you to all break it up right now!"

Everyone froze. Ross climbed off Bret who got up and pointed at Ross, "This has nothing to do with you. Why the hell are you involved?"

Ross brushed himself off. "Well Bret, I'm not about to stand by and watch my sister be harassed by her older brother."

"That's enough everyone. That gaddamn Bruce, he started all this didn't he?" My dad shook his head.

"This had nothing to do with Bruce, Dad. Bret is just jealous of Davey." I yelled.

Bruce heard his name being mentioned and ran down from the porch, "I don't know a thing about this!"

"I saw you go down to the basement and stir Diana up. You instigated this whole gaddamn mess, Bruce," my dad accused.

"Like hell I did!" Bruce retorted.

My dad scolded, "That's why I can never have you running my business Bruce. You can't be in charge. You're a gaddamn trouble-maker."

This seemed to pacify Bret. "Bruce doesn't call the shots around here. Dad does. That's why dad is putting me in charge, Bruce."

"I make the gaddamn decisions around here." My dad thundered. "I'll decide who is going to Japan!"

The fight broke up and everyone dispersed, but it remained a sore spot for years until we eventually learned to laugh about it.

My dad did recognize Davey's talent and Davey did wrestle in Japan. Davey remained loyal to my dad for nearly 20 years.

Davey proposed to me at my sister Alison's wedding to wrestler Ben Bassarab. He approached my mom first and then my dad to ask for my hand. Davey said my mom looked as if she might faint, but they gave their blessing and he asked me to step out onto the huge balcony at my parents' mansion.

Out of his pocket, he hauled a beautiful triple-diamond ring that cost him a month's salary and by the time he slipped it onto my finger, we were both crying with happiness.

CHAPTER NINETEEN

My Wedding Day

Oct. 7, 1984 was our wedding day.

It was marred by an incident that had taken place three weeks earlier. Davey had returned from a match in Edmonton on a Sunday morning and come straight over to see me at my dad's house. He came up to my bedroom and woke me up. He sat on the edge of my bed with his back to me, his shoulders heaving.

"Oh my God," I thought, "something awful has happened." I thought maybe one of his parents had died.

"What's wrong?" I asked gently rubbing his back.

"You're not going to want to marry me," he sobbed.

"Of course I will," I assured him. "What's wrong?"

He shook his head, "No, you won't. Not after what I have to tell you."

"Oh Davey, nothing could stop me. We're a team. We are going to have a wonderful life together. What is it?" I pleaded.

He continued to beat around the bush for half an hour. By that time, I was getting annoyed. I concluded he was trying to break off our engagement and didn't know how to tell me and told him so.

He began crying even harder. "No, that's not it. I'm so happy with you. You are my life. I love you more than anything. This ring rat in Edmonton says I got her pregnant."

This took a moment to digest. "Well Davey, I'm not mad at you for something you might have done a few years ago."

"No. She's about two months pregnant," he replied with his back still to me.

"Oh my God, how could she make up such a vicious lie? Is she trying to blackmail you or something?"

There was a silence.

"I've been seeing her all this time, Di. Right up until she told me about the pregnancy yesterday," he croaked. Then he turned and laid his hands on my forearms. "I don't think it's mine though. She's been with a lot of the wrestlers."

I shook his hands off me. What was he trying to do? Excuse what he had done because he might not be the father?

"You bastard! I could even understand if you were in love with another girl, but she is just some bum you and a bunch of wrestlers were taking turns with. That's despicable. My mom and dad have planned this huge wedding for us in less than a month!"

"Please, please forgive me Di. Forgive me. I'm sorry. I'm so sorry. Don't tell Stu. Don't tell Helen. Just don't say anything to anyone. Let's just move on."

"Well what about this girl? Is she going to come after you and sue you one day? How will we explain this to our future kids?"

He shook his head. "She 'as to prove it's mine first and I don't think it is. Di, it could be anybody's."

I buried my face in my hands. "Oh my God, your life is on the road. How do I know you won't do this again?"

"Because I love you. I don't wanna to be with anyone else. I want to spend the rest of my life with you. If I can't 'ave you I will kill myself. I swear to God, Di. I'll end my life."

I was 20. He was my first love and I believed him. I kept this to myself for 14 years. We had already invited 1,000 people from all over the world to our wedding. I was sick about what Davey had told me, but felt powerless to do anything. I couldn't eat or sleep for the next three weeks and lost more than 15 pounds. Everyone thought I was being a self-indulgent little princess with pre-wedding jitters. Little did they know how tormented I was.

The wedding took place on a beautiful fall Sunday afternoon. A heavy, red velvet tablecloth covered in bone-colored lace was draped over my mom's 18-foot Chippendale dining table. The table was laden with sumptuous finger foods. A harpist plucked gently in the front room, which was decked out like a ballroom. The house was filled with candles and flowers. Waitresses collected dishes and served hors d'oeuvres, while barmen worked in every corner.

I remember my mom surveying the room with her sister Diana Sr. They always had a slight rivalry, but Diana had supplied the wedding menu. There were fried chicken wings, deviled eggs, rare prime rib served with cocktail buns, kielbasa sausage, quiche lorraine, fruit and vegetables.

The menu came from a White House function. Diana's husband, Jock, worked for the Canadian embassy in Washington. My mom glanced outside at my dad tending a rotisserie filled with chickens and ducks and sighed.

"Stu is cooking more chickens. How are we supposed to eat chicken with all this finger food?"

There were 13 cats running around and two or three dogs chasing each other through the guests. My mom rubbed her forehead as she always did and pleaded with no one in particular, "Will someone please put these cats away?"

About 800 people filled the house: dignitaries, relatives, old wrestlers, and wrestling photographers from all over the world. Tom Billington was Davey's best man and a little Japanese reporter holding a video camera upside down was trailing him.

While Dynamite was chowing down on a prime rib bone and guzzling a beer he noticed this cameraman moving closer and zooming in on him. He turned angrily to him and, in a strong accent, he sniped, "That's it, yard dog. I've 'ad enough o' you. Now eff-off."

Just before the ceremony I sat on the porch railing next to my dad. He poked at the meat on the rotisserie. Twenty chickens, two ducks and one large prime rib turned gently, dripping grease. Dad, never a drinker, was holding a cup of tea. I could see he wanted to tell me something, but my dad takes his time.

"Not a bad turnout," he said.

I nodded. "Yeah and the weather looks good for Thanksgiving weekend."

There was a long silence, then I smiled at my dad. "Davey looks good in your suit, too."

My dad nodded, "That's nubby silk."

I brushed his arm. "Thanks for giving it to him, Dad."

My dad modestly shook off any gratitude. "Oh that's fine. It looks nice on him. I can't wear it anymore. I remember when I used to do 1,000 squats non-stop. I'd amateur wrestle one guy after another all day long."

We stared at the chickens slowly spinning.

Then my dad cleared his throat a little. "Di, can I just talk to you for a second here."

I looked up at him.

My dad continued to stare at the meat. "The art of submission wrestling is a lot like life. We always gotta know what the other guy's move is before you move. Then you guzzle 'em."

Guzzle is another way of saying move in for the kill. My dad was trying to tell me that as a married woman I would have to stand on my own and be strong.

Then Davey and Dynamite appeared in the doorway and the talk turned to their careers.

CHAPTER TWENTY

Bruce Allen

Shortly after we became engaged in 1983, Davey was in Tokyo to wrestle as White Tiger. He was in the dressing room getting ready when the Canadian rock singer Bryan Adams and his manager Bruce Allen strode in. Bruce had already had huge success with Heart and Loverboy and was now building a great career for Bryan. Bryan had just released "Cuts Like A Knife" and was on the verge of superstardom.

Davey, dressed as White Tiger, jumped up and demanded to know who they were. They introduced themselves and Davey took his mask off and said, "I'm sorry about that. I just didn't expect to meet you guys in Japan."

Bruce laughed and said he was a big fan of the British Bulldog. Davey explained he was only filling in as White Tiger for a wrestler who was sick. They chatted for a few minutes and hit if off. Then Davey coincidentally ended up sitting right next to Bruce Allen in first class, flying back from Tokyo to Vancouver.

Bruce told Davey, "I'd love to do promotions for Stu. He's got Gene Kiniski doing promotions in Vancouver now and the newspaper ads aren't any bigger than a postage stamp and poor Stu's losing money. If I just had a chance I wouldn't even take a salary for the first show just to prove to him how much money I could make for him."

When Davey got back to Calgary, he immediately talked to my dad. It took quite a bit of convincing because my dad's very loyal. Even though Gene was robbing him blind, he was loath to replace him. Gene was a real bitter, jealous old bastard. He had two sons, Kelly and Nick, and a wife who shot herself. I thought he was unbearable. Gene was a football player for the Edmonton Eskimos before he turned to wrestling. His mother was Julia Kiniski, a longtime Edmonton city alderman. Gene had a voice that sounded like he was chewing gravel and was a world's champion before Vince

McMahon's time. Gene was a "squeaky wheel gets the grease" kind of guy – always complaining and never endearing himself to anyone. His son Kelly was more like his mother and his son Nick played football for the CFL's BC Lions. Kelly got into pro wrestling, but he was quite bull-legged and pigeon-toed. He was much more likable than Nick. Nick used especially offensive language around the female wrestlers.

Bruce Allen ran a show for my dad in Vancouver and he produced an awesome turnout. They sold out the arena. Afterward Bruce said, "Stu, I think I proved myself to you."

Bruce had done what he promised he'd do and didn't make a penny on it.

My dad understood. He said, "Okay Bruce, you did a phenomenal job, you got 10,000 people at the show."

Gene was sick about Bruce's success. My dad had let him run the wrestling in Vancouver for years and he had been only moderately successful. My dad's relationship with him went back to the '50s when my dad coached him a bit in wrestling and helped him with junior football.

But the wrestlers were always complaining to my dad about Gene. They said he treated them like garbage and that there were no people at the shows and no advertising. It was demoralizing to drive 12 hours to Vancouver for nothing.

My dad agreed to let Bruce Allen run the shows in Vancouver and Victoria, but he cut Gene in. Gene began to undermine Bruce's efforts and so did his son Nick. Nick was an absolute beast.

Bruce's secretary and right hand Crystal Harbidge really knew his promotion and put her heart into everything. She arranged all the catering and wrangled the talent. In fact, it was she who taught us to call the wrestlers "talent." They got a kick out of that. She picked them up at the airport and booked them at better hotels and made sure their every need was looked after. Expenses came out of my dad's end of course and now that Bruce had proven himself, it was time for my dad to pay up.

Gene refused to cooperate and made it really difficult in the dressing room. Crystal arranged professionally catered food for the wrestlers: fresh fruit, cheese, buns and vegetables. It was great. They were treated like celebrities. They felt better and the shows looked better. Crystal was used to doing this for rock stars like Bryan Adams, Heart and Loverboy.

Nick Kiniski and Gene helped themselves to the food and tossed aside what they didn't want like a couple of pigs at the trough. They would make a total mess of the buffets.

Finally Crystal intervened. "This food is for the wrestlers."

Nick swore at her, putting her in tears.

"I don't have to listen to you," Nick growled. "There shouldn't be bitches allowed back here anyway."

Bruce, Bret and Davey were upset with the way Nick treated Crystal. But my dad still would not fire Gene. My mom got wind of this story and she flew out to Vancouver to fire Gene herself, but it never happened. My mom never went on the road. It just never happened. It wasn't even like, "Oh, that's unusual." She absolutely never went, but so infuriated was she by the reports about Gene and Nick, she flew out to Vancouver.

"That bastard. I'm going to fire him. He never liked your father anyway."

When she got there, my dad stopped her. Very rarely did he forbid her to do anything, but he could not bring himself or anyone representing him to tell Gene off.

Bruce Allen had a wonderful impact on Stampede Wrestling. He helped our territory a lot. He was getting wrestlers deals on airfares. He lined up Air Canada and Rainier Beer to sponsor the shows. He sent us a disc jockey from Vancouver named Dave Pratt to work as our announcer. Dave, who is now with The Sports Network, was great. He was like a new, improved version of our old commentator, Ed Whalen. Actually I thought he was better than Ed who tended to be pretty corny.

Ed was a big part of the early Stampede Wrestling shows out of Calgary. He had a distinctive nasal voice and some catchy one-liners. He'd talk about a "malfunction at the junction" and a "ringa-ding-dong-dandy." He'd sign off, "in the meantime, in between time." Nothing was too corny for Ed. But he definitely had a following. He was treated like a rock star when he did a publicity tour in the Caribbean.

Ed likes to portray himself as a big friend to our family, but in reality he's not. He never thanked my dad for making him an international celebrity. He'd carefully credit himself with the show's success while pretending to be modest. He treated my dad like a stupid wrestler, when it was my dad's promotional ability that made the whole show go.

When Bret started to get famous, Ed pushed past my dad to stand next to him. He never missed an opportunity to knock anybody he couldn't benefit from. Ed was never there for anybody in our family when they needed something, but he'd show up in a minute when the spotlight was on.

When Owen died and we were all suffering, Ed was doing columns and interviews. I was offended.

My brother Smith used to say Ed's bottom was so flat his underwear was padded. I'm not sure if this was true or just Smith's way of showing how much he disliked the man.

Wrestling was Bruce Allen's real love. He liked it better than the rock business. Bruce promoted these awesome angles and the show grew in popularity. It was seen all over the world. In Uganda, it was one of Idi Amin's favorite shows. He and the guards in his camp watched it regularly.

We found out about this one night while watching the Canadian game show Front Page Challenge. They had a prisoner of war on the show and you could see his silhouette behind a panel of journalist celebrities including Pierre Burton and Betty Kennedy. It was their job to guess who he was and what story he represented.

This fellow told them he'd watched the show every Sunday. I remember how odd this felt. On one hand, it was impressive that the leader of a country liked our show more than any other, but on the other, Idi Amin was a ruthless dictator and an abusive, syphilitic husband with 50 wives.

Vince & the WWF

During the summer of 1984 just before my wedding to Davey, my dad was secretly negotiating the sale of Stampede Wrestling to Titan Sports Inc., owned by Vince McMahon. Bret was the only one of the kids who knew about this.

My dad was 68 years old and, though he liked Bruce Allen, he didn't like the direction my brother Bruce was taking the business. He felt Bruce had a small-man complex. He behaved like Napoleon. He was sadistic with the wrestlers, particularly the bigger guys, and he disregarded my dad's suggestions. My dad would go into the dressing room before each show with specific instructions.

"I don't want to see Bruce getting raped in the corner while I'm standing at ring side looking like an asshole. I don't want to see any more nut shots and I don't want any chairs and I don't want the wrestlers fighting in the crowd. Let's have a good show tonight and not have the fans leaving pissed off at me for a change."

As soon as my dad left the room, Bruce would turn to them and say, "Fuck him. He's senile. I'm the one who calls the shots around here."

It was 1984 when my dad weighed all this out. He decided to sell the wrestling to Vince. The deal included four wrestlers, Davey, Dynamite, Bret and Jim, plus my dad's territory, all the TV rights and a non-compete clause which stipulated that my dad could do nothing wrestling except help promote Vince McMahon's shows for one year.

Vince offered him $1 million and my dad was given a $30,000 down payment. Actually, I've heard different amounts. I've heard it was $15,000, I've heard it was $25,000 and I've heard it was $30,000. No contracts were offered because Vince wasn't giving contracts then, but the four guys were put on the WWF payroll.

Vince offered Bruce a job as the western Canadian representative. He would be able to market and book shows, but not wrestle because he was too small. But where would Wayne and Ross go? Wayne was the best referee in professional wrestling. Ross ran the television show. And where would Ben go? Alison was hysterical over the whole thing. What was Ben going to do? He didn't have a job and he wasn't part of the equation.

"How come nobody sent Ben to New York?" she asked.

It was a fair question. But my dad was always loath to confront anyone in business. Maybe he thought if he insisted the others work with Vince too, the deal would fall through. Vince did say that he would be running shows in western Canada often and would use people like Wayne and Ross for them, but the whole thing turned into a fiasco.

My brother Bruce defied my dad and Vince by approaching Bruce Allen and offering to work together on a new Stampede Wrestling promotion. Then he applied for a license through Calgary's Boxing and Wrestling Commission.

My dad found out and was livid. He knew this could jeopardize his deal with Vince. He called Bruce Allen and explained that WWF now owned Stampede Wrestling and that under no circumstances should his son Bruce be working against them. Bruce Allen was a gentleman about the whole thing. He thanked my dad for the opportunity to work with him and they parted on good terms.

Davey was becoming a star. The big names in Stampede Wrestling at the time were "Rotten" Ron Starr, David Schultz and Leo Burke, but they'd stick to the mat. Davey would do all the high flying. People loved to watch him wrestle for all his acrobatic stunts. He set up his own deal so that he could wrestle in Japan. They loved him there because he really wrestled, full contact. While he was there my dad sold Stampede Wrestling to Vince and the WWF.

When Davey returned, Dad told him, "My deal with Vince was, when I sell, he gets you, Dynamite, Jim and Bret." Davey tried it out for a week, then he and Tom quit. Bret and Jim stayed. Davey said he had never seen so many prima donnas in his life. He came home disgusted.

"What a conceited bunch of assholes," he said. He claimed that except for the real stars-Hulk Hogan, Rowdy Roddy Piper, Jesse Ventura, Big John Studd and Quick Draw Rick McGraw-a lot of Vince's wrestlers spent their time bragging about what bigwigs they were. Davey didn't like going from the main event in Stampede Wrestling to the opening match in WWF.

Vince was astounded at Davey's audacity. Then Dad called Davey up because Bret was furious. Vince was having him beaten in the ring every night and paying him garbage as punishment for Davey's leaving the WWF.

But Davey could not be dissuaded. He loved wrestling in Japan, four weeks on and eight off throughout the year. He and Dynamite were treated like gods over there. The fans in Japan never dreamed the matches were predetermined. The wrestlers were admired for their strength, size and agility. They were akin to samurai.

But the fights in Japan were strenuous. At 21, Davey was beat up and sore. Dynamite had two knee surgeries behind him. Even though they were a tag team, Dynamite still treated Davey very much like the younger cousin. He negotiated all their deals and paid himself twice as much.

Then on one tour in Japan, they faced off against each other. As a finale, Dynamite was supposed to crawl back into the ring after being suplexed over the ropes and beat Davey on the count. Davey held Dynamite by the waist and flipped him above his head over the top rope. But Dynamite missed grabbing it, and fell, hitting the small of his back on the apron of the ring.

As he lay there, Davey could see two big, fist-size lumps growing in Dynamite's back. Davey went over to pick him up. Tom was supposed to pile drive Davey onto the concrete outside the ring, so Dynamite could escape, roll back into the ring and beat Davey on the ten-count. When Davey leaned over, Dynamite croaked, "My back's gone." Davey banged his knee on the ring beside Dynamite's head and pretended to fall. Dynamite rolled into the ring and won, but he had done great damage to his discs.

During that entire year, Vince McMahon tried to convince Davey and Dynamite to come back to the WWF. Dynamite's injury prompted them to accept an invitation to fly to Toronto for a meeting. My dad was pleased. He felt this was the best thing for their careers. He predicted the WWF under Vince's guidance was going to be a huge enterprise someday and he saw it as an opportunity for his family to work together again.

Bret, Jim Neidhart, Ellie and I had all been working on the boys, hoping they'd consider a new offer from Vince. I was pregnant with our son Harry and I missed Davey. Japan is a 20-hour flight from Calgary and he spent 26 weeks a year there. Our phone bills were over $1,000 a month when he was away. When he was home he was often recovering from jet lag or an injury.

Vince sent Frank Tunney, his right-hand man in Toronto, in a limo to the airport to pick the boys up, and Frank guided them into the hotel suite where Vince was talking on the phone.

Davey and Dynamite took a seat and listened for a moment, then Davey nudged his cousin. "Tom, he's talkin' to Mr. T. about working at Wrestlemania." Chicago native Lawrence Tero was a huge star in Hollywood. He had played Sylvester Stallone's nemesis, Clubber Lang, in Rocky III and he had his own successful television series, The A-Team.

Dynamite nodded. "If we can get on that same card, we'll be rich!" he whispered.

Vince hung up and negotiated a good deal that included Dynamite and Davey winning the World's tag-team belts within a year. Davey's salary doubled. He went from making US$120,000 to US$250,000 per year. Mind you he was booked to wrestle twice as much. They were also to receive 0.5% of merchandising with potential for endorsements.

But Tom blew all that. Their first booking was at Vancouver's World of Wheels car show and Tom was a no-show. He continued to miss bookings, leaving Davey with egg on his face. It didn't take long for the WWF to stop calling them for promotional appearances.

The deal with Vince seemed better, and would have been, had we known how to manage our finances. The money Davey made in Japan was all after-tax dollars. An international tax treaty let the Japanese pay taxes to the Japanese government and freed us from Canadian income taxes.

Davey's WWF paycheque was all before-tax dollars. We were paid into our personal accounts and Davey paid his expenses on the road without knowing to deduct expenses through a private company. So rather than paying 18% corporate taxes after expenses, Tom and Davey paid 48% taxes on everything. By the end of each year Davey and I were barely scraping by and Tom ended up declaring bankruptcy.

They did make it to the same card with Mr. T., Wrestmania II. Davey and Dynamite went up against the champions, "The Dream Team," consisting of Brutus Beefcake and Greg "The Hammer" Valentine, for the belt. Davey and Dynamite were assigned heavy-metal singer Ozzy Osbourne as a manager just for that show. Vince told Brutus and Greg to drop the belts to the British cousins. They deserved it. Davey and Dynamite could out-maneuver, out-wrestle and out-fly anybody.

"Nobody can lace our boots up," Davey boasted.

Davey and Dynamite kept the belts nearly a year, longer than anyone in tag-team history. But Dynamite was a big drinker. It was horrible trying to wake him up. And he'd snore so loud Davey couldn't even room with him on the road. Dynamite had stopped training and was starting to lose it. His body was beginning to sag. Davey had to work harder in and out of the ring to cover for him.

Tom's bad back plagued him. In a match against "The Magnificent" Don Muraco and Ace "Cowboy Bob" Orton in Hamilton, Tom hit into the ropes with his back. He stood and appeared to have recovered, then jumped over Don and in mid-air crumpled to the ground as if he'd been shot.

Vince had three seats taken out of Air Canada's first class compartment, so Dynamite could lie down on the way home. He was transported by ambulance to the Holy Cross Hospital in Calgary. Two days later, he had three discs removed from his back. He lost a couple of inches in height.

The problem was he and Davey were still the tag-team champions and, now that Dynamite was out of the picture, they had to lose their belts. Bret and my brother-in-law Jim Neidhart were chosen to succeed them. Vince began grooming them as "The Hart Foundation," the next tag-team sensation.

Davey arrived in New York alone. He loaned Bret his belt for publicity pictures. That way when Bret won the belt, the pictures of him and Jim wearing the belts would be ready. But Dynamite refused to lend his to Jim.

"When I drop the belt, I'll hand it over to him personally."

Bret heard about this and threw a tantrum in the dressing room. He banged chairs against the walls and screamed. "Where's the other belt? I want that other belt!"

Vince walked in and tried to calm him down. "Geez Bret, take it easy. We'll use one belt for the pictures. No big deal."

Dynamite and Davey met Bret and Jim six weeks later in Florida. Dynamite was 40 pounds lighter and could barely walk. As they made their way toward the ring, Davey had his bulldog Matilda on a leash and was walking as slowly as possible for Dynamite's sake. Then as was choreographed, Bret's manager Jimmy Hart pretended to deck Dynamite with a megaphone before Dynamite could even climb into the ring.

Dynamite went down and Davey went into the ring to face his two brothers-in-law alone. The match had to be quick since Dynamite was supposedly unconscious on the floor. Toward the end, Jimmy Hart distracted Davey while Jim Neidhart clobbered him as hard as he could with the megaphone.

In real life, Jim was a dirty brute. He really did hit Davey as hard as he could. Davey saw stars. Then Jim set Davey up for "The Avalanche," their finishing move. He put Davey in a bear hug, lifting him off his feet, while Bret hit the ropes, jumped up in the air and clothes lined him in the face. At that point, Davey let Bret pin him. It was a spectacular finish.

Dependency

Davey was getting frustrated. He was training hard and eating, but he wanted to be bigger. The problem was he was losing weight. It was 1987 and he was wrestling at a remarkable rate. Sometimes he was on the road for 65 days without a day off.

He talked to Jim Neidhart. Jim told him to visit Dr. Dennis (pseudonym) a general practitioner in Calgary. Davey entered his office without much ado and the doctor introduced himself then asked, "What do you need?"

Davey tried to sound cool, "I need steroids."

Dr. Dennis initially refused to give out prescriptions, but he was very generous with shots in his office in exchange for cash. He instructed Davey to pull down his pants and a few minutes later, Davey had his first hit of body-building drugs: 3 cc's of Deca-durbolin, the Cadillac of steroids.

The steroid also helped reduce pain and swelling in his joints. Soon after the injections started, he was bench-pressing 600 pounds-huge weight. Sometimes Dr. Dennis would hit him up with testosterone, which was good for gaining size and strength. But Davey became irritable and aggressive so the doctor gave him Percocet to take the edge off and relieve pain.

Soon Davey learned of a doctor in Hershey, Pennsylvania, John Zoharian. He worked for the athletic commission there. Dr. Zoharian would take your blood pressure, lock the door and offer up almost any drug known to man. While Davey was on the road, he would stop by and stock up: ten bottles of Deca-durbolin with syringes, 300 Halcion to sleep at night, 300 Valium and Placidyl.

Placidyl was a horse pill with 750 milligrams of tranquilizer. It looked like a vitamin e capsule except it was dark green, not gold. It was a favorite among the wrestlers. They'd put it in their mouths and wait for it to dissolve, then bite and chase it with a beer. Later, Davey told me Placidyl tasted like year-old sour milk. Davey stopped taking it because a few wrestlers died on the stuff. He couldn't bring his stash back across the border for fear Customs would spot it, so he'd leave it with wrestlers in the States to hold until his return.

Unbeknownst to me, Davey's daily regimen in 1988 included a coffee, two hits of speed, Ionamin and Fastin-which within 15 minutes made him feel he could run through a brick wall. He'd take two shots of Deca-durbolin per week and hit the gym. When he got back he'd be so wired, he'd take four Valium to settle down.

This would give him a smooth ride and get rid of that speedy feeling so he didn't have to go into the ring wired. He would wrestle at night, then go for something to eat and hit a bar with his wrestling friends. He'd get hammered, then back to his hotel room where he'd take two or three Halcion to sleep. It was bad, but it was kid stuff compared to what he was up to ten years later.

Davey's addiction wasn't the first I was exposed to. My mom is an alcoholic. She started drinking heavily when there were only four of us kids left in the house: Owen, Alison, Ross and me. I think she did fight it off as long as she could and she finally just succumbed. Alison would pour salt in my mom's liquor bottles. Ross emptied them down the sink or diluted them with water. Owen would smash them.

When Mom was drinking, my parents fought constantly. Fighting, fighting, fighting from morning 'til night. You wake up, you hear it, you go to sleep, you hear it.

I remember being with Owen up in the attic where Smith and his son Matt live now, we'd crouch under the pool table and Owen would talk about how we had to get out of there and how we couldn't stand it anymore and wonder how come dad kept buying her the goddamned liquor. Neither of us could understand why we'd get in trouble for throwing it out.

My dad rarely acknowledged that she had a problem. And when he did, he'd say, "I don't know where she's getting the gaddamned stuff."

But we knew he was buying it for her. Sometimes he wouldn't be able to wake her. He would become frantic with worry. He'd drag us into the bedroom. "See if you can wake her," he'd plead.

Owen and I would look at each other. An unspoken question passing between us. "Is she dead or is she alive?" We'd be so disappointed in our mom, drunk at two in the afternoon. We'd shake her and beg her to wake up and my dad would be saying, "Is the poor thing dead?"

She never really liked our house. In fact she hated it. We all grew up listening to her raving when she'd get really drunk about how much she hated the house and hated the life she was living. It took its toll on Owen, me, Ross and Alison.

Owen and I could not bring ourselves to invite friends over. On the rare occasion we did, we'd be very anxious. Were they going to hear the fighting that was going on all the time? Would they see my mom stumbling around drunk? It was such a private thing at the house.

In addition, there was the secret world of the wrestlers that we were warned not to expose. We were not supposed to let anyone see two enemy wrestlers that apparently hated each other on TV, sitting in the same living room sharing a coffee.

"Don't let the wrestling fan see Bulldog Bob Brown in the same room with Chris Benoit. Don't let them see Carey Brown and Jim Neidhart in the same room. Don't let anyone know that Davey and Dynamite are cousins because they're wrestling each other."

It was hard for us younger ones in the family. Bret was a bit older. He didn't really see a lot of it because he was about 17 and he was starting to get out. He was always very popular with girls. Actually, most of the Hart boys were, but Bret had the most girl-friends.

Dean had lots of girlfriends too, but I never saw Dean kissing them or anything. He was always very reserved about things like that. But I remember Bret's girlfriends were so in love with him they couldn't keep their hands off of him. They would pat him on the head or wrap their arms around his waist or hold his hand. I guess, he was irresistible.

In 1988, Vince ran a big European tour and Davey and Tom, being from Great Britain, figured prominently. The night before they were to leave, one of Vince's agents Pat Patterson was doling out tickets for the flight. He called Davey aside to give him instructions.

Tom wandered off for coffee. When Tom was on his way back he met up with another wrestler, Jacques Rougeau. Jacques and Tom had bad blood between them. A few months before Jacques and his brother Raymond or "The Quebecers," asked Curt Hennig aka "Mr. Perfect" to look after their bags while they were in the ring. They were afraid Dynamite was going to pull a rib on them.

Tom was noted for his mean practical jokes and Davey was often guilty by association. Tom would empty an entire can of shaving cream into the bag of anyone who happened to have left it open. Once, he'd handed Sam Houston-Jake "The Snake" Roberts' brother-his cowboy hat on his way out to the ring after covering the entire band with crazy glue. When Sam yanked off his Stetson, a lot of his scalp and hair came with it.

Tom also got a big kick out of substituting Preparation H for toothpaste. And no one would accept a drink from him, because it was sure to be spiked.

Davey's ribs were fairly innocent. One time he had popped a baby mouse into the Ultimate Warrior's wrestling boot. It gave the Warrior a little scare, but the mouse was unharmed.

Curt Hennig was also a notorious ribber. Knowing Tom would be blamed, he padlocked both Rougeaus' bags to the ceiling pipes in their dressing room and made out as if Tom and Davey had done it. It took more than an hour for the Rougeaus to locate bolt cutters and get their stuff back. They were really mad. Jacques complained to Pat Patterson about Tom.

A few days later, Vince asked Tom to apologize to the Rougeaus about the padlocked bags. Tom refused and was furious about being unjustly blamed. He made a beeline for Jacques and confronted him in the dressing room. When Jacques repeated the accusation, Tom sucker punched him in the jaw. Jacques' jaw shattered leaving him unable to wrestle for a month.

Vince had quite a time trying never to schedule them on the same card and they were only together on this eve of this European tour because they were all picking up their plane tickets. Jacques was carrying a roll of quarters and Tom had a coffee in each hand. Still angry over being sucker punched, Jacques took one look at Tom and hauled off and knocked his front teeth out.

Tom never rallied after that. He did the European tour and came back for the Survivor Series where he and Davey were pitted against the Rougeaus. Both the Bulldogs and The Quebecers were professional enough to leave personal issues outside the ring and put on a hell of a show.

The Survivor Series was Tom and Davey's last show together for the WWF. Tom convinced Davey to quit and both Brits went back to Stampede Wrestling, which had started up again. Vince hadn't been able to make a go of it in my dad's territory, so he gave it back to him. My dad was happy to get another crack at it and recruited and trained a new generation of wrestlers including Owen, Chris Benoit, Brian Pilman, Steve Blackman, "Strangler" Steve DiSalvo, Bill Kasmire, Hiro Hasi, Keichi Yamata aka Jushin Liger and Tom McGee.

Tom "Dynamite" Billington was on the road to self-destruction. One night in Calgary, he came down to the ring drunk out of his mind, with his teeth missing and his wrestling boots tied around his neck. He staggered up in front of the TV cameras, grabbed the microphone and demanded to see Chris Benoit,

"The time has come," he slurred, "but I don't know when." His words whistled through the empty gap in his gums. Chris arrived at the microphone totally perplexed. Tom had always been one of his heroes. Tom threw his boots around Chris' neck.

"I'm retiring and I want you to have these. You're the only one who can fill my shoes."

Chris was gracious and tried to cover up for Tom's drunkenness. He skillfully guided Tom back into the dressing room.

This came as a big shock to my dad. He had been building an angle between Tom and Davey, billing it "The Dogfight of the Decade: Bulldog versus Bulldog' and now Tom had made this surprise announcement.

My dad couldn't advertise Tom anymore, not only because he had retired, but also because he never knew when Tom would show up. Tom did take the occasional road trip and my dad let him. But Stampede Wrestling was still struggling to gain a foothold so the wrestlers did not travel in style.

Bruce never lost an opportunity to needle Tom and Davey about how low they had sunk after quitting the WWF. In late June, just before Owen's wedding, Tom confronted Bruce after hearing that he had been badmouthing him. Bruce rolled his eyes.

"I don't know a thing about it Tom." Tom broke Bruce's jaw.

On July 4th Davey, Ross, Chris Benoit and Carl Moffat were in the baby face van waiting to leave for Prince Rupert, British Columbia and then on to the Northwest Territories. All the good guys traveled together and all the bad guys traveled together. The baby face van was in good condition. The heel van was beat up.

The heels didn't respect my dad's property and they slashed the seats and peed all over the floor. It was filthy. My dad decided to go ahead with "Dogfight of the Decade." If Tom didn't' show,

Davey would wrestle Johnny Smith who was billed as Davey's brother. (In reality he was no relation.)

The heel van waited for Tom to show, but my dad finally sent them on their way. The baby face van waited another hour and a half for Tom, but finally everyone got fed up and left. It was a 15-hour journey, and they were cutting it tight. To make up for lost time Ross stepped on it.

They stopped at a gas station in Jasper, Alberta. Davey bought a chocolate ice cream cone, a Diet Coke and a muffin. Ignoring his seatbelt he jumped in on the passenger side beside Ross who was still driving. The van sped through the mountainous terrain in northern British Columbia. Davey spotted a hairpin bend ahead and ordered Ross to slow down.

Ross sighed, "We're fine Davey. I've been driving for years. I am quite aware of what I'm doing."

"Fuck it, Ross. Slow down!"

Ross tried to brake, but it was too late. The van started hydroplaning and the brakes were locked. Ross tried to make the turn on the tight curve, but the van was sailing straight for a 300-foot cliff. Just as they were about to plunge over the cliff, a camper coming in the opposite direction t-boned the van on the passenger side. The camper carried the van to a full stop against the side of the mountain. Davey was thrown onto the road through the front windshield. Carl Moffat, who had recently injured his right knee at a match in Puerto Rico, was hit in the same leg by a loose spare tire. Miraculously no one else in the van was hurt.

The driver of the camper sustained a crushed pelvis, but the parrot traveling in the front seat beside him was unscathed. I got a call from Ross an hour after the accident occurred. He was calm, but grief stricken.

"Diana, I don't know how to tell you this, but there has been a really bad accident. I was driving and we were hydroplaning and we were hit. Davey is unconscious. We can't wake him up. I wish to hell it was me not him. I'd give anything if it was me. You know how tough he is Diana. I know he's going to pull through this."

His voice faltered but I could hear Carl Mofatt whining in the background," My leg, my leg-my career is over, it's over. Davey's dead, oh God he's dead!"

Ross sighed, "Oh and Carl Mofatt got hit with the spare tire."

I hung up the phone and called my dad. Mom and Dad, Ellie and Jim, Georgia, BJ and Alison immediately arrived at my doorstep to comfort me and await more news. I couldn't breathe. We sat at the kitchen table speculating on what had happened. If only they hadn't waited for Dynamite. If only Davey had worn his seatbelt.

When I told them about Carl's background comments Jim, who had known Carl for years, said, "His career is over? Oh my God that'll be a big blow to professional wrestling." This made us all laugh, which relieved the tension a little.

Then the phone rang. Ross told me Davey was conscious. He said when the paramedic finally succeeded in reviving him, Davey was feeling around the road with his left hand searching for his chocolate ice cream cone.

Davey spent the next year recovering. I started training with him to keep him company and I was so proud of him. He had over 135 stitches in his forehead and the doctors said anyone else who had been thrown 25 feet with such force and landed on the pavement on his back the way he had, would have broken his neck. The steroids he had been taking created such muscle mass in his neck it saved his life.

He did have herniated discs at the top of his spine, which limited his head movement and the eyesight in his left eye was impaired. He suffered bad headaches for almost a year, but he was back in the ring five months later.

Meanwhile, I had started some serious bodybuilding. I entered the southern Alberta provincials and came in second in the heavyweight division. At five feet nine, I weighed 144 pounds of solid muscle. I'd borne two children-five-year-old Harry and two-year-old Georgia-and my stomach was as flat as a pancake.

Davey gave me a pill every few days to help me build muscle for the contest. I never knew what it was. I also took one Ionamin in diet-pill form a day and Slow-K, which Dr. Dennis prescribed to help me handle cramping from the lack of potassium. When the contest ended I threw out all the dieting drugs and gained 30 pounds in a month. I didn't look fat. I looked healthy.

Davey and I had no income during his recuperation. That's when he turned to Ben and Hermish for financial help. He also signed on for another Japanese tour with Dynamite. They happened to meet up with Vince McMahon at one of the shows. With five months of solid training behind him, Davey was in peak form. Vince was impressed. He knew Davey was so loyal that if he wanted him back, he'd have to offer Dynamite a job too. He approached Tom and Davey and asked if they would consider working for him again.

Tom told Vince to fuck off and Davey said, "I'd love to come back." They finished their tour. Vince still hadn't called so to keep us going, Davey did independent tours around the world on his own. He wrestled in Africa and the Middle East as the Gulf War began and Tom never spoke to him again.

CHAPTER TWENTYTHREE

Jim & Ellie

My sister Ellie's husband Jim Neidhart is one of the most-wicked people I have ever met. He is a monster.

Ellie is a mere shell of what she once was, both in looks and personality. Her face and body are lumpy from the bruising and scarring she has suffered as Jim's personal punching bag. It is all so sad because Ellie once had a crack at happiness, but my family urged her to turn her back on her soul mate because he was in a wheelchair.

John Hutchinson was born May 2, 1950 and died October 7, 2000. John was about six feet five before his accident. He was a teenage passenger in a car driving home to Calgary from Edmonton's summer Klondike Days celebrations. The driver fell asleep at the wheel and the car swerved across the highway and flew off the overpass near Red Deer. The steering wheel was imbedded in the driver's mouth and ripped his lips from ear to ear, but he survived. John was found unconscious and nearly dead 75 feet from the crash. Paralyzed from the neck down, he lived the rest of his life in a wheelchair.

My brother Wayne introduced Ellie to John and they went out for hot chocolate. John had a special vehicle with hand controls. He was handsome. He looked like a combination of Dick Van Dyke and Alan Alda.

Ellie was a pathological nurturer and I think that was what first drew her to John, but as they got to know each other better, she fell in love with him. They had so much in common. They loved art, animals, children and nature. My parents thought it was a shame that she was wheeling him around. They thought she was too pretty and had too much going for her to be a caretaker. Worst of all, if she married John, Ellie would never be able to have children. But John was Ellie's soul mate and she ignored their advice for four years. Then an incident took place she could not ignore.

One night Alison was helping John do some silk screening-John later claimed Alison was wearing a low-cut sweater and he couldn't help himself-he made a pass at her. Alison went to my parents and told Mom and Dad that John had tried to kiss her. Mom and Dad told Ellie who was terribly hurt. She and John had a huge fight and they broke up. My parents saw it as a blessing in disguise.

John put some effort into trying to get her back. He called for a couple of weeks, but she wouldn't speak to him. Finally, he quit calling and started dating someone else.

John became even more of a hippie after he and Ellie split up. He started taking drugs, something Ellie disapproved of. He just sort of deteriorated. Ironically, he became friends with Smith's former girlfriend Zoe and started using intravenous drugs. He died of cancer 22 years after his romance with Ellie.

Ellie dated a few people, but no one moved the earth. Then she met Jim Neidhart. In 1978, he came up to Calgary from the States. Jim was living with a guy named Maylen who owned a gym in La Jolla, just north of San Diego. Maylen had a bulldog named Taxi and a black cat named Lemieux, this cat that ended up becoming Ellie and Jim's pet. Despite being such a bully, Jim had a soft spot for it.

Maylen, an alcoholic, had heard about my dad. He had a lot of big guys train at his gym, a lot of football players. My dad always says that if Jim hadn't met Ellie, he'd still be squeezing blackheads out of the backs of the homosexuals training at Maylen's Gym. My dad has never ever had any problems with anyone's sexual preference or their race or their religion. He was just stating a fact. Jim worked as a towel boy at the gym and had to rub down the clients after they showered and steamed.

Maylen gave Jim some phone numbers and advised him that his football career wouldn't last forever. Jim had been playing for the Oakland Raiders. In high school, he got a shot with the Dallas Cowboys. He was that good a football player. He wasn't extraordinarily tall-just six feet-but he was fast and stocky.

Unfortunately, the offer from the Cowboys interfered with his shot-putting career. He couldn't play pro football and be an amateur shot-putter at the same time. Jim was hoping to compete in the 1980 Olympics, which were boycotted by the USA because of the Afghanistan war. So he missed out on the Cowboys and the Olympics, but he did go to world championship meets in Poland, the Soviet Union and South Africa.

He was treated like royalty all over the world because he was part of the hopeful Olympians. His best friend Terry Albriton was the world's best shot-putter. He had the record. Unofficially, Jim had broken it, but outside of competition.

This is one of the reasons Ellie uses when she's trying to convince herself why she has to stick with Jim, that he unofficially held the world's record in shot put. Terry and Jim ended up coming to Calgary.

My dad was quite impressed with these two big, educated would-be wrestlers (or at least that's how they represented themselves), because they were both attending UCLA on scholarships.

Terry was legitimately smart, but he had huge mood swings. He was either manic or depressed which often happens with really smart people. He wrote one of his essays on why he hated war on toilet paper. He was heartbroken when the Afghanistan war wiped out the Olympics for the Americans. His professors thought the toilet paper was profound.

As for Jim, he got kicked out of university for trying to extort money from the school. It was bad enough he never did any work, but then he began to demand money in exchange for being on the shot put team. He was thrown in jail and expelled for that.

Then the Oakland Raiders picked him up. He had two seasons with them. The first season he was put on injured reserve. He had thrown out his elbows, which after surgery, resulted in six-inch scars on each elbow. Between getting kicked out of university and Oakland's off season, Jim wanted to explore a life in wrestling. He came up to Calgary thinking, "Okay I'm making career choices. I'm going to get into wrestling after my contract ends with the Raiders."

He arrived at the beginning of the summer and impressed my dad by doing sprints and power lifting in the yard behind the house. He and my dad hit it off quite well. My dad loved being in the gym with this big strong rhinoceros. It was a good challenge for him because Jim was so strong. Every day, my dad stretched the hell out of Jim. My dad would force him into submission and keep him in painful holds for what seemed like an eternity.

"Discipline!" my dad would order. And Jim took it. I've got to give Jim credit for that because he went back day after day and allowed this to happen. It was the only way to become a world-class wrestler.

Coming from California, Jim liked to have marijuana joints and beer on hand. He loved Canadian beer, especially Pilsner. When he first came up to Calgary, he thought he was in for a free ride, free training, free everything and would get some kind of certificate or something and walk away saying he was now qualified to wrestle professionally.

Of course it doesn't work that way. You never really get a certificate or a diploma saying, "So and so has graduated from Stu Hart's Dungeon and now can work as a professional wrestler." You may get that in modeling or acting, but you don't get that in professional wrestling.

But he was right about what it would cost him to train. My dad never charged a single soul to learn to wrestle. My brothers did, but my dad trained hundreds of wrestlers including Archie "The Stomper" Gouldie, "Superstar" Billy Graham, Greg "The Hammer" Valentine, John Helton, Bob Leuck, Rick Martel, Steve Blackman, Nikolai Volkoff and Chris Benoit-all for free.

My dad was quite fond of Terry and Jim, but the one who stuck it out and stayed in Calgary was Jim. My dad didn't take any nonsense from him like Jim's mild-mannered accountant father, Hank did. An accountant with the San Diego Yacht Club, Hank also owned the first hotel right outside of Disneyland called the Lamplighter Inn. He came from the military and had been raised by Poppy Neidhart, the original Hank. Poppy was a lawyer for the Mexican Mafia and received lots of perks. As the only child of Grammy and Poppy Neidhart, Hank Junior was indulged.

My sister Ellie eventually knew them both, but she said Jim's father was nothing like Poppy. Jim's grandfather and Jim are apparently just very alike: German, hot tempered and belligerent. Jim's grandfather, Poppy was extremely possessive of his wife. Her name was Eileen, but Jim called her Grammy. Poppy bought her furs and diamonds. They had a lovely house in Nevada and they vacationed in the Pokonos. But he was brutally possessive, the same way Jim is with Ellie.

Ellie says Grammy was a charming, lovely little lady. They raised Hank, and then Hank had this monster named Jim and a daughter named Debbie. Debbie ended up living with her mother Katie, the one who tried to save Alison from Smith's crazy wife Maria in the brawl in our family's kitchen. Jim stayed with his father when his parents got divorced. Hank eventually lost all his money, unbeknownst to Jim until years later.

Jim had been into steroids and pills and pot and drinking since he was in high school. He was indulged by the coaches and basi-

Stu Hart —
early wrestling days 1935

Helen Smith —
prior to wedding
Stu Hart. Age 19

Lunch at the Hart house — 1963 prior to the birth of Diana and Owen. Left to right: Dean, Georgia, Wayne, Ellie, Alison, Ross, Stu, Helen, Smith, Bruce, Keith and Wayne

Hart family — 1964. Front row, left to right: Smith holding Diana, Bruce, Keith, Wayne, Dean, Ellie, Georgia, Bret, Alison and Ross. Back row, left to right: Helen (pregnant with Owen), Boxing Champion Primo Canera, Stu Hart

Wrestling Legends,
Stu Hart with
Andre the Giant —
Calgary Stampede

Diana Hart with
Andre the Giant at
Clearwater Beach, 1973.

Stu Hart presented
with flowers by
daughter Diana, prior
to a wrestling match —
Calgary 1975

Stu Hart with
Hulk Hogan —
AKA Hollywood
Hogan

Bruce, Bret
and Keith
Hart —
Stampede
Wrestling
1981

Smith Hart —
wrestling in
Germany for the
National
Wrestling
Alliance Tour
— 1981

Davey Smith at
age 17

Davey Smith press
slamming Dynamite Kid
— 1982

Bret in a bloody
wrestling match with
Kerry Brown —
Stampede Wrestling

Bret Hart — wrestling
in Japan 1982

New Japan Pro
Wrestling — 1982
Davey Smith,
Tom Billington
and Bret Hart

Davey Smith and
Diana Hart — recently
engaged 1983

Davey Smith
and Diana Hart —
1983 Victoria Pavilion
Calgary

Davey Smith and Diana Hart
— wedding day October 7th,
1984

Michelle and Tom Billington
May 1983

Owen Hart and
then girlfriend
Martha — 1983

Owen and Martha's wedding reception — July 2nd, 1989
Martha, Owen and Diana

Diana and Jim — The Anvil — Neidhart — 1988

Ellie, Nati, Jenni and Jim Neidhart

Davey Smith, Diana Hart and Owen Hart — Stampede Wrestling

Owen Hart, Davey Smith and his bulldog mascot, Matilda

Brian Pilman and Owen Hart — Stampede Wrestling Days —1987

Diana Hart — March 1990
— professional body
building competition

Davey Smith — AKA The British Bulldog

Davey Smith with Max Crabtree — 1994

Davey Smith and Rick Rude — 1993

Owen Hart, wrestling The Edge and Christian 1999

Smith family in
Florida, Harry, Davey,
Georgina and
Diana Hart Smith —
1994

Diana Hart
Smith with
her children
Harry and
Georgia and
nephew
Matt at
Wrestlemania
XIII in
Anaheim —
March 1996

Mrs. Marty Funk, Dory Funk, Alison Hart, Brian Blair, Hollywood Hogan, Bruce Hart, Diana Hart Smith, Davey Smith, Chris Benoit, Chris Jerico, Nancy, Mike Anthony, Shane Douglas, Bret Hart, Terry Funk. Front row: Bruce Hart Jr. and Stu Hart

cally got away with a lot more than your average student would. My dad had never seen anybody like Jim before. He was always stoned, but could somehow function quite well. My dad was sort of amazed at Jim's metabolism.

Jim had reddish-brown curly hair, dimples and a paunchy stomach. Some thought him quite handsome, but my mom thought he was grotesque. It was odd because he had very good manners, nice teeth, well-manicured hands and neatly combed hair, but my mom never really warmed up to Jim. She thought he was a stupid ass and she was right. My dad admired Jim's athletic ability and his genetics.

Each day, Jim and my dad would push each other around like two bulls for about an hour before they'd even get into amateur wrestling and the stretching and submission holds. Then Jim would come upstairs and my dad had would tell him to help himself to whatever they had. My dad always had beer in this big Coca Cola cooler on the porch.

There were freezers and refrigerators and coolers all over my dad's house-on the porches, under the garage, in the basement and on the balcony. My dad couldn't resist a good deal. If he found a commercial cooler for $3,000 regularly priced at $15,000 my mom would worry, "It's so expensive, it's $3000! We don't need another Coca-Cola cooler!" My dad would argue that it was too good a deal to pass up and he would buy it. Even if they could afford it, my mom would be furious that he was spending money like that.

These issues would cause fierce arguments between them. It was never ever about my dad eyeing another woman or coming home drunk or gambling. It was always about my dad spending money on things like a rotisserie for the porch that could hold 70 chickens. He's probably got $200,000 worth of commercial kitchen equipment. He's also invested in chests of tools, welding equipment to build rings, mechanical hoists, car jacks and air compressors.

Anyway, one day, Jim went upstairs through the kitchen and helped himself to one of these Pilsner beers in the cooler. That's when he spotted Ellie. She was quite spicy. She looked just like my mom's mom who was always yelling at her girls as they grew up, she was especially tough on her daughter Joanie. In fact, Joanie would always say to Ellie, "I just can't look at you Ellie. You remind me too much of Gaga."

Jim fell for this girl who was so independent and saucy, the first girl in our family after five boys. At the time, Ellie was still mooning over John who she hadn't seen in a year and Jim's passion wasn't returned. Like my mom, Ellie couldn't stand him. She thought he was a big, boorish blowhard.

A few weeks later Ellie, who always had a rabbit or chicken or turtle or cat, left her turtle Posy in the grass next to a window. She boxed him in safely with wrestling ring 2 x 12 planks. A couple of hours later she went to retrieve him and the pen was empty. She was frantic and crying.

Jim stepped up. "I'll find your turtle, Elizabeth," he promised. "I'll follow his turtle tracks." A few minutes later Jim returned with Posy. "Found him down by the road." Jim smiled showing his big dimples.

Not used to being deceived, Ellie fell for this and felt apologetic and grateful and accepted his invitation to go out for dinner.

In the fall he had to go back to California and serve two months in jail for extortion. Then he rejoined the Raiders to finish out his contract. He wrote her calling her his "Little Snowflake." She was embarrassed, but had never been romanced. On American Thanksgiving that year he insisted on flying her down to watch him play football. She was swept off her feet. He picked her up in the Raiders' team car. She met all the players and they all made such a fuss over Jim. She felt she had misjudged him all along. They were married within the month on December 26th, Boxing Day. He wrestled that night.

Jenny was born within the year on November 27, 1981. Natty was born just over a year later and Muffy was born the next May. After Muffy's birth, Ellie had to have her tubes tied. My dad and mom were heartbroken, but the doctors insisted. Ellie's uterus was too thin. Jim wasn't pleased because he wanted a son.

Jim became friends with a wrestler who worked for my dad named Sylvester Ritter or "Big Daddy" Ritter, later known as "The Junkyard Dog." Sylvester was a big African American wrestler, six feet four and 300 pounds. When he first started out, he and his wife and little boy lived in Calgary.

Jim and Sylvester were on the road in the late '70s wrestling all over my dad's territory. One Monday while driving from Calgary to Regina for a show, Sly told Jim about a dream he'd had the night before.

"I dreamt my baby, little Sly Junior died." He said it was awful. "It was a nightmare. I don't ever want to go through that again."

A few hours later on the highway, the RCMP flagged them down. There was an all points bulletin out for my dad's 1976 green El Dorado convertible. An officer approached the car and leaned in, first identifying the passengers.

"Are you Sylvester Ritter?" he asked.

"Yes," said Sylvester.

The officer's expression was serious. "I know this is bad news, sir, but your baby died in Calgary last night."

Sylvester immediately called home. The baby had died of the croup.

Sly was devastated and never recovered from it. He came over to the house that Friday and my dad said, "You take all the time off that you need and we will help you in whatever way we can."

Sylvester replied, "You can help me by letting me wrestle in the show tonight. It's a distraction for me and, you know, life has to go on."

I'll never forget that match. Everyone was heartbroken. These big, strong, bulky, burly wrestlers may put on a show that they're invincible, but they were all crying that night.

The Junkyard Dog made a small fortune in the WWF, but never got over the death of his baby and fell victim to cocaine and eventually became a crack addict. Substance abuse came with his success. Sadly, Sylvester died in a car accident in 1998 in Mississippi as he was returning from his daughter's high school graduation. He was only 45 years old.

Sylvester was the reason Jim moved to Baton Rouge, Louisiana in 1983, just before my dad sold to Vince. I remember Ellie and her three little girls driving off in my dad's green Eldorado, loaded down with a U-haul full of possessions, a stereo, some dishes and Jim's training weights. My dad's welder, Hans Gleisner, custom built the racks and dumbbells. Jim never did pay the guy.

In Louisiana, Jim wrestled for a promoter named Bill Watts and lived on the road with Junkyard Dog. Ellie became friends with "The Natural" Butch Reed and his wife. Butch was a 255-pound African American wrestler. His gimmick was that he dyed his hair blonde and claimed it was his natural color.

Ellie said she had never witnessed racism like she saw in Louisiana. In Calgary, people with black skin stood out, but not in a bad way. In Louisiana poor Butch Reed's wife would go into the supermarket to get something and they wouldn't serve her. She would go to another till and they wouldn't serve her there either. She was really dignified and refused to cry. Ellie was appalled. She thought that kind of behavior was despicable.

Butch and Sylvester and Jim wrestled all over-Baton Rouge, New Orleans and most of the southern states. Other than the ignorance regarding race, Ellie enjoyed Louisiana, but little by little, Jim was becoming more controlling. Despite a decent income, Ellie would call home all the time and say she had no money. Jim would go on the road for ten days and give her ten dollars and command her not to leave the house.

What worried her the most was that she couldn't afford to feed her kids. Due to the fact Jim was drugging and raping her-a little trick he taught Davey-she had terrible hemorrhoids and no money to buy hemorrhoid cream. In addition, the electric company was threatening to shut off her power. Jim was not a good provider and was very selfish and greedy with their money.

Even after he joined up with the WWF and his money situation improved drastically, Ellie never saw much of it. He refused to put her name on the bank account, the house title, even the car lease. She'd just get whatever handouts Jim would throw her way. Fortunately, Ellie is creative. Since Jim wouldn't provide money for his little girls to have toys, she learned to make them dolls. It actually seemed to annoy Jim that Ellie was thriving despite how little he was giving her.

They ended up moving back up to Calgary and my dad bought them a house in Bowness, right on the Bow River. My dad got it at a time when the interest rates in Calgary were at 18% so people were walking away from their houses or letting them go for a dollar. My dad bought this house for Ellie and Jim in exchange for a car, one of his Cadillacs.

My mom and dad thought it would be so wonderful to have their daughter Ellie back in the fold. Jim worked on the road for the WWF and with Bret, Dynamite and Davey. My dad had his four boys all together again and his family back in Calgary. He even made the payments on the house for them, though Jim had the money to do it himself. But Jim is a man with no pride. He's a selfish and greedy and Ellie allowed him to be that way.

Jim and Ellie fought like hell all the time. Jim would complain, "I'm not happy up here. I don't like the weather. I want to go back to the States."

For their sixth anniversary my dad gave Jim a pair of new ostrich skin cowboy boots. Jim wanted to wear them out to dinner but he couldn't fit them on his feet. Ellie suggested if he wore a pair of nylons his feet would slide right in. So Jim wriggled into a pair of nylons she wore when she was pregnant and his feet did slide right into the boots.

They went out for dinner and it was a disaster. They fought the whole time, Jim was bitching about how much he hated Calgary and how he wanted to get out of here. He didn't like my dad knowing how he was treating Ellie. Questions were beginning to crop up.

"What the hell are you doing, Jim? You are making all this money and you are not giving my poor daughter anything. How come my daughter and my grandchildren don't have any food? And how come your electricity is getting cut off?"

Jim didn't feel he needed to answer to anybody for his selfish ways. He called his dad, crying that he hated Calgary.

Hank phoned my dad and Ellie and said, "You people are killing poor little Jimmy. How could Ellie do this to him, make him live up in Calgary where he can't stand it?"

Ellie was furious. "You are such a Goddamned baby, Jim."

This all came to a head the night that Jim had the nylons on. I was baby-sitting the girls that night and when Jim and Ellie returned from their anniversary dinner, they continued their fight on the deck in front of the house. Jim had taken the boots off and he was standing outside in nylon stockings. It looked absurd. This big wrestler with these nylons folded over the top of his pants and sticking out underneath his pant legs. The fight ended when Ellie burst out laughing as Jim began stamping his stocking feet.

Eventually Ellie succumbed to Jim's wishes and they ended up leaving Calgary and walking away from their great house, which my dad eventually put my brother Bruce and Andrea in.

Ellie just got so fed up with the fighting. They moved to Florida and bought a place in Tampa in an area called Timber Lane. Then they moved to Land O Lakes and bought an acre in The Oaks. Jim started buying a lot more things for their house. It was an abstract ultra-modern place and Jim loved it. But my dad would still get calls from a crying Ellie, complaining that Jim left her for two weeks without a dime and the gas tank on empty.

Florida

On the first anniversary of Davey's car accident, he got a call from Pat Patterson at the WWF. It was just before SummerSlam 1990. Ed Leslie-better known as Brutus 'The Barber' Beefcake-had been in a boating accident and was just about killed. Brutus was trying to assist a female acquaintance as she made her first parasailing landing and her knee hit him right in the face at over 40 miles per hour. This pushed his nose so far back into his head that it skimmed his brain. The collision also broke his top jaw.

Brutus was in critical condition. His best friend Hulk Hogan got in touch with one of the best plastic surgeons in all of United States and said, "As a favor to me, can you help? Brutus is going to die if you don't." An arrangement was made. Hulk would visit a lot of sick kids at the hospital and the plastic surgeon performed a 12-hour surgery on Brutus

He recovered, but was warned that if he wrestled again, his face could shatter. Needless to say, he eventually wrestled anyway.

Brutus was scheduled to wrestle the 'Texas Tornado' Kerry Von Erich for the Intercontinental Championship Belt at SummerSlam. Brutus was the heel and Kerry was the baby face. But now Brutus was out of commission. The WWF called and asked Davey to replace Brutus even though Vince would have preferred Davey to come back as a baby face. While we waited for the WWF to get Davey's working visa in order, we went to Florida to see Brutus.

We stayed at Jim and Ellie's place. I loved being around Ellie's daughters but Davey and I knew Jim was possessive and didn't really want anyone in his little castle so we made ourselves scarce.

We could hear Jim screaming at Ellie, "When is your family going to leave?"

"You would be nowhere if it wasn't for my family," Ellie fought back. "I never complain when you have your friends over." It was a constant war.

While we were down in Florida, Davey and I rethought our whole situation. We saw a show home about half a mile away from Ellie and Jim's place. I loved it. Besides all the trouble I was having in Calgary with my family, I was worried about Davey's involvement with Hermish and Ben. I hoped we could start a new life again in a new place. If Davey signed with the WWF, we would be closer to his wrestling venues. We bought the home with $1,000 down payment.

Davey's visa could not be processed in time for SummerSlam, but the WWF wanted him back anyway and they started to prepare a story line for his return.

It only took two months of living in Florida to know that I had made a mistake. I wanted to be back in Calgary, living with my family. But two months turned into six years.

I used to think if I were back up in Calgary things would be better. I started to blame Florida for my unhappiness, but it wasn't Florida. Florida's a beautiful state.

Drugging and Rape

Florida is where Davey starting drugging and raping me. Davey told me a Florida wrestler named Duke "The Dumpster" Droesse figured out how to make GHB liquid. The recipe is easy to obtain now, but in those days it was just coming into vogue. Gamma hydroxbutrate is sometimes used by bodybuilders instead of steroids. It's reputed to stimulate human growth hormone. Its most noticeable effect is euphoria but when mixed with alcohol it renders people unconscious. It's extremely dangerous and can lead to coma or death. Colorless, clear, tasteless and odorless, just like Rohypnol or flunitrazepam, it often causes amnesia during the periods it's taken.

Duke introduced it to Davey who told him it was really good for getting to sleep and the beauty of it was it increased your metabolic rate so it burned fat while you slept. Davey began giving it to me without my knowledge. Since then, there have been many incidences reported in the press about perverts using this drug to rape their dates.

At the time all I knew was that unusual things were happening to me. I developed really bad hemorrhoids and woke up with my posterior burning and sore. I felt something had happened to me during the night, but couldn't understand what. I thought maybe I was losing my mind. Part of being married is being able to trust the person you are married to. I never dreamed Davey was slipping me this drug in my nightly glass of orange juice in order to violate me. It just never even occurred to me.

I shared my symptoms with my sister Ellie. Without batting an eye she sighed, "Yeah Jim used to do the same thing to me."

"What!" I swallowed. "What do you mean?"

"He'd give me GHB before bed. He told me it was really great for losing weight. And it was. But it knocked me out and he would take advantage of me while I slept. That way he didn't have to please me and he could do whatever he wanted without any resistance."

I bit my lip. "After taking the orange juice Davey gives me at night, I'll wake up in my bed and not remember how I got there. Davey tells me not to worry. He says, "I took care of you."

I covered my face in my hands. "And sometimes he'll say, "You were really cute last night." And I'll ask him, "What do you mean?" He'll answer, "Oh, you were really cute, you looked really pretty last night," almost as if we'd had incredible sex or something. But I have no idea what the heck he's talking about."

I didn't tell Ellie about how puzzled I had been over finding my housecoat belts tied to the top of our four-poster bed.

Davey was insatiable. Sometimes he'd want sex ten times a day or three or four times in a row. I took it as a compliment, but he was a big guy and fairly aggressive and not very willing to do things that pleased me. Oral sex was rare and unfulfilling because he rushed through it. His idea of foreplay was saying, "Geez you've got great legs, bend over." That was it. He always wanted anal sex, which I found too painful to endure.

Finally, I started to figure things out. To substantiate my theory I decided not to drink my orange juice one night. Instead I surreptitiously poured it down the sink. Davey watched me like a hawk all night with a puzzled look as if to say, "Hmm, what's happening here?" After a couple of hours he brought me another glass of orange juice. I pretended to be grateful for his attentiveness, but when he turned his back I got rid of that one too.

I still had to be careful because he would slip it into my coffee or pretty well anything I was drinking. He was at the point where the only way he wanted to be with me was if I were unconscious. I guess in a really weird up way, I felt flattered that he desired me. I rationalized that he still loved me. What a screwed up relationship.

While we were in Florida we found out Andrea was expecting her third baby. The WWF scheduled a show during Stampede Week in Calgary in July 1991. I stayed home in Florida because Harry had to go to summer school. He had missed so much school due to the move. But Ellie and the girls stayed with my parents and said there was a party at the house after the show. Ellie said Andrea was getting stoned on pot with my brother Wayne and Bret's wife Julie. Even though she was three months pregnant, Andrea was so drunk she was falling all over Julie laughingly claiming she was taking speed to keep her weight down so that she could go to the

Ranchman's Club and not look pregnant. That way she could pick up guys.

Andrea smoked cigarettes all the way through her pregnancies. We knew she drank and smoked pot, but were shocked about the amphetamines. The baby was due in December, but he was born very premature at the end of August. The doctors didn't think he was going to make it. They named him Rhettgher, a combination of the first names of Rhett Butler – even though Andrea has never seen Gone With the Wind – and Rutger Hauer star of the romantic movie, Ladyhawk. Andrea was always telling people she looked like Michelle Pfeiffer.

Bret stopped by to visit me that fall and shook his head. "Andrea is so irresponsible. Bruce has got to put his foot down with her. She's still smoking and she's still drinking. Somebody has to stop her from having more crack babies."

Everyone was aware of her substance abuse but no one wanted to say anything to her face because they all felt so sorry for her having this poor little premature baby. Rhett was in the hospital for three months and then he came home. He was blind and afflicted with severe cerebral palsy. He was a beautiful blonde, blue-eyed moppet and his handicap just wrenched my mom's heart. It was such a shame. He was around five years old when he first started to talk and one of his first words was, "Harry."

I've seen Andrea try to feed Rhett, pulling his hair back and forcing his mouth open. It's horrible. She often puts him on this stupid carrot juice diet to improve his sight. She has no sense. At five years old he only weighed 30 pounds. He should have been on high-calorie shakes, but she has him on carrot juice.

From what I've seen, she leaves him on the bed or strapped into his chair much of the time. Now that he's eight, he goes to a special school each day and when he comes home, she plunks him in an empty bathtub and closes the door to muffle his crying. He sucks his index finger so much it looks like a little red balloon. Ellie has complained to social services numerous times, but the officials never seem to do anything about it.

By December when Rhett should have been born, Andrea was trying to get pregnant again. Tory, short for Torrin, was born the next fall. I used to call him Troy to aggravate her. He is far behind developmentally due to the drugs she took during her pregnancy. Then she had another baby Lara Helen. Lara, she got from the Julie Christie character in Dr. Zhivago. "We have the same eyes," she said. And Helen is for my mom because Andrea's so fond of her signature, especially on a cheque.

When she had Lara in 1995, I was still in Florida. We would come up for summer vacations and I was happy to be home. After Tory was born, I thought, "Why would she have another baby so soon?" She gained very little weight with these babies, usually only around five pounds because she was adamant about wearing her jeans home from the hospital.

I found out through my sister Alison that Andrea did indeed have an agenda. My mom had had a few drinks one night and suggested to Andrea that if she had a large family, she might get the house in the event anything happened to her or my dad. Of course it was a ridiculous conversation prompted by the fact my mom was feeling sentimental due to the liquor, but Andrea took it seriously.

My Wrestling Career

At the WWF's SummerSlam 1992, Davey was wrestling Bret for the Intercontinental Championship Belt. All 80,000 seats at Wembley Stadium in London were sold out 10 hours after the event was announced. Officials at British Telecom sent out press releases stating that at one point 25,000 people simultaneously dialed the credit card ticket number. The speed of the sellout broke records previously held by Michael Jackson, Eric Clapton, Elton John and Madonna.

I remember being escorted by Vince McMahon's son, Shane, from the royal box at Wembley Stadium to the field, and being put right at ringside. The angle of the match was that my brother and husband were at odds and it was tearing the family apart.

The WWF did televised interviews all of July with our whole family. They liked mine in particular and I was front and center for the cameras at the match. I was so excited and felt like this was a real big step for me. I was not going to let anyone down. I was also a complete nervous wreck and my nervousness made it that much more convincing.

A London Daily Mirror article dated August 31 quoted me at ringside saying, "I am so worried they are going to destroy each other." No one but Vince, Bret and Davey knew who was going to win. And in a rare display of trust, Vince told Bret and Davey not to let him in on how they were going to end it. He wanted to be genuinely surprised.

It was an incredible match. My dad, who is the world's greatest judge of good wrestling, proclaimed, "I wouldn't change one iota of that match." He said that match, shown on television around the world, was a fantastic endorsement for wrestling.

The Daily Mirror article described it this way: "His beautiful wife watched helplessly and ashen-faced at ringside as the British Bulldog lay pinned to the canvas, painful defeat staring him in his sweat-streaked face. Davey Boy had dreamed for so long of wearing the gleaming golden belt of champions. He was at the mercy of the opponent he had most dreaded having to meet. The odds looked hopeless. His dream was fading fast.

"Desperately Davey Boy fought his way free, turning the tables on his opponent in a lightning sequence of brilliant moves and it was all over. The 29-year-old Bulldog had been pitted against his own brother-in-law, WWF heartthrob Bret "the Hitman" Hart.

"In a real needle match, tension gripped the family and woman torn between the giant pair, Bulldog's wife and the Hitman's sister. She sat close to tears at ringside.

"The Hitman nonchalantly whizzed the Bulldog from one set of twanging ropes to another. All seemed lost for the Bulldog when the heartless Hitman squatted on his back in a classic Boston Crab, wrenching his legs to force him into submission. In a supreme effort, Davey Boy inched his way painfully to the edge of the ring and forced his way free. Then in a stunning set of moves, perfected by years of relentless training, he took the boastful Bret by surprise, pinned him upside down, shoulders to the mat and that was that.

"As the cheers echoed around the stadium, the Bulldog stuck out his meaty paw in friendship only to have it spurned by his broken-hearted brother-in-law. But finally the paired embraced to the screams of the crowd. Diana leaped into the ring and hugged them. A huge Union Jack waved above the Bulldog's head. Fireworks shot showers of stars into the sky. Rule Britannia thundered out of the speakers. Diana sobbed in Davey Boy's arms."

Vince was so happy with the way the match had gone, he gave Davey a big hug.

Davey was in a fog. The excitement and adrenaline left his mind a blank. I don't know if Davey was working me or not, but he said, "Did I win?"

I was hugging him and checking him over for injuries. "You were wonderful, Davey. Just wonderful."

He said, "Well I can't remember what happened in the match, I really can't. How did it look, Di? Did the fans like it?"

The fans went home delirious and I told him so. They could have watched Bret and Davey wrestle for another hour.

I saw Bret the next morning at breakfast at London's Ramada Hotel. I sat down with him for a moment. "How are you today, Bret?"

He forced a wry grin, "I feel like I got hit by a truck. How's Davey?"

"He's about the same," I told him. Bret, like my dad, is a man of few words unless he's angry.

This whole thing between Bret and Davey was a strong angle. They were set to mix it up again at Wrestlemania in the spring. But Bret never got the return match. Instead he got the WWF World Championship Belt and Davey was let go.

While in England, The Ultimate Warrior asked Davey for the name of a steroid dealer. Davey poked around, got a name and phone number for him and that was that. The Ultimate Warrior made the contact and started getting steroids sent to his house in Arizona. He was receiving delivery after delivery from England. Of course, it stuck out like a big red X when it went through customs and they confiscated the steroids at the post office.

Meanwhile Vince was under grand jury investigation. They were trying to close him down claiming he was basing his business on wrestlers who were using illegal drugs and that he was providing those drugs.

Vince said that if they were going to close him down they'd have to close down every professional sports industry. It was a real witch-hunt. He was working hard on cleaning up his wrestlers. He had them tested weekly and randomly. If their drug levels were dropping, that was acceptable, but if their levels were elevated or TCH (from marijuana) showed up in their urine, they were either fined, suspended or fired. The tests were costing Vince a fortune, but he was determined to prove he was serious about running a drug-free federation.

Vince's medical technicians actually got down on their knees to watch the wrestlers urinate into the receptacle. Otherwise some of the wrestlers would cheat. They'd have a Visine bottle full of someone else's drug free urine tucked up under their testicles. Instead of urine coming out of their penis it was coming out of the eye drops bottle. Sometimes they'd squeeze a bit of Visine into the sample to ruin it. Jim Neidhart's favorite cheat was claiming he had diarrhea so bad he couldn't take the test. If he were made to anyway, he'd make sure fecal matter landed in his sample.

Davey failed his test at the beginning of 1992. They detected Ecstasy or MDMA, a methamphetamine. Vince was concerned and warned Davey.

"If you take that stuff you will kill yourself. That is something people make in bathtubs in their garages." Davey was given six weeks off to clean up.

The Drug Enforcement Agency confronted Vince about the Ultimate Warrior's steroid deliveries. Vince denied any and all knowledge and fired Warrior immediately. Warrior assured the feds that Vince had nothing to do with his $10,000-per-week steroid habit. Then he ratted Davey out. On the advice of his legal team, Vince had Davey's job with the WWF terminated. Privately, Vince assured Davey he would bring him back when the heat cooled down.

I was just sick about it. I could not believe this.

"Vince," I was thinking. "How could you do this to Davey? How could you let him go?" Davey vehemently denied giving Warrior the phone number. I had no doubt he was telling me the truth. But after months of going over it again and again with Davey, "How did Ultimate Warrior get the steroids?" he finally broke down and admitted it.

"Well I introduced him to the guy, but I didn't know he was selling steroids," he confessed. Then a few months later he said, "Well, okay I knew the guy had steroids, but I figured since I wasn't the one using them, what did it have to do with me?"

It's such a shame because Davey may have become the World Champion. Instead they let him go and ended up putting the Belt on Bret.

Vince had Davey lose his Intercontinental title to Shawn Michaels, the Heartbreak Kid, and a week later Bret won the World Belt. He wrestled Rick Flair in Saskatoon and Vince flew my dad out for it. Davey was there and he was happy for Bret. He really felt Bret deserved the win.

We had a long battle with the WWF fighting over the rights to the British Bulldog name. Davey couldn't go anywhere else to wrestle because Vince owned it. It was in their contract. Vince had the rights-including merchandising-after Davey stopped working for him.

For two years after Davey was let go, Vince-not Davey-made a small fortune on British Bulldog bedding, wallpaper, teddy bears, videos, Super Nintendo games, running shoes, coffee cups, action figures, night clothes, boxer shorts, watches, playing cards, TV trays, birthday cards, lunch boxes, scarves, Halloween masks, calculators, t-shirts, hats, ice cream bars, foam hands, wall clocks, posters, windbreakers, umbrellas, erasers, paper dolls, slippers, pins, badges and backpacks.

There was a long, costly legal battle and it caused a lot of animosity between Vince and Davey.

Davey returned to the WCW, the rival federation to the WWF, as Davey Boy Smith. He signed a contract with Bill Watts, but he never really liked it there. It was way too cliquey and the management never treated Davey like one of their own. Instead, Eric Bischoff focused on Steve Borden aka Sting.

Steve began as Ultimate Warrior's tag-team partner back when Ultimate Warrior was the Dingo Warrior and together they were The Blade Runners. I always thought Sting was overrated. But what really got me was that Eric was having Davey beaten by Leon White aka Van Vader in violent, dangerous matches. Vader was clumsy and unskilled. I got the impression he was trying to knock Davey out cold. It reached the point where our son Harry and I couldn't even watch these matches on TV. When Davey tried to retaliate he was called on the carpet by WCW management.

"What the hell are you doing Davey? Vader is our World Champion!"

Eventually Davey and Sting tagged against Vader and Sid Eudy aka Sid Vicious. Sid and Vader would handle Sting like he was porcelain china, but when Davey stepped into the ring, they'd powerbomb him with all their might. They were destroying his health, hurting him in every match. Thankfully Davey was the best wrestler out there, and could legitimately take care of himself. He continued to be professional and do what he was told.

In February and March of 1993, the WCW sent Davey to Europe. He was a huge hit and took the WCW from 700 seats in The King's Court in London to selling out The Royal Albert hall twice in one day.

Aggravated Assault

In July of that year Davey was facing a seven-to-14-year jail sentence over an altercation in a bar with a guy named with Kody Light. Kody claimed Davey manhandled him. Specifically he alleged Davey smashed his head into the wall, pile-drived him into the floor, and powerbombed him. All these accusations were untrue. You cannot put these moves on a civilian. It takes two to create certain holds.

It's not like Davey was looking for a fight that night. But we were in the wrong place at the wrong time. It was a Saturday night. We were tired from a day trip to the Rockyford Rodeo. This was during the time he was working at the WCW and wrestling in title shots against Van Vader. He said like he felt his back was going to shatter.

Davey and I had stopped into the Back Alley Night Club. We rarely went out to nightclubs because fans would pester us, but this night a friend of ours wanted to buy us a drink in order to impress her friends. I don't drink so I got up to dance with Adam, our friend's teenage son.

A complete stranger named Kody Light who had been drinking there since the bar opened that evening and had a blood alcohol level six times the legal driving limit, approached us on the dance floor and began harassing us. He was slurring his words.

"When a beautiful chick like you and a geek like that are screwing, who's on top?"

Adam looked embarrassed and I told him to ignore this idiot. Kody began lunging at my chest. Meanwhile, Davey had wandered over to find me. Totally unaware of what Kody was doing, he tapped his watch to indicate we had to get going.

Light confronted Davey. "Hey, I'm talking to the lady."

"That's my husband," I snapped.

"That's my wife," Davey added.

Light smirked. "You've got a nice fucking wife." Then he grabbed Davey's hand and squeezed. Davey tried to free his hand, but Light wouldn't let go. Enough was enough. Davey put him in a front face lock and walked him ten feet over to the bouncers. Then abruptly let him go. Light stood up and as the blood rushed back to his head, he weaved and fell backward. There was glass from broken beer bottles all over the floor and some of it became embedded in the back of his skull.

An ambulance came, and while we waited, Kody's friends began taunting Davey, challenging him to fight. The bouncers instructed us to leave before things got out of hand.

We returned to Florida Monday night as planned and it wasn't until four months later, during a Christmas phone call to Bret, that we found out the police were looking for Davey. Davey flew back to Calgary and turned himself in. He was locked up on charges of aggravated assault. He spent the weekend at the Remand Center and I posted $7,000 bail. My dad had to put up a $500,000 assurety bond for Davey to get his passport back.

By November, Davey still had not received his promised bonus for his European tour. Eric Bischoff took Davey up to a suite at the Marriott Residence Inn in Orlando to meet with him, Bob Dhue, one of WCW's top managers, and Bill Shaw, another suit. I was there because the WCW had rented the whole courtyard at the Marriott for a wrestling party.

I remember talking to Brian Pilman and his new bride Melanie. She was expecting Brian's first son. I felt like a third wheel hanging around them because they were sort of in that newlywed stage.

Davey came back fuming. He said when he asked for his bonus, Eric pulled out his false teeth and slapped them on the table and said, "I have my black belt in karate and I know you killed a man up in Calgary, but if you want to fight me over your money, then let's do it right now."

Davey said that initially Eric had been leaning toward paying him but that Bob Dhue refused and had acted like a complete asshole. Eric worked for Bob and Bill, so he switched horses and challenged Davey to a fight.

Davey left the WCW shortly after that. They claimed he failed his drug test for steroids and cocaine and insisted he either enter rehab on Peach Tree Street in Atlanta or leave. Davey refused. He didn't want to work for them anymore anyway. The only thing

Davey felt bad about was that the previous November Davey had beaten Rick Rood aka Rick Rude. Davey was scheduled to return the favor and in the time-honored tradition lose to Rick at Starcade. He called Rick to apologize but Rick said, "Ahh, don't worry about it."

By January of 1994, Davey was on his way to England to work for Max Crabtree.

In August 1994, Vince won his grand jury case ending their quest to indict him and shut him down. In my opinion they never had a case against Vince. They were using him to make it look like the US government wanted to get tough on drugs.

Owen had wrestled Bret at Madison Square Garden at Wrestlmania Ten, "Brother Versus Brother." By August they were facing each other again at the brand new United Center in Chicago. WWF was looking at ways to intensify this big match so they flew our whole family down and included Davey and me. Davey was over the moon. They wanted him back.

Ironically Hulk Hogan reached Davey on his cell phone while he was on the landline in his mom's kitchen in England with J.J. Dillion of the WWF. He had both federations on the phone simultaneously, one talking into each ear. Hulk had recently split from the WWF and was trying to recruit Davey for the WCW. Davey flatly refused.

"I 'ad nothing but trouble with them. No way."

Hulk was persistent. "I'll look after you Davey Boy, even if I have to pay you out of my own bank account." Hulk was always good to Davey. He had even landed him a guest spot on The A Team television series in 1985.

Davey was tempted because he liked and trusted Hulk, but his heart was with the WWF and my family.

Davey and I, my mom and dad, Smith and his son Chad, Bruce, Wayne, Georgia, Ross, Martha, Oje, Jim Neidhart and Ellie were all placed at ringside. The angle was that Jim, Martha and Oje were to cheer for Owen while the rest of us rooted for Bret. When Bret won the match, we all stood and cheered and Jim as planned, went ballistic and clotheslined Davey and me from behind over the railing into the ring.

This set the scene for the tag matches between Jim and Owen and Davey and Bret. It was an excellent way to reintroduce Davey back into the WWF after his two-year hiatus. He was 265 pounds and ripped. His hair was long and curly. He never looked better.

Bret had been pushed as their main event since Davey left and he had developed quite an ego. The first thing Bret said to Davey in the dressing room just before the show was, "Cut your hair and lose some weight."

Because Bret and Davey hadn't yet had a return match after Davey's win at Wembley in 1992, the seed was planted for them to wrestle each other. Davey called me up in the fall of 1995 and said, "Vince wants you to come out. We're going to do this angle again with Bret and me. This time I'm going over as super heel."

I was just delighted. I was thrilled. I remember Bret sitting me down quite sternly saying, "Are you ready? Are you prepared? Are you prepared to get a nanny? Are you prepared to go on the road with this?"

I said, "Oh yeah, but what are you talking about Bret?"

Bret didn't like it, but what the WWF wanted me to do was present a bouquet of thorny roses to Bret and then turn on him, going berserk, attacking him and getting him all scratched up. Davey was to come in and finish him off leaving him in a heap of stems and petals. The idea was that I was a really villainous, rotten female heel jealous of my brother Bret.

My mom was aghast and my dad, though he saw the potential, didn't think it was a good idea either. Bret didn't go for the idea of his sister or anyone in his family not liking him even though he had milked the angle between him and Owen for all it was worth. I think Bret thought that people would start thinking he was an asshole, because his little sister and brother didn't like him.

I was willing to go ahead and so was Davey, but Bret had more juice with the WWF than we did so they modified my participation to interviews where I bragged about how great Davey was.

Just before the WWF "In Your House" pay-per-view which pitted Davey against Bret, Bruce and Ross gave them a trial run up in Calgary at the tribute show they held for my dad's 80th birthday.

It was held for cerebral palsy although I gather Bruce slipped Andrea a fair amount of cash from the merchandising. The show was chock full of wrestling stars: "Razor" Ramon, "1-2-3 Kid," Keith, Owen, Mike Shaw aka Makhan Singh, Chris Benoit, Louie Spicoli aka "Rad Radford," Terry and Dory Funk, Dan Kroffat, Rhonda Sing, aka "Bertha Faye." The main event featured Bret and Davey.

Several dignitaries including Premier Ralph Klein came to the show. Ralph's father Phil Klein refereed for years for my dad and they were dear friends. Bruce went overboard while tagging with Brian Pilman against Terry and Dory Funk. By the end of the match, Bruce and Brian were bleeding profusely. They staggered around the crowd, throwing garbage and chairs and Bruce instructed Brian to go over to Premier Klein and bleed all over him.

My dad was absolutely livid. Later he gave Bruce hell in the dressing room. "That's the very gaddamn reason I got out of this business!"

Bret and Davey were also mad at Bruce because it's tough to follow a blood bath with a technical bout.

Two days later on December 17, 1995 Davey and Bret were the main event at WWF's pay-per-view in Hershey, Pennsylvania. Bret and Davey met before the match at a German restaurant to plan the bout. I was with Davey. Bret asked Davey for a hit of speed because he didn't want to be tired while he was wrestling. They went over their spots. Again Vince allowed them to create their own finish as long as Bret was the winner.

Owen had wrestled one of the Hog Men just before the main event so there was slop, salad dressing and milk, all over the ring. The caretakers had tried to mop it up, but the mat was still slick. Davey threw Bret outside the ring, then jumped over the ropes and threw Bret into the metal stairs. But Bret lost his footing and fell head first on to the bottom stair. Just like Bruce two days before, when he stood up Bret was covered in blood.

The TV cameras kept cutting to me, in order to censor all the blood. I was straining my neck to get a better look, but it appeared from where I sat that Bret had split his eye open. I thought he had lost an eye. I was horrified. My parents would never forgive Davey for this. I began weeping. Thankfully it wasn't Bret's eye that was bleeding-it was his hard head.

Bruce Pritchard, one of the WWF bookers told me he was captivated by my facial expressions and remarked how, while Davey was such a blatant heel, I in contrast looked so innocent and fooled by it all. They started flying me out on a regular basis for TV tapings and for pay-per-views, but not for regular shows. That way I stayed home with Harry and Georgia, but I went on the road with Davey when it was televised. I had the best of both worlds.

It took three years for the Kody Light case to come to trial. It lasted 10 days. Crown prosecutor Gary Belecki's courtroom theatrics would have been laughable if the situation hadn't been so serious. He screamed and yelled so much, our seven-year-old daughter Georgia, nine-year-old son Harry and their 12-year-old cousin Matt fled the courtroom in tears. He questioned my testimony, accusing me of lying to keep Davey out of jail so he could continue earning a lot of money.

"He makes a pretty good living. You and your husband live very comfortably in your Tampa home don't you?"

"We have a nice home, because we make it a nice home," I answered.

Mr. Belecki's skewed logic put Davey on the spot. He asked Davey whether wrestling was fake, expecting Davey to deny it was. He wanted to show that Davey was capable of picking someone up and throwing them across a room. But Davey reluctantly threw Mr. Belecki a curve ball when he admitted it wasn't all real.

Mr. Bilecki fumbled around a moment and then accused Davey of making his living based on lies and suggested Davey was lying on the stand.

Justice Waite interjected, reminding Mr. Bilecki that Davey took an oath and that to suggest he was lying, belittled that oath. Of course the next day's headlines around the world reported, "Davey Boy Smith exposes wrestling!"

Carl Moffat, the wrestler who had been whimpering about the spare tire hitting his leg in Davey's 1989 car accident, called the prosecutor and volunteered to come down and testify that Davey was capable of throwing a man 30 feet. So we had to call my brother Ross as a rebuttal witness to testify that Carl was vindictive because Davey wouldn't support him in a lawsuit against Ross and my dad relating to the 1989 accident.

We also asked Ed Whalen to write a character reference for Davey. Ed had made thousands of dollars over the years with the family's wrestling promotion and it was the first time any of us had asked a favor in return. But he turned us down. He said he couldn't get involved because he might want to run for politics some day and it could come back to haunt him.

It cost us half a million of our hard-earned US dollars to defend Davey. In the end, Justice John Waite acquitted him. He was adamant in his opinion that if anyone was victimized it was Davey.

"Light's actions could be properly characterized as an assault on Smith. The rights of a professional wrestler are no different than any other citizen and Smith's conduct throughout was entirely justified."

CHAPTER TWENTYEIGHT

More Adventures

At the end of October in 1995, I began accompanying Davey to the ring as his devoted wife. He was still a heel, but my gimmick was that I would stick by him no matter what. The fans hated me. I was like Sandy Scott, the ref who used to look the other way when wrestlers were cheating.

Then the WWF decided to pair Davey with Owen. They were terrific together. Owen became the flyer and Davey the power-house. I was the common link, the wife and sister. We were a heel trio.

Owen and Davey often tagged against Jake Roberts and Ahmed Johnson. Both Davey and Owen hated being slammed by Ahmed. He didn't know his own strength. They said that he'd slam them so hard; they'd see little birds. When Ahmed bodyslammed him, 'Stone Cold' Steve Austin said he'd have to wiggle his fingers to make sure he wasn't paralyzed.

Ahmed had a move called 'The Pearl River Plunge,' a move where he would scissor kick the back of his opponent's head. His heel would knock the guy face-first into the mat, then he'd pick up his opponent and powerbomb him. I was watching from the sides when he gave Owen a concussion doing this move. After getting kicked in the head, Owen's eyes went vacant and he ran flat-footed away from Ahmed, obviously unaware of his surroundings. He was wrestling on instinct. Owen ricocheted off the ropes and Ahmed threw him over the top rope. He landed like a rag doll on the concrete floor next to the ring. This wrestling was real all right.

Then they added Van Vader to our team of heels. They gave us Jim Cornette as our on-stage wrestling manager. We were a little army and Jim was our general. Jim would lead our way to the ring followed by Vader, then Davey and I would walk up, talking to-gether. Owen's hands were full because he would always carry two Slammies – wrestling Oscars – and his World Tag Team Belt.

155

He'd run up from behind and budge in front of Davey and me, sticking his face right in front of Davey's face for the camera and smiling approvingly and pointing his fingers at me, as if he were putting me over.

Davey would then run in front of Owen and flex his biceps, which would propel Owen to run in front of Davey.

I always worried when the boys had to go in with Jake 'The Snake' Roberts because at the time I thought he was a drunk but later I learned he was a drug addict. I remember one night Jake came to the show and the next day he disappeared because he was on a crack binge. Meanwhile Vince was trying to get a live TV taping done and he was asking, "Where the hell is Jake? Where is he? He's in a six-man tag, where is he?" It turned out Jake was in jail. He got caught with some girl who was the daughter of someone in the police force.

I felt bad for Vince McMahon because he seemed to have a lot of disloyalty in his company and he was trying to get his show off the ground.

He reminded me of my dad, especially the times when my dad had struggled.

Jake was a brilliant man, with maybe a genius IQ, but he was troubled. He had a great gimmick. He would carry a burlap sack with him into the ring and stash it in the corner. When he was the victor, he'd empty a huge yellow boa constrictor from the sack onto his downed opponent. Jake's snake provided the inspiration for a story line that was cooked up for us. Jim Cornette was absolutely terrified of snakes. One night they had me sitting in the crowd rather than at ringside because I was going to be told Jim Cornette had had a heart attack after Jake scared him with his snake. Davey and Owen were supposed to be frightened too and run out of the ring instead of resuscitating their dying manager.

But instead of just teasing Jim with the snake, Jake dumped it right on Jim and it began threading itself around his body. Jim came close to genuinely having a cardiac arrest, and this made Davey and Owen laugh so hard they forgot to run out of the ring. In addition, the story line had me leaving my seat to tend to Jim in the back and getting distracted by a handsome Shawn Michaels. Then to cover my flirtatious behavior with Shawn, I leaned over Jim and said, "Did you see that Jim? Shawn just made a pass at me."

The cameras caught Jim pulling Davey and me into a locker room. Then they cut to Davey throwing a chair across the room yelling, "I'm going to kill that Shawn Michaels!" This angle was built for the big pay-per-view event in Savannah, Georgia, three months later in May of 1996. Vince split Owen and Davey up and had Davey wrestling as a single. Owen was paired with Vader and Jim Cornette managed them.

Much like the soap opera Vince McMahon eventually created with his daughter Stephanie and WWF superstar Triple H, I was supposedly getting involved with Shawn Michaels. Davey was supposed to be concerned that Shawn was making advances. This would lead to a big fight. Then I found out that part of the big angle had me getting on a closed-circuit camera seducing Shawn. It would have been so good if I had just gone with it. But I talked to my dad about it.

Bret had just lost the World's Belt at Wrestlemania 13, in a 60-minute hard-fought match with Shawn who had entered the ring on a harness from the ceiling of the Anaheim Duck Pond. He wasn't crazy about losing the belt to Shawn. He wouldn't have minded losing to Steve Austin or Diesel, but Bret and Shawn were always vying for Vince's attention. So he had a chip on his shoulder. He decided to put wrestling on hiatus while he pursued an acting career.

The WWF's booking agent Bruce Pritchard and Jim Cornette approached me. Jim said, "You know, this is going to be great! You're going to be making the moves on Shawn, trying to ram your tongue down his throat and undo his belt buckle while Shawn tries to resist. Your feelings will be hurt because he has spurned your advances, so you go back to Davey and say, 'That SOB, that goddamn Shawn Michaels, he's been making passes at me and I want you to put a stop to it. I want you to finish him.'"

Davey hated this. He said, "It makes me look like an asshole because my wife is making moves on Shawn and I'm going after Shawn. I should be going after her!"

Jim rolled his eyes. "Uh you see, Davey, you don't know she is the bad one. You love her and believe her when she says Shawn is trying to grope her." But Davey didn't like it. I was uncomfortable with it because I'm Diana Hart, not Sable. For one thing, I was using my real name. I was nervous about acting out the scene on TV, but I would have trusted Shawn to help me through that. It would have been really good for me to get that kind of exposure. It was what I'd been waiting for my whole life.

I was so stupid and stubborn. I should have thought of it like the Undertaker. He's not an undertaker, he's not really a funeral home director, but that's his role on TV. I guess it was the way Jim Cornette told me about it. He was so coarse. He was really laughing and I thought maybe it was a joke on me. I didn't really comprehend the potential of the whole thing. I could have been such a good bad sister. I got back to my hotel room and I called Bret. He was absolutely against it. I think at that time Bret did care about what I did in wrestling and he was concerned about the way I would be perceived. But at the same time he was mad at the WWF because he had to lose to Shawn at Wrestlemania. Bret said, "You can't do that, you're Stu Hart's daughter. When dad goes to the IGA or the Safeway store and some guy says, 'Hey, Stu, I saw your daughter on TV. God what's happening there?' Well you just can't put dad through that."

I understood what he was saying. We were Stu Hart's kids and we didn't want anyone to think we were brought up to take advantage of our father's name. My mother has always said, "Dahling, we'd never want anyone to think your father's daughter was that kind of girl." Bret advised me to take the first plane out of there. Then I called my dad. He was furious about this angle. I could hear him yelling to my mother in the kitchen. "That gaddamned Bruce Pritchard wants Diana to appear as some sort of tramp, some and I think that's gaddamned disgusting. Would he want his mother to be watching his daughter doing a role like that?" My dad was going ballistic.

Then Owen pulled one of his ribs, which didn't help. Vince had these 1-800 phone line rooms set up where wrestlers talked to wrestling fans and answered questions at so much money per minute. Owen and Jim were working the phones when Owen discreetly dialed my dad who answered. "Oh hi, it's Owen," he said. Right away my dad started yelling about, "that gaddamned Bruce Pritchard and Jim Cornette and what kind of perverts are they?" He ranted, "I'm so gaddamned mad I could rip their nuts out!" Owen couldn't resist this golden opportunity. Without saying who he was talking to, he handed the phone to Jim, "It's for you." Jim Cornette grabbed the phone. "Yeah, Jim Cornette here."

In wrestling terminology, my dad cut a promo on him. But Bruce Pritchard was notorious for his impersonations so Jim assumed

Owen and Bruce were trying to pull one over on him. He decided to go along. He really hammed it up. "Yeah, we're going to have your daughter go up there and it's going to look like a Goddamned orgy by the time we're finished. We're going to have her French kissing her brother and we're going to have Owen with his hands all over her ass and Davey Boy will be in there for a three-way." My dad was just going nuts on the other end. He screamed, "Gaddamnit, I don't want ... that's gaddamned horseshit and I don't want my daughter being a part of that."

Jim Cornette held the phone away from his ear laughing and looked at Owen saying, "Okay who the hell is this anyway?"

Owen was trying to keep his laughter in check. "It's Stu Hart, my dad." Jim laughed again, "Yeah right."

Then Bruce Pritchard walked into the room. Jim turned white as a sheet and started back-pedaling and apologizing to my dad, who was way beyond being pacified. To this day my dad thinks that Jim Cornette and Bruce Pritchard are really warped guys who wanted a perverted, incestuous orgy to be portrayed on TV with his kids.

My TV flirtation with Shawn was toned down considerably due to my reticence and because my dad objected so strenuously. Jim Cornette was sincerely afraid of my dad. Shawn was good about it. I told him I was really uncomfortable with the scenario and he said that was fine, we'd do something else. But I wonder what would have happened had I gone through with it as planned. Maybe it was my last chance to star in wrestling and I blew it. Maybe my being such a square cost me.

Davey gave notice to the WWF. He had to give three months" written notice through a lawyer by registered mail to WWF Titans Sports in Stanford, Connecticut. At that time Vince was losing guys to the WCW. Hulk Hogan still wanted Davey to join him there but Davey had only given notice so he could negotiate a better deal with Vince. Vince called Owen, Davey and me into his office and said, "Davey, I don't want to lose you. Come on, you're family." He was really decent about it. Owen had already signed. He had no intention of leaving. He had the good sense to stay in one spot.

Matt

It was then a terrible tragedy befell our family. My son Harry's cousin and best friend in the world, my sister Georgia's middle son, Matt, died of flesh-eating disease.

Davey and I had had enough of Florida. I was horribly homesick. Davey could see how miserable I was and I think he missed my family too. So we sold our house and packed up. The school year was due to end in one week and we were scheduled to move back home to Calgary on the sixth of July. On the Saturday night two weeks before our move, 13-year-old Matt, his brother Ted and some of their friends were wrestling in the outdoor ring set up in my dad's yard for the KWA, the Kid's Wrestling Alliance. This was a club Harry and Matt started just before we moved to Florida. All 30 cousins belonged. The girls were managers and the boys were wrestlers and commentators. They had costumes, sets, music and animals. It was a children's version of Monday Night Raw.

Alison called on Monday. She said a head butt to the groin had hurt Matt. He was at The Alberta Children's Hospital because he had developed some strange symptoms. He was itchy, had a fever and chills and he was doubled over in pain. Georgia thought he had pulled his groin muscle. X-rays showed nothing. But the hospital diagnosed the flu and sent him home with codeine. Later that morning, his dad, BJ, came home from a weekend shift at the fire hall. He felt Matt's pulse and rushed him to the hospital.

Alison called again Tuesday. She wanted us to come home immediately. She said Matt had turned the color of an eggplant and was having trouble breathing. She also said he was repeatedly asking for Harry. The doctors were baffled. Specialists from all over were called to consult. The family was told that Matt was the sickest boy in the whole country. By Wednesday he was on life support. Everything was shutting down except his heart and brain. His fingers had shriveled up into long, skinny raisins. His whole body was cold and hard. Matt and Harry lived for wrestling and even in his weakened condition it was still the number-one thing on Matt's mind. Owen visited with Matt and heard Matt's final words before he lapsed into a coma.

Owen had told him, "You're going to be okay. You are such a strong, healthy boy. Harry and Davey and Diana and Baby Georgia are on their way to see you. Hang in there, Matt."

Matt whispered, "I hope Davey will stay with the WWF. I want to talk to him about that. Harry and I have to get ready for our next KWA match. Baby Georgia's going to be my manager. Harry just faxed me."

"Yeah we'll all be wrestling for the WWF together someday. You and Harry, me and Davey and Jim."

"Bret needs to come back to the WWF too."

Owen nodded gravely. "Bret will be coming in to see you soon, Matt. Why don't you talk to him about that?"

That night Matt fell asleep and never opened his eyes again. The doctors finally found a diagnosis, flesh-eating disease.

A friend of our family, Danny McCullough was acquainted with Mother Teresa. He got in touch with her in India and she and her nuns began praying for Matt.

Davey, the kids and I arrived the next day. We went straight from the airport to Matt's hospital room. Anyone who visited Matt got a prescription for antibiotics and had to be disinfected and swathed in a hospital gown before going into his room. Although he was only ten years old, Harry marched right up to Matt and took his hand. He didn't bat an eye at Matt's shriveled limbs and distended stomach. He ignored the fact Matt was in a coma and started right into the KWA, making plans for their summer. He was so happy to see Matt again.

Harry was such a big wrestling fan he had always called his dad Davey. "What kind of car should Davey get? You're still going to wrestle as The Canadian Cougar, aren't you Matt?"

Harry sat by Matt's bedside daily. He heard the doctors discussing how they might save Matt by cutting off his legs and his arms below the elbow with a saw and it would have to be quick because oxygen would promote the speed of the flesh-eating disease to his heart. They hoped he would get stronger so that he could withstand the amputation.

The whole family came to see Matt. Bret and Davey hadn't spoken to Bruce for five months since my dad's 80th birthday tribute and now they all stood side by side praying for a miracle.

Thirteen days after he had been admitted to the hospital, Matt died. Matt's 16-year-old brother Ted called me just after midnight. He was crying, "Can you get to the hospital right away? Matt has taken a turn for the worse."

Harry and I raced to Matt's bedside. Georgia, BJ and Ross were right on our heels. We all stood quietly in an adjoining room with a glass partition and watched as the doctors and nurses flew around his ravaged figure. He was drowning in his own blood. One of the doctors joined us and with tears in his eyes, he told us they couldn't save Matt. He said we had perhaps two minutes to say goodbye.

We all kissed Matt on the forehead. Everyone held a part of him. Harry had his hand. I stroked his atrophied foot. It was cold as ice. Georgia was crying. "You are such a nice boy. We love you so much."

BJ had been a fireman for 20 years. He was accustomed to death. But now he was sobbing, "How could they take my little boy?" he gulped. "When I die Matt, promise you'll meet me at the gates."

Ross said, "That's right, you're going to heaven."

Georgia wept, "There is no heaven. God would never let this happen to you, Matt."

We were all crying. "We love you. You are the best."

Harry leaned over and kissed him whispering, "I'll never forget you."

As Matt's heart beat for the last time, blood poured out of his mouth like a waterfall. When the blood ceased, Matt was gone.

I went into the mourning room and called my dad. I couldn't bring myself to say that Matt was dead. I said, "Matt has gone to heaven Dad."

"Poor little guy," he said.

CHAPTER THIRTY

Family Outing

I finished my run with the WWF at "The International Incident" in Vancouver four days after Matt's funeral in July of 1996. The match pitted Davey, Owen, Vader and Jim Cornette against Ultimate Warrior, Ahmed and Shawn Michaels. It was the first "In Your House" pay-per-view that they had done in Canada.

They hired me one more time in July 1997, for The Canadian Stampede. I had been crowned Mrs. Calgary so my picture was often in the paper and the WWF decided to capitalize on that. The Canadian Stampede pitted Ken Shamrock, Steve Austin, Mike Hegstrandt aka Hawk and Joe Laurentis aka Animal-together they were The Legion of Doom-along with Dustin Runnels better known as, Goldust, against the entire Hart Foundation: Brian Pilman, Jim Neidhart, Bret, Owen and Davey.

I walked them out to the ring. We cheated and won and the fans were crazy about us. Maybe it was because Bret had said that the United States needed an enema and should be flushed down the toilet. My mom was really offended lest her American sisters hear what he had said.

We got a standing ovation and I remember Brian Pilman turning to me in awe. "Ten years ago, who would have dreamed we'd all be here starring in the Saddledome in front of the world on pay-per-view!"

The whole family jumped up from their front row seats and clambered on stage. There were over 50 of us including Bret's 14-year-old daughter, Jade.

Bret turned to a strange teenage boy standing beside him and snapped, "Who the hell are you?"

The kid was grinning from ear to ear and waving enthusiastically at the crowd, "I'm Jade's boyfriend."

Owen and Martha

Owen always told me he met Martha and her sister, Virginia, at the wrestling matches in the early eighties at the Victorian Pavilion. I won't say Martha was a ring rat, but that's where she first laid eyes on Owen. Virginia was being frisked at the match because a police officer thought she had drugs in her purse. Virginia was super straight. There was no way she had any drugs with her, but she was so shaken by the police officer that she fled to the bathroom crying.

In later years Virginia did go a little wild. She and her husband Ronnie had five kids. Virginia would drive Chad, one of her sons, to hockey and that's where she started an affair with his coach, George. She eventually left Ron for George and Owen was just furious about it. He didn't want anything to do with them.

In 1983, Owen was working at the door selling programs and taking tickets and witnessed the scene with the officer and the girls. Taking pity on them he introduced himself and tried to ease the situation with a few jokes. He began to look forward to bumping into Martha at the matches. One thing led to another and before long they were dating.

Owen and Martha had been dating a few years when he went to wrestle in England. There, he met a girl named Luisa Edo Juan, the daughter of Anne Relwysko. Anne Relwysko was married to Ad Nankasey who had wrestled in the WWF, and later became a manager. Luisa was adorable. She looked like actress Melissa Sue Anderson who played Mary Ingalls on the television series Little House On The Prairie. Luisa loved wrestling, grew up in wrestling and understood wrestling. Luisa's mother was very protective of her. She made sure Luisa was well educated. Luisa knew three languages. She had a pilot's license and was enrolled in university. On top of all this, Luisa was very pretty and very funny. Almost too good to be true, she and Owen hit it off right way. Owen was staying with Luisa's family because they were involved in promoting his tour.

When Owen returned to Calgary a couple of months later at the beginning of 1987, he confided to me he had very strong feelings for Luisa. She was everything he wanted. He'd thought about it and he was ready to break up with Martha. He gave it his best shot, but Martha wouldn't have it. I saw them fighting on my dad's lawn and Martha was crying and yelling at him, "I waited for you while you left to wrestle in Europe. I was loyal and you were screwing around with some British wrestling slut? How dare you do this to me? What kind of lowlife are you?"

Owen was devastated. He had never broken up with a girl before and the last thing he wanted to do was hurt anyone. He began to backtrack.

"No, no it's not like that. I'm sorry, just calm down, calm down." He was so like my mom. He'd rather switch than fight. My dad has said he sometimes thinks that if my mom had known how to say no, she would not have married him.

When Owen talked to me later that day he clenched his jaw, "I just can't hurt her so I'll live with it then. Christ."

There was no way Martha was going to let him out of her sights as a free man again. She kept at him night and day and two weeks later they were engaged.

Martha was the dominating and controlling partner in their relationship. She wanted a traditional wedding yet neither of her parents was willing to contribute any money to the celebration, not one red cent.

Martha wanted a sit-down turkey and ham dinner with potato salad and Jell-O for about 500 people. My mom cringed. She confided to us that it sounded like the menu from some 4-H club dinner, not a proper menu for a wedding. But of course my mom refused to say anything to Martha. She didn't want Owen angry with her.

My mom, Georgia, my dad, Owen, Martha and her mother all sat down. My mom urged Georgia to speak on their behalf. Georgia began, "Perhaps the ham and turkey thing would be better suited to a Victoria Park community hall," she smiled. Victoria Park was the grungy area near the Stampede Grounds where Martha grew up so it wasn't the most politic thing to say.

"When Diana married Davey-Boy, our menu came directly from the White House," Georgia continued. "Our aunt Diana's husband

Jock was the former Canadian Prime Minister Joe Clark's press secretary."

Martha was furious. She literally stamped her feet on the ground. "This is my wedding! I want a sit-down dinner. I don't see anything wrong with potato salad and paper plates!"

My mom swallowed. "We're only trying to think about the guests, dahling. For a group this large, hors d'oeuvres really would be better. They can mingle that way. A sit-down dinner restricts them to their table.

And Martha, dahling, where would we seat 500 people? And where will we get the tables?"

Martha clenched her fists and accused my parents of being cheap. Martha's mother stood up angrily, "Nobody's going to ruin my baby's wedding! What Martha wants, Martha should get."

The meeting ended with my mom and dad compromising. They agreed to serve ham and turkey along with finger foods. The food would be served on bone china, not paper plates and there would be some tables set up.

The encounter drove my mom to her room and the bottle for two days. She was just sick about the conflict and Martha's lack of wedding etiquette.

"This is what my son is marrying. What will my sisters think?"

My mom's worries were valid. At the wedding, Martha's aunt drank too much red wine. She became nauseous and Georgia guided her into the bathroom on the second landing. As she bent over the toilet her false teeth dislodged and landed in the bowl. Her plate broke in half and Georgia was forced to fish for the fragments. She carefully rinsed each half under the tap before Martha's aunt snatched them out of her hand and popped them back in her mouth backward.

Martha's mother Joan danced with her boyfriend Frenchy Joe, who lived in a camper outside her home. Frenchy Joe became homeless later, after Owen achieved financial success and was able to help her out, but at the wedding the couple swayed drunkenly on the dance floor, grinding their cigarette butts into the antique Persian carpets. Eventually, Davey confronted them and told them to cut it out. The mother of the bride sneered and shouted at him to "Fuck off."

To Owen, Martha became the damsel in distress. She was always complaining that she was being victimized. In order to protect her from criticism, he became secretive about their relationship. Owen and I maintained some closeness throughout his marriage to Martha. He saw me quite often, but only when she was out and he never told her about our clandestine visits.

When I was on the road with Owen and Davey in 1995 and 1996, Owen and I had long talks. The odd time Savio Vega would be in the car with us, or Duke Droese or Brian Pilman. Then we would talk about other things. But if it were just Davey, Owen and me, we would get into our family politics. He told me he was unhappy about Martha's mother's drinking problem. He wasn't comfortable with her being at the house all the time and he didn't want Martha getting a job. Not because he was a chauvinist but because he thought one of them should be home with the kids. Martha got a job at the post office and he was very upset. I remember him complaining.

"She's got to leave for work at four in the morning and she does that every day and she says it makes her feel good, but I'm thinking how come I can't make her feel good? I'm supporting her. I'm doing quite well in my career and she still wants this little job at the post office. Yet she never stops complaining that she doesn't see me enough. What am I supposed to do, quit wrestling so we can live off her post office salary?"

It hurt him that Martha was never happy, never satisfied. She always wanted more and more-a bigger house, private schools for the kids, opera tickets. It was if she thought she could buy class. Owen was distressed by her demands that they work as much as they could while they were young and strong and that he do all the autograph sessions that he could possibly make time for and save all the money so that, when they retired at the end of his contract, they could both take it easy.

Anyway once Martha put her foot down, which is what she always did, Owen went along.

"I'm keeping this job," she declared. "And on top of that, my mother is going to live with us to baby-sit our kids while I go back to university and take courses to become a psychologist."

But Owen didn't like it because he said Martha's mother was a heavy drinker and he didn't like that his kids were around her more than they were around Martha.

Owen and Martha's son was named Oje because it was Owen's nickname. Martha is Jewish, but doesn't advertise that fact. They had a christening for Oje at St. Mary's, the big Catholic Cathedral where we went as kids. Conspicuously absent was anyone from our side of the family. None of us was invited. My mom was very hurt. Owen defended their decision.

"Well, you all would have shown up late anyway."

Athena Christy was born in September 1995. Martha hadn't told us she was pregnant until that July. She said she felt it would curse the baby and warned Owen not to say anything, so it was quite a surprise. Again, none of us were invited to the baptism.

Now that Owen isn't here, Martha doesn't hold back from saying whatever she wants to about the family. My parents supported her in her lawsuit against the WWF and she won an $18-million settlement. They received $2 million. Once the case was over, she dropped them like a hot potato. So what are we going to do, sue her?

Bret

In 1996, Davey signed a five-year contract with the WWF that guaranteed him US $300,000 a year. Vince said he would create a belt specifically for him called The European Championship Belt and Davey was wily enough to insist it be written into his contract.

Bret came back less than three months later and signed for 17 years at around $1million dollars a year. The idea was that, when he quit wrestling, he would become part of Vince's office. Another stipulation in Bret's deal was that he was to have main-event billing, so he was furious when Davey and Shawn were the main event at a pay-per-view called, "One Night Only," in Birmingham, England. There, Davey was supposed to drop his European Championship Belt to Shawn.

Bret wrestled in the Birmingham show but he was beside himself because he wasn't the headliner. Bret grumbled the whole night and I finally said, "Bret, you're not the hero here, Davey is."

Vince pulled Davey aside just before the show and said, "Davey, Shawn is going to beat you tonight, but we are going to have a return match in Manchester in the spring at the G-MEX and you will win your belt back." Davey was a little disappointed about having to lose in his home country, but he agreed.

"Fine, whatever you want, Vince, no complaints."

Bret grabbed me for a quick conference. "You know Dave is putting Shawn over tonight. He's jobbing for him. So when you're in the ring with Davey after the finish, Owen and I are supposed to do a run-in to save you and Davey against Rick Rude, Hunter Hearst Helmsley, Shawn and Chyna. I have a feeling that Chyna will go after me, and I can't hit a girl so you go after her."

I was skeptical. "She's not going to go near you, Bret."

Bret was impatient with me. "Of course she will. They'll do anything to make me look bad."

I was astounded. Just because he was not headlining this once, he had decided the WWF was out to ruin him. In my opinion, he was so successful – perhaps the biggest wrestler in the world at the time – that he became paranoid and terrified he would lose his status.

Chyna didn't go near Bret; but she ran straight for me. She bear-hugged me and took me right off my feet. I couldn't believe how strong she was.

"Geez," I thought, "if she does turn from me and go after Bret, I'm not sure what he expects me to do?"

In the dressing room, Bret confronted Vince. "Undertaker and I should have been the main event tonight!"

Vince replied, "No, this was an exception, Bret. Davey is a huge star in England and we wanted to capitalize on that."

So Bret said, "really? Why did you have him lose then?"

Vince said, "We wanted the crowd to sympathize with him. Everyone expected him to win. We had him beat by four guys."

The match coincided with the recent death of Princess Diana so when Davey walked down into the arena with his sister Tracy who was recovering from a terrible bout with cancer, it had a huge emotional impact, just as Vince knew it would.

Bret threatened to quit over the snub.

By the end of that month Bret and Vince were constantly arguing. Bret swore he wanted out of his contract and Vince said he was welcome to leave. They worked it out where Bret negotiated a deal with the WCW and got US$3 three million dollars each year for three years, plus a percentage of the merchandising. He was going to finish up November ninth at the Survivor Series. Vince needed Bret to drop the World's Belt and he wanted it to be to Shawn.

Bret was in the midst of making a big documentary called "Wrestling With Shadows: The Bret Hart Story." Bret didn't like Shawn, so in his documentary, he edited a match in which Shawn was the guest referee in a bout between Bret and Undertaker. Seemingly unprovoked, Shawn took a chair, and tried to hit Bret over the head with it. Bret ducked and the chair clocked Undertaker. But what Bret didn't show in that segment was that he had spit right in Shawn's face and Shawn was retaliating with the chair.

Vince's big worry was that Bret was going to quit with the belt and go to the WCW and perhaps throw Vince's World Belt in the garbage. Alundra Blaze – who had been the world female champion for the WWF – had gone on TV for the WCW and done that. Vince was fed up with ex-employees going on to the WCW and calling the WWF the toilet bowl of wrestling. He wanted to cover himself and the most valuable prize in his federation, his World's Belt. There was no way he wanted Bret to leave with it.

The cities where the pay-per-views are held are booked well in advance. The Survivor Series '97 happened to be Montreal. So Bret said, "No I can't lose in my home country." Even though Davey just lost to Shawn in Birmingham, England.

Vince said, "Well, Bret, let's think of some ideas then, how are we going about this?" So a group of wrestler's – Jim Neidhart, Davey, Owen and Shawn – came up with various ideas. Everyone was trying to figure out a way in which Bret could lose his belt to Shawn, leaving Bret happy and Vince with his belt. One of Bret's solutions was not to have Shawn beat him at the Survivor Series, but to bring Shawn on TV's Monday Night Raw, and Bret would just hand the belt over to him.

Vince said, "Well I don't really see how that helps me out. Where do I go from there? You give the belt to Shawn like he couldn't beat you. So my champion is the WCW's newest import."

They worked on different scenarios all month – though it was going nowhere. Unbeknownst to Vince, Bret was attending all these meetings wearing a wiretap, hoping to record his discussion with Vince for use in his forthcoming documentary.

It was ironic that Bret would later make such a fuss about how Vince had been dishonest with him and here Bret was sneaking tape recordings out of private meetings for his own documentary project.

On the Saturday night before the Survivor Series, Bret came to Vince and Vince finally said, "Okay Bret, I agree to that." He was pacifying Bret. But Bret had Vince on tape giving his word that he would go along with Bret's idea involving Davey and Owen. Davey and Owen were to interfere in a kind of hodge-podge in the end.

Meanwhile, right after he made that deal with Bret, Vince had a clandestine meeting with Triple H, two of Vince's agents – Pat Patterson and Jerry Brisco – and referee Earl Hebner. They agreed to double-cross Bret.

Vince always commentated wearing a tuxedo, but the day of the Survivor Series he wore casual clothes. Davey thought that was kind of strange.

As the match neared the end, Davey and Owen were in the gorilla position, named for the late Gorilla Monsoon, a former Hungarian wrestler and one of Vince's closest friends. Gorilla used to sit watching the TV monitor, so that he could give the wrestlers their cues. In another few minutes Davey and Owen were to run down into the ring to create confusion.

Vince was ringside. Shawn put Bret in Bret's own finishing move, The Sharpshooter. Bret was getting in position to kick him off and grab the ropes so the referee would have to break the hold when suddenly Earl yelled to Vince and the timekeeper, "Ring the bell! Ring the bell!" Then he waved his arms and the match was over. Vince snatched up the belt and handed it to Earl. Earl presented it to a confused looking Shawn.

Davey ran in the ring, "What the fuck happened, Bret?"

Bret said, "I don't know."

And Davey said, "I think Vince got you, Bret." Owen had joined them. All three were furious. Bret went berserk. He spit in Vince's face and started smashing the TV monitors all around the ring. He headed to the dressing room warning, "If Vince comes in here, tell him I'm going to punch him out."

Vince started looking for Bret and found Davey. He asked, "Where's Bret?"

Davey answered, "Well, he's just got out of the shower, but if I was you, I wouldn't go in and see him."

Vince replied, "Well, thanks for the warning, but I'll do what I have to do."

Vince stuck his head in the dressing room and said that he wanted to talk. Bret angrily replied, "I'm getting dressed and if you're still around when I'm done, I'm going to punch you out."

Vince nodded, "Okay, I'll take my chances."

Bret got dressed and, sure enough, Bret cold-cocked Vince right in the eye and broke his knuckle doing it. Bret was so mad it took both Davey and Shane McMahon to pull him off Vince. While he was helping out, Davey tore his knee ligaments, which were already hurting from wrestling Shawn in England for the Intercontinental Belt.

After the big blowout, Davey and Owen took a stand. They didn't show up at Monday Night Raw and Owen stayed off the road for a week, but then decided to return to work. He told Bret, "I'm not going to quit my job, I'm not going to pay a fine, and I'm not going to go to the WCW. Martha wants me to finish my career here and retire, and that's it. I'm sick about what happened to you, Bret. I think it was horrible, but I've got to do what I have to do for my family."

Bret was just furious about that. He swore, "That fucking Martha. She's got Owen so pussy-whipped. He can't do anything without getting her permission. She doesn't understand. She doesn't like wrestling. She doesn't understand this at all. The family's got to stick together."

Bret went back to Owen and told him that if he didn't leave, he would never think of Owen as his brother again. Owen didn't leave.

Bret assumed a lot of guys were going to quit in protest, but they didn't.

I remember my dad asking if this Survivor Series thing was all work or was it legitimate? Did Bret actually punch Vince McMahon in the face in the dressing room? The WWF had shown it all on camera, even Bret spitting in Vince's face, right in his eye.

The ratings carried over to the next night so Vince used Monday Night Raw as a platform to promote his next star, Steve Austin. And boy, Steve did an excellent job. He was awesome. He started out as the guy who hated his boss, and so many people shared his feelings because of what they thought Vince had done to Bret. Vince made a superb heel.

Bret never seemed to get over Survivor Series '97. In his eyes, everybody who didn't follow him, betrayed him. Owen told Vince Russo, the WWF's booker at that time, that Bret was hounding him to quit all the time. Owen told me he was sick of Bret at this point. He was fed up with Bret phoning him and Martha and hammering away.

"I'll never forgive you if you don't leave. This is your brother we're talking about. I can't believe you're gonna stay with Vince McMahon over your own brother."

Owen said, "Bret I want to finish my career. I'm actually disgusted by this whole incident. I'm sick of you, I'm sick of all of it. I just want to finish my time here and retire from wrestling and go some place where nobody even knows my name or bothers me. That's the point I'm at right now – and quit bothering Martha!"

Vince Russo assured Owen that they were going to do something with him and not squash him or have him jobbed out (beaten by every Tom, Dick and Harry who comes along.) He pledged they would not make a mockery out of him just because he was Bret Hart's brother.

Vince Russo called Bret. "Bret, you've got to leave Owen alone right now. He's trying to provide for his family and he doesn't want to leave and he just wants to do his job. You keep calling him and you're confusing him. You're not making it easy for Owen. He has never done anything to hurt you. As your friend, and as Owen's friend, I'm asking you to leave him alone."

Meanwhile, Bret was calling Davey and me just as often. He was determined to get Davey to move to the WCW with him.

"Vince is going to bury you," Bret told Davey. "He's going to do to you what he did to me." Bret had Carlo D'Marco – his best friend and WWF Canadian representative – talk to Davey.

"Davey, I have been sitting in on the meetings and I know they are going to job you out." Carl said, "I know this Davey. I heard it. I sat in at the meetings. We had conference calls and round-table decisions. Vince is going to have you and Owen beaten by anyone and everyone. They'll have you beaten by midgets just to get back at Bret. If I were you, I would leave before they have a chance to do it."

Though Bret didn't have a gun to Davey's head, he was in his ear constantly. "The deal over here can't last for long. Eric (Bischoff, the president of the WCW) is getting fed up. He can't hold his breath much longer."

Bret would call me too. "What is Davey doing? He is going to blow this fucking deal. I'm doing everything I can to keep Eric from walking away."

The trouble was if Davey left the WWF he would have to pay a US $100,000 fine. Davey did put his lawyers on it and Bret was relentless.

"What's your lawyer doing? You're going to lose this deal." Eric Bischoff had assigned the head of his legal department Nick Lambrose to handle it. Nick Lambrose was going back and forth with the WWF lawyer Ed Kaufman and Davey's lawyer. The WCW was offering a three-year contract. He'd make US $333,000 the first year, US $383,000 the second, and US $433,000 the third year. They also agreed to pay half of the US $100,000 up front and then take it out of his first year's salary.

Davey left the WWF for the third time on January 19th, 1998. He was recovering from knee surgery. He'd blown out his knee that November at the Survivor Series incident in Montreal, when he and Shane had pulled Bret off Vince. Owen told me that he got US $100,000 for staying. We wired US $100,000 into a WWF bank account and the WWF paid one lump sum of US $100,000 to Owen and further rewarded Owen with two more years on his contract. Owen used that money to buy the lot to build his dream home where Martha now lives.

I wasn't mad at Owen for getting the money that we had been fined, but the irony of the situation wasn't lost on me. Bret swore that he would never think of Owen as his brother again because he saw Owen's loyalty with the WWF as a betrayal against him.

Bret never seemed happy at the WCW. Everything I read about him, every time we talked, all I heard was how Vince screwed him. He pulled his groin early in the fall of 1998, but kept wrestling. Finally, he had to have surgery. He returned to the ring after mending and faced Goldberg – WCW's biggest star.

Bret claimed Goldberg kicked him in the head because he was so unskilled. I've seen Goldberg, a six-foot-five athlete, turn a somersault in the air, so I was surprised to hear Bret knock him like that.

Bret told Keith, "My brain is mush from that kick, so I'm going to retire." According to my sister Ellie, Bret got a five million dollar insurance settlement, but sadly he left with a whisper not a bang – unbefitting of such an admired athlete.

Davey and Drugs

Davey told me Eric Bischoff talked to him in February, in the dressing room before his first match back at the WCW. Davey was pitted against Steve 'Mondo' McMichael. Eric was trying to get rid of Steve, an ex-NFL player, because he was a junkie. Steve's arm was sore and bandaged up.

Eric told Davey, "Break his arm. I want to get rid of him for awhile."

Davey looked at Eric. "Are you serious?"

Eric nodded.

Just before he went into the ring, Davey overheard WCW agent Arn Anderson say to Steve, "Mondo, go do your rails."

Davey turned to Arn, "What are rails?"

"He's gotta do coke because he's so slow," Arn replied.

Davey was disgusted. Vince took care of his wrestlers. Davey had never heard a WWF agent tell a guy to get stoned before he entered the ring. It's dangerous for him and his opponent. Wrestling requires a lot of trust. Davey was worried. He was putting his body in the hands of a guy who was totally fucked up. Ironically, Davey ended up with the shoe on the other foot within the year.

Davey says he tried morphine for the first time the year before his return to the WCW, around the time of the Canadian Stampede. He claimed Akim Albrecht introduced it to him. That's what my son Harry told me. During a 'father-son chat' Davey told my 13-year-old that Akim shot him up in the shoulder explaining to Davey, "Damn, it's really good for stress and it takes the pain away."

In the early '90s, Akim placed in the Mr. Olympia bodybuilding contest. He was in his mid 30s and figured he had peaked, so he decided to get into wrestling. He met Davey and told him he used to box a little bit when he traveled with the circus.

Akim said he left home when he was 15, and joined a circus in Germany and then started boxing. From there he got into weight-lifting, then steroids and bodybuilding. He began competing in the United States and placed in a few competitions. He had a few little endorsements and he modeled occasionally, but he has spent more money on bodybuilding drugs than he made. He also started to dabble in morphine and cocaine.

In 1996 he met Shane McMahon at a gym when the WWF was doing a TV taping in California. Shane thought Akim was a pretty impressive looking guy and had wrestling potential. He sent Akim to Calgary to be trained by Bret.

Bret ran the training camp from the swimming-pool area of his house. The area was huge-2,000 square feet-and it held a ring, the pool and a weight-lifting gym. Akim came for training, along with Ken Shamrock, from the Ultimate Fighting Challenge, a fierce, no-rules-barred competition.

Ken had a reputation as an awesome shooter, which means he was a legitimate submission wrestler. Matches took place in a cage and no competitor could leave until one of them tapped out. Ken was a world champ. He would always make the other guy tap out. It's devastating to fight to the finish and then forced to leave through submission.

I met Ken and Akim in Calgary in May of 1997 at a birthday party for my dad at Bret's house. It was my dad's 82nd birthday. Initially, Owen didn't like either of the new recruits. He complained that Ken often bragged to them that he was a real wrestler whereas Owen and Davey were just showman.

I felt that Ken lacked integrity. He was portrayed on TV as a real family man. WWF profiles showed him walking in the grass with his wife and son, but while he was in Calgary, he spent a lot of nights falling in love with strippers and waitresses. Owen called them Ken's bimbo girlfriends.

Bret arranged for Akim to stay at Mom and Dad's house. Akim had a rental car and a nice fat contract with the WWF called a developmental deal. He was so spoiled; he had the world by the tail. My dad was really impressed with him. He had huge calves and huge hands. His hands were actually growing because he was on so much growth hormone.

His fingers and toes looked like Fred Flintstone's and you could see the protrusions in his eyebrows and his nose from those hormones. He was exceptionally good looking in a freakish sort of way, but not as healthy as he appeared. Every time he got hurt or banged up, it would turn into an abscess.

One day while training in the dungeon, he fell on his hip and his leg turned a funny color. Because of what happened with Matt, my dad rushed him to the hospital. The doctors told him his liver was shutting down because it couldn't handle all the drugs he was taking.

In early 1998, just a month after he had jumped to the WCW, Davey realized he'd made a big mistake. He approached Bret for help, but Bret, who had been Davey's buddy while lobbying for him to quit the WWF, treated him like a leper. Davey broke down at our kitchen table and he started crying.

"I wish I never fucking left Vince. I wish I never fucking left him. I hate your brother Bret. I hate him. He doesn't do anything for me. He doesn't want anything to do with me. Now he tells me I'm getting jobbed out at the WCW. I don't know what I'm doing. I've got no friends there. I left Owen. I left a good company. I wish I'd never left."

Little did I know that some part of Davey's unhappiness was attributed to a growing morphine habit he acquired. Bret knew and so did Owen, but no one told me. The Halloween party the year before was the first indication I had had that Davey was using, but I had no idea it was morphine.

I said, "I know, Davey, I know. I didn't want you to leave either." I wasn't trying to say "I told you so," but I had tried to convince him not to leave and he wouldn't listen. Davey is so loyal to the wrong people sometimes. He had been loyal to Dynamite and Bret and now he was loyal to his drug dealers and fellow users. He kept them on the payroll and bought them dinner. But Owen and I were his true friends and instead of listening to us, he took us for granted.

With no other friends, Davey began hanging out with Jim and Mondo McMichael. Davey's morphine addiction started to envelope him. He stopped flying home from matches to be with us. He even stopped calling me from the road.

Bret called me a few times during that spring and told me Davey was on thin ice and Jim was on wet toilet paper with the WCW and they were going to be let go.

"I don't think Vince will ever take Davey back. He's burned his bridges, so he better straighten out. I heard that him and Jim were so screwed up they couldn't even put their boots on at last week's TV tapings in Orlando."

Things got worse after he hurt his back at the WCW Fall Brawl in 1998 and stayed home to recuperate. Jim Neidhart introduced

Davey to a Dr. Joe in Calgary. Davey got him to prescribe morphine, Percocet, Soma, Noverol, and anti inflammatory drugs, Toradol and Tolwin. Dr. Joe also gave him steroids.

I pleaded with my family for help. At Sunday dinners, I'd point to him. "There's something wrong with him," I'd insist. "Am I the only person here who notices he can't feed himself?"

Everyone would tell me to leave him alone. I even took a water pistol with me one time and squirted him every time he dropped the food off his fork. He was so stoned he barely flinched. My sisters Georgia and Alison leaped to his defense, telling me to stop it. And my mom said she wouldn't tolerate one of her guests being treated that way.

Harry and Georgia were beside themselves with worry. Why was their daddy staggering around the house? What were those big sore-looking marks on his arms? Why did he always hide them with long-sleeved shirts? Why was he slurring his words like that?

They were terrified to drive with him. Davey had always loved to take us out to eat, but now he was a public embarrassment. People would stare as in his doped-up state he'd knock into tables while stumbling to the bathroom. He'd take forever in there, often shooting up again. He began to look bloated and purple, like Elvis just before he died.

It all became too much for me and that's when I attempted suicide.

When Davey first entered rehab they checked him into the hospital in Grand Prairie for three weeks to dry out. Going off morphine and all the other drugs made him vomit and suffer delirium tremens, but the steroid withdrawal made him psychotic. He'd call me a couple of times a day.

Sometimes he'd tell me about his little green pet dragons that were sitting on his lap while he was talking to me. He'd give the nurse heck for scaring them away. He hallucinated constantly. He told me he received the $50,000 I'd sent him and that he had to sleep with a gun next to his pillow because the other patients were trying to kill him.

He thought Bret, Razor Ramon and Eric Bischoff had been up to see him and wondered where I was. He sounded so rational sometimes that I got confused about what he was imagining and what was really happening.

One day, he called and said he'd been watching Monday Night Raw and congratulated me on the big angle Shawn and I were doing. I thought maybe they had shown a rerun of me and Shawn and Davey, but it turned out this was another of his drug-with-drawal fantasies.

When he was finally out of the hospital and in the treatment center, he was given day passes and would sneak to a nearby bar and down vodka and orange juice. Then he'd take one of the wait-resses to a nearby motel. I didn't learn of this until later.

I got up the nerve to call Vince's secretary Beth Zazza at the WWF. I asked if they could fit me into the program, possibly with Owen. I also mentioned how unhappy Davey was at the WCW. Beth was sympathetic and thanked me for calling and said she'd talk to Vince about it.

I hung up and called Owen. Owen was opposed to my involve-ment with him because he had been working with Mondo's ex wife, Deborah McMichael. "Diana, I know it's your dream," he said. "I know, I can't tell you what to do, but you don't want to be a part of wrestling right now. I don't think you'll fit in. You don't want to be wearing little bikini bathing suits."

I replied that I didn't have to wear a bikini to be his manager.

He said his tag-team partner Jeff Jarret and he already had a manager, Deborah. He went on to say he felt really sorry for Deborah. Owen told me what a horrible life Deborah had with drug addict Steve McMichael. He said Steve was physically abu-sive, that he threw her out without any money and she went to Vince and his wife Linda and they gave her a job. Owen was com-mitted to helping Deborah out. Besides, he genuinely liked Jeff, Deborah and the angle. He suggested I try to free Davey from the WCW and make a comeback with him.

I hoped Owen could see my misfortune as well as he could see Deborah's. Our conversation ended with Owen promising to see what he could find for me.

In the meantime, Davey was rushed to hospital with an awful staph infection that had been spreading for about six months in his spine. Almost immediately, the news was all over the world. The British Bulldog's career was over. It eclipsed Bret's retirement.

Davey was in the hospital for a month. Everything was collaps-ing on him, including his veins. He looked terrible. He had lost a lot of weight. The WCW sent Davey a letter releasing him. Now we had no income.

Owen came to see Davey in the hospital. He said, "Davey, you know you've been let go, fired, released, exterminated, terminated by the WCW. Would you ever want to come back to the WWF? You could bring Di with you."

Owen was always saying how much fun the WWF was now that Bret was gone. He told us how he loved his job and that Vince had resurrected one of his first characters, the Blue Blazer. Back in 1988, Owen hadn't liked this gimmick, but now it was hip. He loved spoofing the action heroes. Over coffee with me, he told me he liked flying around on this little harness in a ratty-tatty old cape with broken feathers and a mask on, yelling, "Eat your vitamins and drink your milk."

"The fans get so mad because they know that it's me under the mask. Then when I come out as Owen Hart and say, 'You stupid fans, that wasn't me,' Vince just wipes the tears out of his eyes, he's laughing so hard." Owen started chuckling. "I get such a kick out of it." He went on to say how he thought the WWF had such a good team at the time because everyone got along and there were no big egos on board.

Once Owen put the word out, Davey started getting calls left and right from everyone in the WWF, from the merchandise people to the agents. 'Mankind' Mick Foley came up to see Davey when they were in Calgary. Vince McMahon called Davey. He said, "You know, pal, what happened with me and Bret, I wish you had come to me and talked to me about it before you quit. We'd like you to finish your career off here with your family."

Davey began to feel hopeful. When he was released from the hospital, he even refused their offer of a prescription for morphine.

My main concern was getting Davey fit and healthy, but we had no money. Vince offered that even if Davey couldn't wrestle again, perhaps he could work in the office or commentate. Davey agreed, but only as a last resort.

"You know me Vince. I've come back from worse things. I'll be back in the ring before you know it, as long as you've got a place for me."

Davey started back on steroids to get his weight up.

Owen's Fall

I was watching the WWF May pay-per-view, 'Over The Edge,' by eerie coincidence. I was in our living room with Harry and Georgia. Davey was out on a steroid run with Ben Bassarab. I was glued to the set, knowing Davey would be joining soon. I wanted to brush up on all the storylines and find out who was doing what with whom.

Owen had just done his interview as the Blue Blazer. We laughed as he reminded kids to drink their milk and say their prayers and then ran off. I went upstairs for a moment and the phone rang. I picked it up. It was a reporter from 'Off The Record,' a popular television sports show on The Sports Network. He asked me if I had just seen something happen to Owen on TV.

I said, "No."

He said, "So you didn't see him fall?"

I was stunned, "What do you mean? Just now?"

"We're praying for him," he answered.

"I need to go!" I hung up and rushed toward the stairway. Harry met me on the stairs and hugged me. He said, "Something has happened to Owen."

The television showed a darkened arena. The camera was on a wide shot locked on the ring. The commentators Jim Ross and Jerry Lawlor kept repeating over and over again that this was for real. They said there was a freak accident and that emergency personnel were working on Owen and that everyone was praying for him.

I called my dad whose phone had been ringing off the hook. He said he'd been contacted and was waiting for an update. For what seemed like an eternity we held our breath. Ellie came through the door.

Then my dad called. "We've lost Owen."

"I'm sorry Dad," I said, stunned.

Ellie heard me say this and started running on the spot, screaming and crying. "No! Not Owen! Poor Mom and Dad!"

My dad was really brave about it. His voice never quavers or cracks. He's such a complete man. He has to hold everything together for his family, so that's what he did. My dad called me first because he knew what kind of relationship I had with Owen – we were always so close. We were the babies of the family.

After I hung up the phone I cried and cried. I sank to the floor and wept.

Finally, I managed the strength to call Davey at Ben's. I said, "Owen's gone. They say he's dead."

Davey said, "No, no, that's impossible."

Then the funeral took place.

The morning of the funeral, Vince called and apologized profusely, "I'm sorry Diana. It was a terrible accident. Owen was truly a great man. What a joy it was to know him."

He was grief stricken and struggling to get the words out. "If I had the power to change things, I would take his place right now. I want to do what I can for Martha, Oje and Athena. Linda and I want to make things right with your mom and dad. Nothing can bring Owen back. I know that, but I want to help. I am so, so sorry."

Vince, his wife Linda, son Shane and daughter Stephanie were quite emotional at the service. My father and Vince hadn't seen each other in a long time and when they came face to face it was an affecting moment for both of them. They embraced.

Vince is surprisingly charming compared to his onscreen persona. His voice is soft and he is milder and more subdued. At the wake, on my parent's lawn under a big canvas tent, he said, "The thing about Owen was just when you thought you were getting the joke he had pulled on you and you were laughing together, he was actually hooking you for another one. He'd take it to a new level."

Vince chuckled as he told me that one time Owen and Davey borrowed some baby farm animals and pygmy goats from the Hog Men and herded them into Vince's office. When he walked in, they had eaten most of the papers on his desk.

"But no matter how hard I tried, I couldn't get mad at the guy."

Hollywood 'Hulk' Hogan also showed up to pay his respects to our family. He told us how one time Owen leased a rental car and offered him a ride.

"I said sure. So I get in and we start driving when suddenly he starts slurring his words and weaving on the road, like he's smashed. I was terrified. I thought he was drunk. I yelled at him to pull over. And he starts crying like this crazy drunk. It was so convincing! My heart was pounding and I thought I was in the car with a nutty drunk driver when suddenly he turns to me and smiles, sober as a judge. "Terry, you know I don't drink.""

Hollywood shook his head. "He had more energy than anyone I ever knew. I sure hope he left some for us to spread around."

Other wrestlers flew into Calgary to be with us: The Edge and his partner Christian Cage, Triple H, Chyna, Ken Shamrock, Chris Jericho, Brian Blair, Mark Henry, Melanie Pilman, Jeff Jarrett and his wife, Deborah McMichael, Mick Foley, Shane Douglas, Chris Benoit and his wife Nancy, Johnny Smith, Animal, Dory and Terry Funk and their wives and Kane, the Rock and the Undertaker.

It was heartwarming to watch Dad sit in a metal chair on the lawn near the porch, holding court as they gathered around listening to his war stories. Mick Foley, better known as Mankind, is a bit of a maniac in the ring. He used to stuff Mr. Socko, his pet sock, into the mouths of his opponents after he'd beaten them to a pulp. He always wore a leather mask reminiscent of Hannibal Lechter in The Silence of The Lambs.

But in person, though he's missing his front teeth and his forehead is terribly scarred, he comes across as a gentle, intellectual, very thoughtful man. The bond he shared with Owen was they were both family men very dedicated to their wives and children.

He was teary-eyed when he told me about a time Owen pulled one of his famous pranks. "We were flying into some Northern location in the Maritimes and waiting at the luggage carousal when I noticed this guy with one of those video cameras. You know the kind with the fold-out viewing screen.

"He was aiming it at Chyna and I could see he was zoomed in on her chest. This made me mad so I went over to the guy and I said, "Hey, you can't do that. That's disrespectful. I want you to rewind that tape and erase that right now." I was angry.

"While this was going on, Owen saw me arguing with this guy and he came over and said, "Hey give me that thing." He took the camera and said, "Now Mick, stand next to this fellow and put your arm around him." I said, "Go away Owen, this guy..." But Owen tried to put my arm around him again and said, "Hey, I'll tape you two together. C'mon Mick, put your arm around him.""

"So I end up in this jerk's video tape, looking like his pal, with my arm around him."

Mick shook his head. "He was always doing the ribs. Another time, I was bragging to him how I got a good rate at this hotel. Well, I get unpacked and the phone rings. It's this hotel manager with a British accent. He says, 'I'm sorry Mr. Foley, but we made a mistake on your rate and we'll have to charge you more.'

"I said, 'What do you mean? We agreed on the rate!'

"And the British guy says, 'I'm sorry sir, we are going to have to charge you more. By the way, are you from that WWF?'

"I said, 'Yes I am.'

"He says, "Is wrestling fake?"

"I replied, 'Well, 62% of it is real. But one time a guy got down to 57% and he was fired.'

"The Englishman laughed and said, "Ho ho ho, you are very funny sir, but we're still going to have to charge you more.'

"Of course it turned out to be Owen."

The only people from our family allowed to speak at the funeral were Bret and Ross. Even my parents weren't invited to say anything.

Smith prepared a poem that went unread. It was particularly touching:

"Once you were here
What a difference you made, dearest of dear brothers.
To the hell that was raised when a dozen then played without any others.
Only heaven knows why you got chose, and that you'll await us is our belief.
I smell lily and rose and read each and every heartfelt card, through flows of grief.
What is spoken is tasted and what is heard of your greatness is felt deep within our heavy hearts and certainly all around this solemn gathering.
As I still try to write in this, the 13th hour, Owen
And search for words of praise and worth,
I sense your presence pure and sweet.
Owen, don't think I don't know that you are haunting our house already."

Ellie had hoped to read the congregation these words:

"No words can express the deep and profound loss of our dear brother, Owen. All of our lives will be forever changed because of this awful, fateful day. Our family will endure because of who we are and because of the great strength, courage and compassion our wonderful parents have instilled in us. My father is my great hero for so many reasons. It is not his way to blame, nor is it mine. We can't change what has happened so we must all try to move on. They say time heals all wounds. I'm not sure it will this time, but I find great comfort in knowing, Owen, Matthew and Dean are together. They will always watch over us."

Bruce wrote:

"They say the true mark of a man is judged by the number of lives he has touched, I have no reservation in saying that my kid brother was a man among men. We'll miss you and never forget you."

Davey and I were featured in a two-page spread in The Calgary Herald and I spoke to a reporter at the funeral, telling her that I thought Vince felt badly because he was somewhat of a father figure to Owen and my dad was a father figure to Vince. When Bret read this he came positively unglued. He called me on the phone. "What's going on with you? What is the deal between you and Vince?"

I was puzzled. "What do you mean what's the deal between me and Vince?"

"Well, are you working for him, do you have a job?" he demanded.

I said, "Why? What are you talking about?"

"What's Davey doing right now?" he wanted to know.

I replied that Davey was vomiting over our deck railing. He had just had a CAT scan and the dye shot was making him sick. "Why are you screaming, Bret?"

Then he ranted about my quote in the newspaper. He said I was blowing this deal for Martha. "It's a $500-five hundred million dollar lawsuit that we are trying to file against WWF for negligence! Vince McMahon is a murderer."

I said, "Bret, all I said was that Vince McMahon thinks of Dad as a father figure and thought of Owen as one of his own sons."

This seemed to infuriate him more. "What was I then? What was I at Survivor Series?"

"Well I don't know, Bret," I shrugged. It seemed so ridiculous talking about what happened to him at Survivor Series compared to Owen's death. How did that relate to the quote I made about Vince at Owen's funeral? I don't know, maybe he needed somewhere to vent, but he just exploded.

"Listen, you bitch, if I see you, I'll kill you. If I see you walking across the street, I'll run you down with my car! I'm going to tear you and Davey to shreds, if I ever see you at Mom's house. If I ever see you two..." I kept holding the phone away from my ear, but his screaming could easily be heard from several feet away. Both Davey and Ellie were in the kitchen listening.

Bret has a newspaper column in The Calgary Sun and he used it to threaten us. "I am going to put in my column how Davey was in rehab for seven weeks, and how you tried to kill yourself. You need to see a shrink, you bitch. You're nuts! Vince McMahon murdered my brother."

"He was my brother too, Bret," I interjected.

"Obviously he wasn't."

I didn't want to let Bret know that he was getting to me, hurting me, so I remained calm.

"Bret, Mom and Dad do not want to get into a lawsuit with Vince McMahon right now. It was an accident. Owen didn't do anything that he didn't want to do. And if anybody thought that it would have ended up the way it did, if we all had a gift to foresee the future, then Vince McMahon would never have allowed it. But Owen was capable of making his own decisions. He got strapped into the harness and got hoisted up above the ring on his own accord. He had done it before."

"He couldn't say no. He would have been fired. He would have lost his job," Bret yelled.

"No," I replied, "he wouldn't have, Bret."

He started reaming me out again so I put the phone next to the radio, just to aggravate him.

He called back about half an hour later. Ellie was still at the house with me. This time she got on the phone. Bret's started all over again. He said, "I just got off the phone with Mom and she told me to do whatever I want. So I'm going to make sure Mom and Dad file a lawsuit against Vince and the WWF."

Ellie sighed, "Vince didn't push Owen off a ladder, Bret, so why don't you just calm down?"

I got on the extension phone just as Bret started laying into Ellie. "You know what, Ellie? Owen thought you were a loser."

Ellie started to cry.

I tried to defend her, "Why are you saying this, Bret?"

"You shut up. Owen never even liked you anyway."

I said, "I don't think that's true, Bret. I had a relationship with Owen you would never understand."

"Really?" he sneered. "Martha told me Owen had no use for you. He didn't even like you."

Ellie interrupted. "Stop it, Bret! Diana and Owen were... I think that Owen's death out of everyone in the family will affect her and Ross and Bruce more than anyone."

"Well Martha didn't know Owen the way I did!" I cried.

Now that he could hear how upset I was, he sounded more self-assured, "If Owen liked you, Martha would have thanked you in her speech at the funeral. Who did she thank?" His voice started to escalate. "Who did she thank? Who did she thank?" He was yelling again. "She thanked me, and Alison and Ross. She didn't mention you at all. You were nothing to Owen!"

It was true. Martha had left me out of her thank-yous and it had hurt. I gulped, "Well, Bret, I have my own memories of Owen and a lot of my memories don't involve Martha, so whatever Martha and Owen have is their deal and I'll treasure what I had with him."

Just before the funeral, Davey and I did an interview for Good Morning America. I was asked if Owen's death was staged just for ratings. "Absolutely not. Owen's match wasn't even the main event. No one knew he was coming down on a harness. How are they going to get ratings when it wasn't even publicized?" It was an absurd question.

This set Bret off again. He called a family meeting in our kitchen and gave us all our agenda. At first he was patronizing.

"Maybe Diana doesn't understand what's really going on. This wasn't an accident. Deep down, Vince always wanted to destroy the family. We have to band together to help Martha, Oje and Athena. We must support her in whatever she chooses to do. Dad, Diana and Davey are forbidden to speak in public about this accident any longer. You are going to blow this whole thing for Martha. You've got to think of her kids. This is what Owen would want."

"I never said anything wrong. Of course it was an accident," I defended myself. "And I don't think this is what Owen would want."

It wasn't an accident," he roared. "Can't you get that through your thick skull? You are so fucking stupid. Why are you trying to kiss McMahon's ass?"

My dad interrupted, "That's enough, Bret. This thing is tragedy enough. It was just a tragic accident. I wish they had tested it before they put Owen in it. I am capable of doing my own gaddamn talking. I don't want Bret, Diana, Ellie, your mother or Alison talking for me. Your poor mother can't take much more."

My dad leaned over, picked a piece of buttered bread off the counter, tore pieces from it and began feeding Bear, his German Shepherd cross. "Owen was a hell of a wrestler."

Agitated, Bret left the room.

But what Bret had said started to eat at me. I decided to talk to Martha, to try to get her to understand that Davey would continue to work for the WWF – not because we didn't support her – but because we had to make a living. I thought Bret's threats of a lawsuit were just hot air. I felt sure she would want to wait to see what Vince was going to offer her first.

I drove to her and Owen's house later that night. Her Mom wouldn't let me in. She opened the door about half an inch and peeked her nose out. "Martha can't see you right now. Martha's not here."

I said, "Oh, I just wanted to know if she needed any help with anything. I just wanted to see how she is doing."

"I've got to go. Oje and Athena are in the bathtub. Martha is not here and she doesn't need anything from you." She closed the door.

I turned around and headed for my car just as Virginia's new husband George, the hockey coach, pulled up in Owen's teal metallic green Lumina van. I knew Owen couldn't stand him because of the affair he'd had with Virginia behind her husband's back, so I hated to see him driving Owen's new vehicle. And I felt even worse when I saw that Oje was with him. I knew right then and there that Martha was going to cut Owen's kids out of our lives.

I found out Bret spent the night after Owen died at Martha's house, consoling her. I know it was purely platonic, but the last words that she heard before she went to sleep and the first words she heard in the morning were that she had to sue Vince McMahon. She had to close him down, finish him off. She couldn't just let it go. Basically, as Martha put it at the funeral, "I have yet to have my day of reckoning."

Vince didn't even have a chance to offer a settlement to Martha.

My New Life

I was now at a point where I felt my life had been put on hold for the 20 years I had known Davey. The WWF had never been more successful and, as they promised before Owen's death, they welcomed Davey's return a few months later. But no matter how many good angles they gave him, he fumbled the ball. They offered him stock options and the chance to market a workout video we had made, but he didn't pursue any of these avenues. He couldn't worry about business. He was too preoccupied with getting his next fix. His drug addiction was impairing his judgment and his wrestling. He was lethargic in the ring and confrontational at home. On a freezing cold day in December 1999, I caught him shooting up morphine. I followed him into our garage and found him injecting it into his arm. I went berserk. I stood there swearing and screaming, "You son of a bitch, you bastard. How can you do this to Harry and Georgia? It's obvious you don't care about me, but what about our kids? I should have left you a year ago. I hate you. You have ruined my life!"

He looked up at me, his eyes at half-mast, "Don't tell Vince."

I ran into the house and slammed the door. Moments later, he came into the house and fell on the couch, blinking at me like some kind of frog on a lily pad. I returned to the garage and grabbed his paraphernalia, which included both used and full syringes. I drove to my doctor's office. She directed me to my lawyer and warned me not to hurt myself. She gave me a phone number for women in crisis. I arrived at my lawyer's office in tears, gave him the drugs and told him to begin divorce proceedings. While I waited to hear back from him, Davey and I continued to live under the same roof. When he was home, Davey was passed out in front of the television. Ellie stopped by to see me. She was worried. We hadn't talked for a week or so. I told her what had been going on and Davey happened into the kitchen. "Show her your arms, Davey!" I ordered, yanking on his sleeves and exposing his track marks. Ellie's hands flew to her face. "No, Davey, no!" she exclaimed. "How could you do this to yourself? You just got over your infection! You're going to die. Think of Harry and Georgia and Di! "Davey calmly rolled his sleeves back in place. "I don't have a problem, Ellie. I can stop anytime time I want."

By January of 2000, my lawyer had served him with divorce papers. Davey reacted by going over to my mom and dad's and sobbing in their kitchen.

"Why is she doing this to me? To our kids? I've done nothing wrong. I've given her everything."

My parents gave him the benefit of the doubt and confronted me. My dad berated me. His logic was, rather than buy a new car, I should get the old one fixed. Taking into consideration my age, "You are no spring chicken!" he said. That, in combination with my long history with Davey, he felt were reason enough to try again.

"But Dad, "I protested, "he's a drug addict."

"My dad frowned. "He says he doesn't have a problem."

"Dahling, think of Harry and Georgia and what a divorce will do to them," my mom counseled.

"Mom, I would never tell Georgia to stay with a drug addict. And I certainly don't want her growing up around one. Harry wants to go into wrestling. I don't want him to think this is OK. You get married, you become a wrestler, then you become a drug addict and you piss it all away. "But they were sure I was exaggerating and over-reacting.

I called Vince at home on a Sunday night. Stephanie answered. She was cheerful. She was having a ball working with her dad. She brought Vince to the phone. I and spilled out my story. I told him everything. I talked about my suicide attempt, about our marriage and about Davey's drug addiction. He told me he would investigate and that I should stay strong for Harry and Georgia. Within a month Vince insisted Davey check into the Talbot Recovery Center in Atlanta. He would pick up the tab and continue to give Davey his paycheck.

Davey called me during the TV tapings that night. "I hope you're happy. I got pulled today. I know about your little phone call to Vince. Nobody's going to make me go to another rehab. I'll show you! I'm booking myself on the first flight to England and I'm going to become a bouncer. That's what you want isn't it? You don't know what withdrawal is like, you stupid bitch. You have no idea. I don't have a problem."

"Well, if you don't have a problem then why will you have to go through withdrawal?" I asked.

He hung up.

The next day he flew from Nashville to Atlanta. He called me from the airport and told me he wouldn't check into the recovery center unless I dropped the divorce proceedings. Then he hung up again. He was in the dry-out facility for nearly two weeks. This time, instead of green dragons he saw red. He called me every day, at least 20 times, yelling, screaming, threatening, "Who are you sleeping with now? I don't belong here! It's your fault you whore!" Then he'd call back and say, "I'm sorry, I didn't mean that. I just can't wait to get out of here. I just want to come home so much and I'm really sorry. I've just got to get through this detox part and then I want to get home and I just want to see you and Harry and Georgia."

His phone calls terrified me. He sounded so violent. I quietly bought my own my house and moved the kids in with me with just before he entered rehab, and now I was glad I did. He began to call and brief me on what I was to tell the nurses when they called me to discuss his progress. I was to say he didn't take steroids and that the only pills he had been on were Percocet and Soma. I didn't argue. The center did call, but only to tell me not to accept more than one phone call per day from him.

At the end of the first week of his stay, he told me he had tried to kill himself on the plane. He said that just before he boarded, he had taken every pill in his possession and had shot up all the morphine he could get his hands on. He said he wanted his death hanging over me for the rest of my life. He said he had to be carried off the plane on a stretcher.

When he couldn't get hold of me 20 times a day, he called everyone in my family. He'd complain that I refused to drop divorce proceedings even though he was trying so hard to get better. He was right. I still wanted a divorce. I did not want to live with him anymore. I decided to take the advice Owen gave me right after I tried to kill myself, "When a person gets to the point where they want to kill themselves because they are married to a drug addict, it's time to leave. You have your kids to think about."

I started dating again. I met a young, upcoming wrestler named James Trimble who made me laugh again. It started with a handshake. I have a fair grip and he teased me about it.

We went to movies and out for the occasional dinner. I was determined not to sneak around. So I told Davey I was going through with the divorce and dating. Davey immediately contacted some of Hermish's friends and James started getting death threats. Through this entire calamity, James and I became closer.

Davey was scheduled to stay at the Atlanta facility for four months. It was going to cost Vince in the neighborhood of US $100,000. But after just three weeks, Davey checked himself out and came home. Hoping to smooth things out, I picked him up at the airport. He was sullen. I showed him my new home and he insisted on coming in. When he refused to leave, I called the police. They arrived and told me to leave before the situation escalated. Davey began living at my new home and I had nowhere to go. I moved in with James in a high-security apartment building with underground parking, cameras and security guards.

Davey's last wrestling match for the WWF took place in Calgary in May. According to my brother Smith, it was pitiful. It was hard on his opponent Steve Blackman because he broke into wrestling in Calgary and Davey was so out of it all he could do was suplex Steve and pose. People who knew Davey felt sorry for him, and those who didn't thought he was a joke. The match was a complete aberration.

The next night he was booked in Edmonton. He left late because he was hung over from too much ecstasy the night before. Harry heard the alarm around 11:00 am and could not wake him. A drug-dealing hanger-on named Jaden Spencer told Harry to "bugger off" and "let Davey sleep." A couple of hours later, Harry watched them get up and give each other a shot in the rear end.

Jaden was injected with Davey's used needle. Then they each grabbed a handful of ephedrine or Hydroxy Cut, which is a caffeine pill designed to clean you out. They smoked some pot, popped some Percocets and hopped in the car. Harry and Georgia were ordered to squeeze in the back with Davey's wrestling bag and then he downed some Soma so he could nap during the three-and-a-half hour drive.

Jaden stopped in Red Deer to pick up a prescription of Percocet from his dad. Harry said Jaden bragged that he told his dad to visit the doctor and complain of a backache. Harry said Jaden was angry with his dad for getting only 15 pills. Ten minutes outside of Edmonton, Jaden fed Davey 30 ephedrine to wake him up. Davey arrived at the match late, incoherent and wired. Harry said WWF agents Jack Lanza and Tony Garea told Harry to take him home and not to let Davey or Jaden drive.

They stopped Davey from getting his blood pressure taken lest he lose his wrestling license. Steve Blackman who was scheduled to wrestle Davey for the second night in a row was annoyed.

"I can't believe you did this to me, Davey."

"This is all my fucking wife's fault," Davey replied. "She's playing games with my 'ead. She's fucking with me. She's causing me so much stress I'm all screwed up. Fucking bitch."

Harry and Georgia fell asleep on the ride home while Jaden drove again. When they awoke they were in the parking lot outside the apartment building where James and I were living. Georgia watched as Jaden stuffed a tire iron down the back of his pants.

"What are you doing?" she mumbled sleepily.

"Shut up and go back to sleep," she was told.

The closed-circuit camera in James's building caught them pulling their hoods over their faces while sneaking through the underground parkade toward the elevator. They were stopped by security guards. Davey claimed he was just dropping our kids off, then he and Jaden bolted for the door, made it out the building to the car and took off with the kids demanding to know what happened. The next day Davey and Jaden flew to Vancouver for Monday Night Raw. Vince took one look at Davey and sent him home. Davey took a leave of absence from wrestling, but remained on the payroll. He threatened the kids that if they didn't live with him he'd never speak to them again.

"Mummy has no money," he cautioned. "I'm the only one who can take care of you."

Jaden moved in with him. Davey was so verbally violent with me I didn't know what to do. I thought if I opposed him, he would kill me. On the rare occasion I was allowed near the kids they told me Davey and Jaden spent their days taking drugs. Harry would hide their pills because he was fed up with seeing his dad messed up. But Jaden would grab Harry and shake him, demanding he hand them over. They trashed my little house and then Davey found a two-bedroom townhouse over near my dad's place. There was another for sale four doors down. Davey told me that he wanted the kids to live near both of us. He was going to buy one for me and one for him, provided I sell my little ruined house. I almost agreed to this. But while I was cleaning up the little house they had trashed I found Caverjact, a drug that promotes erection when injected into the penis. I was fine with the idea that he might have a girlfriend until I found out who it was. He had started seeing Bruce's wife Andrea. Harry and Georgia told me she had moved her new furniture and clothing into his condo. She ordered Harry into the garage and Georgia onto the living room floor and her own kids into the bedroom Harry and Georgia had occupied. I was stunned and so was Bruce.

He called me and told me to try to get back with Davey so Andrea would, "haul her scrawny polluted carcass back home."

I told Bruce he was crazy, Davey hadn't changed. I wouldn't dream of going back. Meanwhile, Harry and Georgia watched Davey overdose over and over again. The ambulance was called six times between March and September. He phoned me repeatedly and warned me he was going to kill me.

"You'll never see your kids again. I'm going to bootfuck you and James. I'm going to slit your throat."

Davey was totally irrational because I was dating again. Of course it didn't help that James was 13 years younger than Davey. I called the police many times but all they did was advise me to stay away from him.

One time Davey kicked my front door in. I called 911 and the police rushed over. One of the officers asked Davey for his autograph. I felt like Nicole Simpson. I finally managed a restraining order against Davey after he left the following hysterical message on Ellie's answering machine:

"You douche bag, whore, cunt. I'm going to do you. I'm going to do your whole family, Stu and Stu's family, and that goes for my fucking wife. I'm going to skull drag every one of you."

Ellie emailed it to Jerry McDevitt, one of the lawyers at the WWF, and told him that though they were paying Davey US $50,000 a month, I was not seeing any of it. I had nothing. My lawyer told me Davey owed Revenue Canada and the Internal Revenue Service more than $400,000 and that if I accepted alimony, half that debt could belong to me. So I walked away from any settlement. I put my little house up for sale and moved back home with my parents. Harry and Georgia were with me. Davey came screaming up the driveway in his BMW and ordered the kids into his car.

"Georgia, Harry, your mummy's fucking nuts. If you don't get in, don't ever bother calling me again. I'll never speak to you again!"

My heart was breaking for them. They'd been through so much and now they feared losing their dad forever. Georgia started toward the car. "I've got to go, Mummy. He might kill himself if I don't."

Davey stalked up the driveway and stormed into my dad's house. My dad was itching to speak with him. He hadn't been able to talk with him in months. When he saw Davey, he tapped him in the leg with his cane. "Davey, can I just have a word with you? Would you just be quiet and let me talk? I'm gaddamned disgusted with you. And that little bum Andrea should be ashamed of herself, too. What you are doing with Andrea would be no different then if Harry's wife left him for Georgia's husband. I think it's gaddamned sickening. I can't blame Diana for not wanting anything to do with you. I feel for the poor kids. Poor little Georgia." My dad has always loved Baby Georgia. If he has a favorite, it's her. She looks just like Davey but my dad has always said how much she reminds him of me when I was young.

"She can see around corners," he'll say. Or "Her eyes are dazzling." Davey interrupted my dad and said, "Lick me, Stu!" My dad looked at me, frowning, "What did he say?" I leaned over and, in my dad's good ear, repeated, "He said for you to lick him. "My dad looked puzzled. "He wants me to kiss him? "I shook my head, "No, lick him." My dad still didn't understand. "Kiss him?"

Davey threw up his hands and stormed down the driveway, but through the dungeon windows he spotted James working-out. Bruce, Smith and my dad were emerging from the house. My dad was still trying to figure out what Davey had said to him. Harry was standing by the car. Davey looked around and as if he were addressing his fans at Wembley he pointed at the window where James was visible and he said, "I'm begging you. Just give me two minutes with him. I wanna see what kind of man he is. I looked over at Bruce who was watching with keen interest and I suddenly figured out who had called Davey over knowing that James was there. Davey charged down the stone steps leading to the dungeon. Smith and I were hot on his heels. When he entered the dungeon, Davey went after James from behind and shoved him into the weights. I grabbed a two-pound pipe and screamed for someone to get Dad.

"If you don't stop it, Davey, I'm going to throw this at your car."
I ran up the steps and hurled the pipe against his windshield. It
simply glanced off. Davey grabbed me and suplexed me on the
lawn. I struggled free and picked up a large rock. By this time, my
dad had reached us and was wheezing from the effort. He was
furious. "If you would all calm down, I'd like to talk to both of
you. Diana put the gaddamned rock down! I want this all to stop."
Davey ordered Harry into the car and, with Baby Georgia wide-
eyed in the back, Davey got into his BMW, and wheeled around
the house and pulled up beside my Volkswagen Beetle. He kicked
out the passenger window and drove away with the kids waving
to me sadly out the back window. The police arrested Davey shortly
after for threatening to "slit my fucking throat" yet again. The
judge let him go on the condition he enter rehab for a week and
take some anger-management courses.

Vince finally let him go at the end of November. Davey hadn't
wrestled in over six months.

Deborah McMichael wound up marrying Steve Austin in 2000.
When I ran into her seven months after her wedding, she behaved
abominably toward me, especially considering how well Owen had
treated her.

Two years to the day after Owen's death, I was backstage at the
WWF SMACKDOWN show in Edmonton using the bathroom when
Deborah's angry voice berated me from outside the stall I was
using.

"These bathrooms are for talent! You use the bathroom in the
cafeteria. None of us wants to catch something from you!"

When I exited the stall, Terry Runnells Goldust's ex-wife, a petite
blonde bombshell who manages several wrestlers and occasionally
enters the ring herself, had come into the bathroom with me. She
stared in astonishment.

"Was that Deborah?" I asked.

Terry nodded, "Yeah, just ignore her. I don't know what gets into
her."

Deborah had been cold when I ran into her the day before at the
RAW taping in Calgary. I was chatting amiably with Steve and he
formally introduced her to me. I congratulated her on their marriage and told her how fond Owen had been of her. She gave me a
curt "thank you," turned on her heel and commanded Steve to
follow her.

"I need to see you right now," she ordered, through clenched teeth.

I have no idea why she is so mad at me. I'm Steve's age and she is almost ten years older. Maybe that threatens her or makes her feel insecure. Or maybe before she and Steve got together Owen mentioned to her that he thought Steve and I might make a good couple. In any case, she doesn't appear to be my biggest fan.

That same RAW show in Calgary in May of 2001 was the reason Bret promised my mother the next time he sets foot in their house will be at my dad's funeral. My dad was introduced at ringside to a huge ovation from the Saddledome crowd. Me, my sister Ellie and two of my brothers, Smith and Bruce, were with him. Bruce made sure I was seated behind them, somewhat out of sight.

Chris Jericho and Chris Benoit delivered a beautiful, moving tribute to my dad on tape, and then approached my dad in person to thank him for helping make their dreams come true. I could see emotion swell in Benoit's eyes when my dad returned his hug. After that appearance, Bret wheeled into my parents' driveway in his red Durango. He stormed into the house and yanked photos of Owen and him off the walls.

The sign Smith had held up at the tapings, which read, "Hello Bret," prompted part of Bret's anger.

My mother was broken hearted that Bret was robbing her of pictures of her precious blonde palomino. It was almost too much for her. Then the phone rang. It was Martha.

"Helen, I think you are disgusting and pathetic and despicable! Go to hell!" she screamed, then hung up.

My Mom sank slowly into the nearest chair and buried her face in her hands. Martha and Bret's callousness toward my parents regarding Owen continues to take its toll.

Harry and Georgia have migrated back into my arms. I now have a new home with bedrooms for each of them. Georgia has organized all her things there and is beginning to shine again. She is rekindling her relationships with her cousins and seeing my mom and dad on a regular basis.

Both are huge wrestling fans and are already planning careers in the WWF. At only 15, Harry is six foot four and knows more about wrestling than anyone I know except for my dad. The kids are the best of both Davey and me. Despite all they have been through, they remain sweet, gentle and stoic. I am so proud of them.

As for me, I've learned that life is like the art of submission wrestling. You've gotta know what the other guy's move is before you move. And now I'm finally ready to guzzle 'em.